Strassels' Tax Savers

Strassels' Tax Savers

How to Hold On to More
of What You Earn by Paying Less in Taxes
for the Rest of Your Life

Paul N. Strassels and
William B. Mead

BOOKS

Library of Congress Cataloging in Publication Data

Strassels, Paul N.
    Strassels' tax savers.

    Includes index.
        1. Tax planning—United States—Popular works.
I. Mead, William B.   II. Title.
KF6297.Z9S774   1985   343.7305'2   84-40434
ISBN 0-8129-1162-8   347.30352

Designed by Robert Bull

Manufactured in the United States of America

9 8 7 6 5 4 3 2 1

First Edition

To Bernard Strassels and Bob Burkitt

Contents

Contents

Introduction

*M*illions of Americans desperately want to save on their income taxes, but they don't know how. Millions more overpay their taxes and don't even know it.

I should know. For five years, I worked for the Internal Revenue Service, and I saw the mistakes—grievous, repeated, expensive mistakes—that lead so many of us to overpay our taxes. Since leaving the IRS ten years ago, I have been telling people how to understand their taxes and how to pay less. I don't counsel the fat cats; in fact, I accept no private clients. I talk to people through books, magazines, television, and radio.

And I hear back. Through the mail and on radio and television talk shows, I hear from hundreds of taxpayers every year. Their questions and comments concern every facet of the income tax, but they are alike in one important respect: Every question, every comment, every plea for help, is personal.

A taxpayer is not the cross-section that gets analyzed and dissected in stories about tax policy, and gets "advised" in weighty tax manuals and workbooks.

A taxpayer is the retired man in Dayton, Ohio, who happened to watch while I was filming a tax show for television. "You don't know what you're talking about," he told me. "I'm seventy-two, so I don't have to pay tax anymore." He was wrong, but I could see where he got that impression.

A taxpayer is the young musician who hadn't filed a tax return for four years. He was getting married and wanted to come clean, but he was afraid he'd get thrown in jail. Without giving his name, he called me on a radio talk show in St. Louis. A short conversation made it clear that this young man faced no trouble at all. In fact, he was eligible for tax refunds.

A taxpayer is the woman in Tennessee who couldn't understand how the bank could withhold 10 percent of her interest, since the interest rate on her account was only 7 percent.

The more I heard, the more I became convinced that Americans need income tax help targeted to their own private and personal situations. I began to talk about this with my colleague, Bill Mead, with whom I co-author a magazine column. I'm thirty-eight, with a wife and two young children. Bill is fifty; he and his wife are becoming empty-nesters, as their three children finish college. Our problems and perspectives differ because of this very normal difference in our stages of life.

That was the glimmer that became the inspiration for this book. Our tax needs evolve. No tax manual—none of the scores that have been written, many of which are technically very good—address people in this personal way.

When you stop to think about it, a taxpayer is also a young single who is facing adult responsibilities for the first time; a young couple merging their lives—and their finances and tax returns; parents saving for their children's education; employees, the self-employed, homeowners, investors, senior citizens, the divorced.

These are real, personal situations, and we wrote this tax book for each one of them. While we were writing this book, in the summer of 1984, Congress once again amended the income tax laws, changing dozens of rules that apply to people in every stage of life and at every level of income. We wove these changes into the book—not all in one place but rather as they apply in the situations that all of us confront at one time or another.

This book will not teach you every detail of the U.S. Tax Code. It *will* teach you what you need to know so that you can understand your taxes, relate them to your own very personal situation, and pay less.

—Paul N. Strassels

Part One

TAXES
SIMPLIFIED

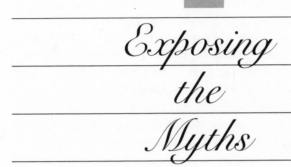

Exposing the Myths

E very year, tens of millions of Americans cheat on their income taxes, but it is not the government they are cheating. They are cheating themselves by paying more tax than the law requires—often thousands of dollars more.

No one overpays his or her taxes deliberately, but far too few Americans take advantage of every tax break available to them. They overpay not because they fill out their tax forms incorrectly but because they fail to work taxes into their financial planning in an intelligent way. The Tax Code contains literally dozens of provisions that can reduce your taxes, whatever your age and income level. These provisions are opportunities; we call them *Tax Savers.*

A Tax Saver is not something that descends upon you from heaven on April 15. It is something you plan for and figure into your financial growth. Some Tax Savers work best when you are young and single, others when you are starting a family, still others when you are looking toward retirement. The key to using Tax Savers—to cashing in on them—is understanding them, relating them to your own situation, and working them into your life.

We offer you no secret tips. The provisions of the U.S. Tax Code are public knowledge. But we will show you how to remove the mystery, fear, and resentment that keep most people from turning the Tax Code to their personal advantage. We will help you understand what a Tax Saver is and tell you which ones are likely to save you the most money at various stages of your life. We will bring you up to date on Tax Savers that are new, Tax Savers that have been discontinued, and Tax Savers that have changed, many as a result of the 1984 Tax Reform Act passed by Congress.

It's time you found out whether you are overpaying your taxes and learned how to enhance your prosperity by the honest use of Tax Savers.

GETTING STARTED

The first step is to ignore all the tax jargon that's bandied about over the office water fountain and in the lunchroom. Sure, you may be able to pick up a tip or two, but chances are the information you get won't apply to you, or, just as likely, it will be downright wrong. The second step is to worry less about your tax forms and think more about your income, expenses, and investments—the elements that determine how much tax you have to pay. And the third step is to tailor those elements into Tax Savers that fit your income level, your financial situation, your family, your goals, your stage of life. The Individual Income Tax is just what its name implies—individual. Work with the rules to cut your taxes to manageable levels. Take advantage of your Tax Savers.

Chances are you are a self-help taxpayer, or you would not have bought this book. That's fine. After all, no one else knows your financial situation as well as you do, and certainly no one else cares as much. Besides, the federal income tax is not as complicated as many people would have you believe. And the Tax Savers it offers—some call them deductions, credits, shelters, or loopholes—are not available solely to the wealthy. You should reap Tax Savers if you have any discretionary income at all—that is, if you earn enough to maintain a savings account, to buy a home, or to qualify for a loan.

Human nature being what it is, most people would

rather turn their taxes over to someone else to handle—someone who will tell them what to do: Invest in this, sell that, make a charitable contribution, open an IRA. But there's a catch: To afford the services of a financial manager, you have to be in the upper strata of the superrich. Tax planning takes time, and only the wealthy can afford to pay someone else to devote that kind of time to sort through the intricacies of an individual tax situation. We feel that you are financially better off taking an active role in handling your own taxes, whether you work with a tax professional or not.

In taxes, those who stand still pay the bill. Let's say you're salaried, and your wages have been rising steadily. In addition, you've been pretty good at picking profitable investments over the past couple of years. You hate even to think about taxes (the IRS loves you), so you leave that to the guy who fills out your tax form every April. That's financial suicide. You're throwing your money away. Whether your personal financial situation is expansive or so tight that you're about to strangle, you should incorporate Tax Savers into your plans. You'll be well paid for your time.

It's easy to be lulled. The Internal Revenue Service counts on you to report your income, assess your taxes, and pay up. By the same token, it's up to you to take advantage of reasonable Tax Savers so that you pay as little in tax as you honestly have to. No one at the IRS will tell you about Tax Savers you failed to take.

Nor should you depend upon the tax professional who fills out your tax return. Contrary to what most people think, very little in real tax savings results from the way your form is filled out. Real Tax Savers—the kind that can reduce your tax bill by hundreds, even thousands, of dollars—come from steps and strategies planned ahead and applied to your everyday financial life.

THE MYTHS

First, let's dispel ten myths that tend to paralyze taxpayers—and to keep them paying too much.

5

Myth 1: All 85,000 employees of the
Internal Revenue Service are eagerly awaiting your
return, with knives drawn.

In fact, the IRS does not take a personal interest in you or anyone else. Chances are no one at the IRS will ever look at your return with a critical eye. Your envelope—the one you sealed so carefully and with such fear and loathing—will be opened by a machine. You can't get less personal than that.

A clerk will check the bottom line to see whether you owed money, broke even, or claimed a refund. If you owed, the clerk will make sure your check is for the right amount. Your check will quickly be cashed; if you didn't pay in full, you'll be billed.

Your return will be scanned for mathematical accuracy, and to see whether you made any of about eighty-five relatively common errors. Did you use the wrong tax table? In figuring your deduction for medical expenses, did you fail to use the formula that limits the deduction to medical expenses exceeding 5 percent of your adjusted gross income? Did you deduct your Social Security taxes? (Better not; they're not deductible.) If you made any of these errors, or if you simply added the numbers wrong, the computer will recalculate your taxes. You'll be sent a notice telling you how much more (or less) you owe, or why your refund is different from what you claimed. If your numbers add up, and you didn't make any of the eighty-five common errors, your refund check will be mailed, assuming you claimed one.

Still, no one—and no machine—has scrutinized your return for tax evasion, fraud, or even to consider an audit. That comes next, and that process, too, is entirely impersonal.

Your return, just like all the other 96 million individual returns, is fed through computers, which give it a grade. On this test you want a low grade, because the higher your score, the more likely it is you'll be audited. But the computer doesn't know you. It only knows, for example, what taxpayers at various income levels typically deduct for charitable contributions, state and local taxes, interest, and so forth. If your deductions, exclusions, credits—whatever—are way out of the ordinary on the high side, you'll get a high grade, and your return may be audited.

So what? Audits aren't so bad.

Myth 2: It's better to pay more income tax than to risk an audit.

True, a tax audit isn't fun, but it isn't the modern version of the Spanish Inquisition, either. When your IRS auditor reaches into his or her briefcase, it's for a calculator, not a thumbscrew. He is there to measure the reality of the numbers on your tax return. He's not your enemy—he probably would make a fine neighbor—but he's not your ally, either. He wants more of your money. You want to keep your money. *In order to keep your money, you must keep good records.* The burden of proof is yours. If you can persuade the auditor that your tax return is accurate, he will give you a handshake, not a shakedown. Even among taxpayers who report more than $50,000 of income, more than a quarter come out of their audits unscathed. A few even come out ahead, with a refund.

Both of us have been audited in recent years—Strassels in person, Mead by mail—and neither of us bears permanent scars. Strassels paid nothing. Mead coughed up a couple of hundred bucks out of four-thousand-and-some that the IRS initially claimed. We'll tell you about our audit experiences in Chapter 18, in which we lay out detailed strategies for surviving an audit.

Myth 3: Our federal income tax is unfair, and the Form 1040 is my opportunity to express opposition.

Curiously, this myth infects people of various political persuasions. Certain conservatives consider the income tax unconstitutional and refuse to pay it. They tell one another that their constitutional stand protects them against prosecution. They're wrong. The IRS is sick to death of these illegal tax protesters and will go after one for as little as $25 in unpaid taxes. The courts back up the IRS. A growing number of tax protesters are being sentenced to prison.

Many liberals disapprove of tax "loopholes" designed to encourage investments of various kinds. They argue that only people with relatively high incomes can take advantage of these loopholes. Some people refuse to use these loopholes on moral grounds. That's the kind of protest the IRS likes: All contributions are gratefully accepted.

In planning and figuring your taxes, put politics and emotion aside. You're dealing with money—*your* money. Our political process gives you plenty of opportunities to express your views on the income tax and all its provisions. Write to your congressman. Join lobbying organizations that will press your views. But don't bat your head against the IRS; it's a stone wall. Besides, the IRS has nothing to do with the provisions in the Tax Code. Congress writes the tax laws, and the President signs them. The IRS is merely a collection agency.

Anyway, few of us would prefer the old English system, whereby the king's tax collector traveled from farm to farm, taking a cow from this household and a sheep from the next. For all its maddening flaws, inconsistencies, and complexities, our tax system is still based on voluntary self-assessment. If you refuse to participate, the IRS will figure your taxes for you and penalize you. You'll pay dearly, and your political gesture won't accomplish a thing. If you pay your taxes, but refuse to take advantage of Tax Savers that would reduce your tax bill, you are volunteering for more than your fair share.

If the U.S. Treasury is your idea of a charity, why not simply make a contribution? Some people do. We quote from *Your Federal Income Tax*, published by the IRS itself: "You can make a voluntary contribution to reduce the public debt. If you wish to do so, enclose a separate check in the envelope with your income tax return." We prefer the United Way, the Heart Fund, and the Cancer Society, but the choice is yours.

━━━━━

*Myth 4: With so many people taking
advantage of sleazy loopholes and shelters, a good
honest citizen like me can't be blamed for fudging
on my tax return.*

Not only can you be blamed; you can be prosecuted. It's one thing to avoid taxes by taking advantage of Tax Savers in the law. It's quite another to *evade* taxes by cheating. The difference between tax *avoidance* and tax *evasion* can be ten years and $10,000. We didn't make up that line, but we subscribe to it.

Besides, it isn't necessary. Each of us makes a pretty good income, and neither of us pays as much as 15 percent of it in federal income tax. You shouldn't either. And we stay legal.

*Myth 5: Due to bracket creep, I'm getting
close to the 50 percent tax bracket, so nearly half
my income is going to Uncle Sam.*

Nonsense. Almost no one pays half his income in federal income tax. Your "marginal" tax bracket may be 50 percent, but there's a big difference between your marginal bracket and your "real" tax bracket. Your marginal bracket is the rate you pay on your last dollar of taxable income. Your real bracket is the rate you pay on your gross income.

Let's say you're married and filing a joint 1984 tax return. You report income of $152,000 and claim four $1,000 personal exemptions, $20,350 in itemized deductions over the standard amount, $2,250 for your IRA, and $16,000 in various tax shelter deductions. Your taxable income totals $109,400. Congratulations! That's the threshold for the 49 percent bracket.

Your marginal bracket is 49 percent. But your taxes are $36,630—33 percent of your taxable income and only 24 percent of your gross income. And that doesn't even take into account any income you may have received from tax-exempt bonds, gifts, Social Security, the tax-free portion of long-term capital gains, and other sources of income that you don't have to mention on your tax return.

To find your real tax bracket, add up your gross income

and divide it into your tax bill. Then let's work together to cut it.

Myth 6: I don't make enough money to
invest in tax shelters. Besides, tax shelters are
shady.

If your income comes to, say, $25,000 or more, you should be sheltering some of it from the IRS. We'll lead you to the right shelters.

First, let's demystify the subject. If this book does nothing else for you, we hope it will take the mystery out of taxes, and tax shelters provide a good starting place.

Here are some tax shelters: Tell us how mysterious or shady it is to

1. Buy a house.
2. Save money in an IRA.
3. Shop on credit.
4. Buy life insurance.
5. Save for your children's education.

If they are handled properly, all those steps save on taxes by sheltering part of your income from the tax bite. By definition, that makes them tax shelters. But when Americans use the term "tax shelter," they tend to think of certain investments that generate large deductions and credits in relation to the amount they invest. The most common are partnerships involved in real estate development or drilling for oil and gas.

Shelters of that kind may or may not be right for you. But tax shelters of some kind will help you—for example, the ones we listed above, starting with the purchase of a house. We deliberately use the term "Tax Saver" because we think it's less scary and mysterious than "tax shelter." But for now let's talk about the investments that are commonly referred to as tax shelters.

Every tax-shelter loophole was deliberately written into the law by Congress to serve a national purpose. Most of them have been in the law for decades. In recent years, Congress has extended the tax-shelter awning still further—so much further, in fact, that in the 1984 tax bill, Congress reversed itself and enacted provisions that will curb some of the more flagrant tax-shelter abuses. Politically, some tax shelters are still controversial. But as long as they are in the law, there is nothing unsavory or shady about using them. After all, William French Smith, President Reagan's attorney general, invested in oil and gas tax shelters. What about investing in refrigerated railroad rolling stock? The IRS commissioner, Roscoe Egger, reportedly basked in that particular shelter.

The best tax shelters make good investments, too. The Reagan tax cuts have been criticized for catering to the very rich, but in fact they brought certain tax shelters within reach of many more Americans. For example, you can shelter income—and save on taxes—by buying a small share of a housing project or a shopping center. If chosen wisely, those can be good investments. But they're hard to analyze. We'll show you how to find better shelters, closer to home.

Don't expect miracles, and don't buy trouble. Tax shelters often are sold with high-pressure tactics. Some salesmen make exorbitant claims—for example, that for every dollar you invest, you get six dollars in tax deductions. If a claim sounds too good to be true, it probably is. The IRS clamps down hard on "abusive" tax shelters—that's what the government calls them. But even the IRS assumes that any tax shelter is okay if you claim no more than two dollars in deductions for every dollar you invest.

Is there a master key to tax shelters? You bet. Any tax shelter should fit your goals, your temperament, and your financial situation, and it should be easy for you to understand. You forge that key, and we'll lead you to tax shelters it will fit.

Myth 7: The bigger my refund, the more I've saved on taxes.

The best tax refund is no tax refund. People can't seem to get that through their heads. We know a man named Joe who proudly claims that he pays no income tax. Last year, he got a refund of $2,000.

In fact, this guy had $17,000 withheld from his pay. His tax bill was $15,000, so he got $2,000 back. Joe not only paid a hefty tax; he also lent the government money, interest-free.

But most Americans are like Joe. Three quarters of American taxpayers get refunds, and the refunds average more than $800. That's wasteful. If you want to lend the government money, buy a U.S. bond or Treasury bill and collect interest. But don't plan your taxes so that you'll be entitled to a refund. Reduce the amount that's being withheld from your paycheck—your employer will give you a Form W-4 to fill out. Or if you pay quarterly estimated taxes, pay less, so you and the IRS break even at the end of the year.

Myth 8: I realize now that I overpaid my income taxes last year and the year before, but there's no use crying over spilled milk.

You can file amended returns as far back as three years, and doing so will not arouse the IRS's suspicions or increase your risk of audit. If you have money coming, you'll get it.

For example, let's say you had one big year of income, sandwiched among years of much lower income. You can file an amended return and take advantage of Income Averaging—a provision that lets you average your income over a period of years.

Taxpayers often overlook Tax Savers like that, and the IRS isn't about to tell us about them. For example, in 1982 working couples got a brand-new tax deduction. They could deduct 5 percent of the earnings of the secondary wage earner from their joint income. The IRS determined that 15 percent of couples eligible for the deduction failed to take advantage of it. Did the agency write to them? No. It did issue a press release, but you probably didn't see it, and neither did the thousands of couples who could have filed amended returns to cash in on the new Tax Saver.

Filing an amended return does not increase your risk of being audited, nor will filing for an automatic four-month extension of the April 15 deadline. To the IRS, those procedures are routine; nothing suspicious about them.

███████████

*Myth 9: The IRS knows more about my
income and deductions than I do.*

About your income, it knows a great deal. About your deductions, it knows little or nothing.

The IRS is overwhelmed with data. Every employer tells the IRS how much it paid each employee and how much it withheld. Every corporation reports dividends and interest paid to stockholders and bondholders, respectively, and every bank, savings institution, and credit union reports interest payments to the IRS, person by person. If your savings account earned interest of say, $14.72 last year, the IRS was told about it. States now tell the IRS about tax refunds they send out. To help the IRS keep track of capital gains, brokers now have to report all securities sales. Even barter exchanges file similar reports.

Does the IRS really match all that data against the income you report on your tax form? That depends largely on whether you get your income from big companies or little companies. Larger firms report to the IRS by computer. That makes it easy for the IRS; it just runs the data through its own computer. Every bit of that material is matched against income reported on individual tax forms.

But smaller companies report to the IRS on paper. The IRS matches less than half of that data against taxpayers' returns.

You might expect the IRS to exercise the same care in tracking your deductions. For example, it could get cities and counties to report how much people paid in real estate taxes. It could get tax preparers to report their fees. It could get hospitals, doctors, and dentists to report their fees.

But why should it? Put yourself in the shoes of the IRS commissioner. It's his job to collect taxes, so he's darned sure going to find out as much as he can about the income of every American. But it's not his job to trim your tax bill. If you don't claim your deductions, he doesn't mind. That's your job, not his. So you'd better keep track of your own deductible expenses.

The IRS cares about your deductions—as we said before, if you're challenged, it's up to you to prove them—but it cares more about your income. The agency figures that of every dollar it should collect but doesn't, 85 cents is from income that taxpayers hid from Uncle Sam. Only 15 cents is lost because of phony or inflated deductions, exclusions, and the like.

*Myth 10: In a dispute, the IRS fights fair,
and a determined taxpayer can win.*

The IRS has extraordinary powers. It can muscle you to the ground. It can attach your wages, seize your house, and sell your investments. The IRS doesn't have to prove that you're wrong. You have to prove that you're right.

If you are determined to fight the IRS, remember that you have to fight by the agency's rules. You can demand an interview with an auditor. You can appeal to the Federal District Court or the U.S. Tax Court, and if you lose there, you can appeal to a Federal Appeals Court. But don't forget, the IRS is impersonal. If you let your emotions overcome your better judgment, you're cutting off your nose to spite your face.

In other words, if you fight the IRS out of anger, you'll probably get beat up.

But if logic and the law appear to be on your side, by all means take a tough stand. Congress writes the tax laws, but the IRS interprets them, and all too often the agency over-reaches. For example, a few years ago the IRS arbitrarily and unilaterally ruled that you couldn't deduct the costs of an office in your home unless you used it for your primary business. Lots of people moonlight at home in addition to their regular 9 to 5 jobs; the IRS told them they could no longer deduct home-office costs.

But the law didn't really say that. Lots of taxpayers complained, and Congress started considering an amendment to clarify the issue. The IRS suggested that until Congress made up its mind, moonlighters should skip the home-office deduction. If Congress finally voted to allow the deduction for moonlighters, they could file amended tax returns.

The catch: The clarification took some time to wend its

way through Congress, and you can't amend a return that's more than three years old. So taxpayers who took the IRS's advice lost out on one or more years of a perfectly legitimate Tax Saver. Instead of heeding the IRS's self-serving advice, they should have claimed the home-office deduction. The IRS could deny it, but the eventual decision by Congress would resolve the issue in the taxpayer's favor— and give him the money to show for it.

We believe in that kind of reasonably aggressive tax strategy. Don't be a kamikaze taxpayer. Don't fight for the sake of a fight. But do aggressively pursue what's coming to you in the way of Tax Savers.

THE STRATEGY

With the mythology laid aside, let's figure out how you can reduce your tax bill. Tax planning is like career planning and investment planning—in fact, all three should be woven together, as part of an overall personal plan. Tax strategies differ greatly according to whether you are single or married, young or old, bold or conservative. Some people enjoy spending time on their finances, while others prefer a system that requires little time. Your approach to taxes should reflect your investment preferences, too. All these personal differences can be accommodated in a prudent money-saving approach to income taxes.

We'll show you how to key your benefits to your situation today, while planning for tomorrow. That's why we organized this book the way we did. Find yourself in our chapter headings in Part Two. Read those chapters, and then read the chapters that are likely to fit your situation a year or five years from now. Plan your strategies so that your tax savings will evolve with the changes in your life. Tax Savers are like a huge smorgasbord—more than any taxpayer can digest all at once. We've filled a plate for every stage of your life. Enjoy them, one by one.

2

Record Keeping Made Easy

*I*n North Carolina, the IRS denied a taxpayer $90,000 in deductions and credits spread over a three-year period because he lacked the records to prove his claims. The records had burned in a fire that had destroyed his house, but the IRS was not impressed. The tax agency stood firm, demanding its taxes. The taxpayer went to court, but the U.S. Tax Court ruled in the IRS's favor, on grounds that it is the taxpayer's obligation to prove his claimed deductions and credits, no matter what the circumstances are.

In Oregon, a woman's act of anger against her husband returned to haunt them both. In a quarrel that eventually led to divorce, she destroyed all her husband's meticulously maintained records. Two years later their joint income tax return was audited, and all their deductions and credits were denied for lack of verification. Both complained—he that his wife had destroyed the records and then divorced him; she that the income had been his, and they were no longer married—but neither was successful. The IRS held them jointly responsible for the unpaid tax because both of them had signed the joint tax return, and neither could produce the records to prove the case.

These cases are extreme, but they serve to illustrate the

importance of backing up your Tax Savers with persuasive evidence. The most serious and widespread misconception among taxpayers is the assumption that the IRS has to prove you wrong. Too often, we've heard comments like, "How can the IRS prove that we weren't on a real business trip?" Or as a big spender picks up a check after an expensive lunch with friends, "Let the bureaucrats try to prove that you aren't my customers!"

The IRS does not have to prove a thing. That's your responsibility. Unless you can persuade the tax collector that what you claim on your return is truthful, you lose. If the IRS goes after you for additional tax, it is instituting a civil proceeding. The burden rests on you to demonstrate that everything on your tax return is accurate.

Only if the IRS accuses you of a criminal tax violation does it have to prove its case. Most criminal tax cases have to do with intentional and willful failure to report income. That's criminal fraud, tax evasion, the stuff you go to jail for. For honest taxpayers—even those of us who shelter a great deal of our income from taxes with the use of effective Tax Savers—the risk is not criminal action on the part of the IRS but rather an audit at which we would have to persuade the IRS that every Tax Saver on our return was correct.

A PAPER TRAIL

There is just one way to do that: Keep records. Record keeping has always been important, and in 1984 Congress made it even more so by adding stiff provisions penalizing taxpayers whose records fall short. Beginning in 1985, if you deduct business expenses for travel, entertainment, or use of equipment such as a car or a home computer, you will have to certify that you have records that substantiate those expenses. If you are audited and are found to lack those records, you are liable for a heavy negligence penalty.

If you prepare your own tax return, you'll have to check a box on the form certifying that you have the proper records. If you fail to check the box, the IRS won't allow those business deductions. If you have your tax return prepared by an accountant or some other professional, he'll give you a form that you must sign, certifying that the records are on hand. Once again, no certification, no business deductions.

Record keeping is not really difficult. Your system need not be elaborate or even particularly well organized. You need not spend much time on it. But you must do it regularly. If you do, you can beat the system, because the IRS relies on the fact that few taxpayers keep enough records to verify everything claimed on their tax returns. If you have been audited, you probably have suffered through the unpleasant experience of having to pay more tax because your records weren't good enough. You knew that a certain deduction or credit was honest and accurate, but because you couldn't prove it, you had to pay.

In fact, "prove" is too strong a word for the records you need to support most of your claimed Tax Savers. Take a typical overnight business trip. You spend $20 on a taxi to the airport, 50 cents for a newspaper to read on the airplane, $1.50 to tip a redcap, $15 for a taxi to your hotel, $2 for a shoeshine, and $1.50 for a glass of orange juice and a cup of coffee. It's not yet noon, and you've laid out $40.50, none of it for the kind of expense that usually produces a receipt. If you wait until you get home, you won't remember those expenses; besides, the IRS will disallow them if it thinks you reconstructed them later.

So how do you protect yourself? You simply keep a pocket diary and jot down the expenses as you incur them. That's not "proof," but it's persuasive evidence. Most of us keep the big, obvious receipts—for example, copies of airplane tickets and hotel bills. You should, because the rule is that you need a receipt for anything costing $25 or more. For anything less, a note in your pocket diary is perfectly acceptable.

To be sure, your pocket diary has to be believable. Don't take a business trip to Sioux Falls and jot down that you spent $100 for dinner alone (although that might be believable if you were visiting New York and your income and life-style were tailored to expensive meals). If your income is $40,000 a year, don't try to deduct the cost of a trip to Hawaii to consult with an investment adviser, although that might be perfectly fine if your income was in the $400,000 range. Don't forget: The purpose of your records is to persuade the IRS.

Many people fail to keep the right records because they don't know what they will eventually need. These are people who have not taken charge of their tax situations. They are passive taxpayers. Passive taxpayers pay more tax than they have to. We advocate that you plan your taxes, picking Tax Savers that fit your situation and your stage and station in life. As you do so, you'll know what records you need. It's simple: You need records to support every Tax Saver you plan to claim on your return.

Keeping records may sound time-consuming, but as you plan your Tax Savers and work with them, you will learn not only what you need to keep but also what you can throw away. For example, state and local sales taxes are deductible as an itemized deduction on Schedule A, so many taxpayers keep every store receipt they get during the year. Frankly, it is very rarely worth the time and effort. If you use the sales tax table that's in the instructions of your annual tax package to calculate your deduction, you'll come out ahead in almost every case. As you become familiar with Tax Savers, you'll know that you need keep a record of only the sales tax you paid on a car or truck, not on day-to-day purchases.

Another example: The deduction for medical expenses is no longer the Tax Saver it once was because you can now deduct only those medical expenses that exceed 5 percent of your adjusted gross income, after taking insurance reimbursements into account. Nevertheless, many taxpayers still keep track of every dollar they spend on doctor bills, prescriptions, and the like. We do, too, until late in the year. Once we're sure we're not going to reach that 5 percent threshold, we stop keeping receipts.

Many records having to do with Tax Savers come to you in the mail, without your asking. Mortgage statements, credit card statements, and car payment booklets show the amounts of interest you paid. Bank statements and canceled checks note the precise amounts of many expenditures. Oftentimes you get several documents supporting the same item. For example, let's say you write a check for $2,000 to a mutual fund for your annual IRA contribution. You'll get the canceled check, a confirmation from the mutual fund, and regular statements from the fund as well. Keep everything. If you're ever audited, you may need it. There's no sense in gambling when you don't have to; it's easy enough to stick those pieces of paper in your file.

That's particularly true when traveling on business. If you fail to keep track of your meal expenses, the IRS allows you to deduct $14 a day for meals—not nearly so much as you probably spend but nevertheless an amount that you don't have to prove. But here's the rub: If for a single day you fail to keep track and instead elect to use that $14 daily allowance, you're limited to $14 a day for meal expenses every day of the year you were away from home on business. Frankly, that is a rotten deal, and that's precisely why financially sophisticated business travelers are not a bit shy about pulling out their pocket diaries and jotting down expenses as they incur them, even while their guests are still sitting at the dinner table. While a monthly credit card statement will list the date, place, and amount of the meal, that's not enough; the IRS will insist on knowing who was being entertained and why, and you must record that information the day of the event or shortly thereafter.

Anyone can lose a receipt, so it is helpful to build a trail of paper. Take the case of a New Jersey businessman who entertained five customers at an expensive restaurant in New York and misplaced his receipt. He kept his receipts for driving through the Lincoln Tunnel and for parking at a garage near the restaurant. His pocket diary listed the customers by name, and he was smart enough to write down the amount of the tab. His office calendar listed the luncheon engagement. And the expense was in line with his normal business practices. The IRS allowed the deduction, taking his word for the amount. Once again, it's not hard to cram those slips of paper into a file. You'll probably never need them, but if you do, you'll be well paid for having kept them.

THE BEST SYSTEM

The best record-keeping system is whatever system comes naturally to you. Toss everything in a shoebox if you like. We keep ours in file folders—one for work-related expenses, one covering IRA and Keogh contributions, another for investments, yet another for miscellaneous expenses that are deductible or that otherwise fit our Tax Savers. Of course, we have one set aside for income items. Whatever system you use for keeping records and receipts, you should maintain a day-by-day calendar. Every taxpayer needs that. Make your system as simple as possible, but it should be comprehensive enough to take care of all your financial activities.

Set up permanent files to store information about your house, and another for investments and gifts you receive. That's because if you sell them, you have to prove what you paid for them, or what a gift was worth when you received it, even if those events took place decades before.

When you buy securities, your broker sends you a transaction slip stating the price. When you sell that stock, you'll get another transaction slip. Staple the two together. That is your record. Keep it in an Investment file.

When you buy a house, you'll get a settlement sheet and contract stating the price and closing costs. Keep them, and as the years go by, put a note or a receipt in your House file every time you spend money to improve your home. In a typical year, you might spend hundreds of dollars on storm windows, shrubs, a burglar alarm system. Anything that improves your home adds to your "Basis"—the amount you paid for the house, plus adjustments. If you keep your home for five or ten or fifteen years, these expenses can amount to a good deal of money even if you don't undertake any major improvement such as an additional room, central air conditioning, or a swimming pool.

These days it's not unusual to sell a house for several times what you paid for it years ago. If you don't buy a more expensive home, 40 percent of your profit is taxable. But you can reduce that potential tax by adding in the thousands of dollars you spent over the years on capital improvements. (Repairs and regular maintenance do not count.)

While House, Investment, and similar files are permanent, you need to keep most tax records only three years from the due date of the return they apply to—that is, receipts used in computing your 1982 tax should be saved until April 1986. Under the law, the IRS cannot audit a return that is more than three years old, except in extremely unusual circumstances: In the case of fraud, the IRS can go back six years; if you failed to file a tax return, the IRS can reach back as far as it wants.

After three years, you can throw away most of your records. Keep a copy of your tax return; you may need it for Income Averaging, one of the best Tax Savers. Keep your copies of W-2 and 1099 forms, which show income, and keep canceled checks for tax payments made to the federal, state, and local governments. You can pitch the rest, although many taxpayers find it easier simply to keep the whole thing and store it away, hoping they will never, ever need to dig it out.

Chances are you won't, since the IRS audits less than 1.5 percent of all individual tax returns filed. But when you do need tax records, you need them badly. It's not an exaggeration to say that Tax Savers become a gamble if you fail to back them up with proper records. With those records, Tax Savers are money in the bank.

3

Our Four-Looks-a-Year Tax Savers Plan

*T*ax Savers have to be planned, and they have to be nourished and pruned to fit your financial situation. You might liken Tax Savers to crops. You plant them early in the year, tend them as the year progresses, and reap their benefits when you file your income tax return.

No one wants or even needs to think about taxes every day. We recommend that you take good, long looks at your Tax Savers four times during the year. At the same time, go over your income prospects, your investments, and other parts of your finances. If you tend your Tax Savers properly, you can't help but review these other important items at the same time, because Tax Savers are related to them.

In this short chapter we'll describe the steps you should take at each of these four annual sessions, and we'll mention some of the Tax Savers you can use with the help of this advance planning. You'll find each of these Tax Savers described in detail in Part Two.

PRELIMINARIES

The preliminaries start in January. Mark key tax dates on your calendar. Pick a couple of days—perhaps a weekend—

to prepare your tax return for last year, and reserve that time. Make it early in the year—perhaps early February. By then you should have your W-2 forms and other reports of your income and expenses. Mark the dates for filing your quarterly estimated tax payments. And mark dates, at least approximately, for your four tax reviews of the year. Think of them as days devoted to saving you money. If you use them properly, they'll pay you handsomely.

FIRST LOOK

The date is, say, February 10, and you are preparing last year's income tax return. This is also your first tax-planning session for the new year. Everything is before you—your previous year's salary, your other income, the Tax Savers you used, your tax bill. You may be frustrated, even angry at yourself, about failing to take advantage of certain Tax Savers. On the other hand, you may be pleased with the effects of the Tax Savers that you used for the first time.

Translate this knowledge into plans for the new year. Get a copy of the current year's tax tables, which list the income tax rates. They're published way in advance, and any tax professional will have them. Mock up a tax return for the current year, using your best estimates of your salary and other income, your expenses, your Tax Savers.

The mocked-up tax return will show you if withholding from your salary will be sufficient to cover your tax bill. If you are being overwithheld by a substantial amount, you should have the amount adjusted downward. If you owe a lot, have more taken out each payday.

Don't gear your estimates for the current year too closely to the numbers from last year. For example, you may have deducted job-related moving expenses last year. Chances are you won't have the same expenses this year, too. Or you might have an adjustable-rate home mortgage. Last year, the interest rate was a low 10½ percent. Then in December you were notified that it was being boosted to 12½ percent. If so, your home mortgage interest deduction will be larger this year. Take that into account in your estimates.

Now look for new Tax Savers that fit into your financial situation and figure them into your plans for the year.

Consider law changes that will affect this year's tax return. You'll have to do this later, too, but at this first session, consider the time bombs that are ticking away in the Tax Code. Congress often passes laws that go into effect years later. For example, beginning in 1985 an inflation formula takes hold. Based on the Consumer Price Index, increases in three important items will take place automatically every year—tax brackets; the personal exemption, which has stood at $1,000 for several years; and the so-called zero bracket amounts, which form the threshold for deciding whether it is worthwhile to itemize deductions. That change was enacted in 1981, effective January 1, 1985. The 1984 Tax Reform Act contains some provisions that are retroactive, some that take effect in 1985, and others that click into place in later years.

Usually the IRS, in its annual Publication 17, *Your Federal Income Tax*, provides a rundown of changes that affect the past year and the current year. This helpful publication is available free from the IRS.

Investments affect your taxes in several ways, and the early months of the year are the best time to review them. If you want to cash in the profit you've made on a stock, a piece of land, or some other investment, early in the year is a good time. That way you get the benefit of the profit all year, and you don't have to pay income tax on it until the following year.

Make sure you've owned the property long enough so that your profit counts as a long-term capital gain. On long-term capital gains, only 40 percent of the profit is subject to income tax; the other 60 percent is tax-free. In 1984, Congress sweetened this Tax Saver by cutting the "long-term" period in half. The rule now works like this: If you acquired the asset before June 23, 1984, you have to own it more than one year before selling; otherwise your gain won't count as long-term. But if you acquire an asset after June 22, 1984, you need own it only six months before selling. In other words, the definition of "long-term" was changed from one year to six months.

If you have not already done so, make last year's contribution to your Individual Retirement Account. You can make the contribution as late as April 15. The earlier you make your tax-deductible contribution, the more it will earn in dividends or interest on a tax-deferred basis.

In fact, if you can afford it, make your IRA contributions for the new year, too. If you can't afford to contribute the entire $2,000 now, contribute as much as you can—even just $50 or $100—and chip away at the rest of the contribution as quickly as you can. Many people think they have to wait until they have the full $2,000 in hand, but that's not so; the contribution can be made gradually. If you are self-employed (part-time or full-time), make your contributions now to your Keogh retirement account, too, for the past year and the current year.

If tax shelter investments are appropriate, plan them now and buy them if you have the money available. Early in the year, good tax shelters are plentiful. By late in the year, the best ones often have been snapped up.

Even if you're pleased with all your investments, you may want to switch some around to take advantage of Tax Savers. Let's say you own shares in four mutual funds. Two of them pay almost nothing in dividends but are designed to produce long-term capital gains. The third is a fund owning municipal bonds, which produce tax-free income. The fourth is a stock fund with a nice dividend yield. If any of those four is in your IRA or Keogh account, it should be the fourth one. The funds that produce capital gains don't need the tax-saving protection of an IRA or Keogh account; neither does the fund owning tax-exempt municipal bonds. But the fund yielding dividends does need that protection. As you plan your taxes for the new year, shape your investments into Tax Savers.

SECOND LOOK

Schedule this one about the time school lets out. This is an easy one. Make sure your Tax Savers are in place and working. Plan new ones and get them started. Review your income prospects for the year and revise your mocked-up tax return if any changes look significant. Organize your receipts and other tax records if you haven't already done so. Bring your calendar up to date, making sure you've noted deductible expenses: mileage for driving to the doctor or for a charity; money spent on child care so that both you and your spouse can work; the cost of storm windows. (For driving to the doctor, you can deduct 9 cents a mile. For charitable driving, the deduction increases in 1985 from 9 to 12 cents a mile.)

Two Tax Savers that should be carefully planned during this tax review are combining a business trip with a personal vacation and summer entertainment.

Review the rules on what is deductible on business trips, meetings, and conventions, the records and receipts you'll need to keep, and how to tack on personal vacations. (You'll find those rules in Chapters 8 and 9.) It is quite easy to deduct the lion's share of the tab when you combine business with pleasure; all you have to do is plan ahead and keep meticulous records.

The cost of summer entertainment is deductible when you get together with business associates and clients. Although this is true all year long, it is primarily during the summer months when people get together for a backyard cookout, attend sporting events, and the like.

THIRD LOOK

Labor Day is gone, the children are back in school, and the end of the year is only four months away. Now is the time to start planning year-end Tax Savers. Get advance copies of tax forms for the current year from a tax professional. The forms become available to professionals in about August, although they aren't mailed to taxpayers until December. Make sure you're using the current year's tax tables. It doesn't make sense to plan for the current year with last year's rates and forms.

If you took some capital gains early in the year, look now for losses to offset them. For example, let's say you sold stock in February and made a capital gain of $5,000. Forty percent of that—$2,000—is taxable. But maybe you own other stocks or bonds that are worth $5,000 less than you paid for them. If you sell them, you can use the $5,000 loss to offset your $5,000 gain. Furthermore, you can take the proceeds from that sale and reinvest them. For example, let's say that in order to get the $5,000 loss, you sell bonds issued by your home state. You can reinvest the money in other municipal bonds—even other issues of your home state. That's called a bond swap. Sophisticated investors do it routinely.

On the other hand, let's say that during the year you sold some stock at a loss. So, for example, if you own some stock that's gained handsomely in value and you've hesitated to sell it for fear of paying a substantial capital gains tax, this may be the time; you can offset the potential gain against the capital loss that is already on your books for this year. (For more year-end Tax Savers having to do with investments, see Part Two, Chapter 12, Tax Savers for Investors.)

Again, check your mocked-up tax return. Revise it to bring in the financial events that have occurred so far this year and the year-end Tax Savers you've planned.

FOURTH LOOK

We like to schedule this one the weekend after Thanksgiving. You have one month to put your final Tax Savers in place—not just to plan them, but to act on them. That's not too much time. Year-end Tax Savers may save you several hundred dollars or even several thousand, but most of them require more than a stroke of the pen.

If you use a tax professional, this is a good time to talk to him or her and make sure you've done everything you can to reduce your taxes. Bring yourself up to date on any changes in the tax laws, rulings, or regulations that might affect your finances. Tell your tax professional when you'll have your tax work sheets ready and ask him to put you on his schedule for that time.

Most of us benefit by deflecting income from the current year into the next year and at the same time accelerating deductible expenses. That way we reduce our taxable income from two directions—less total income, more deductions. But you have to think about the following year, too. So we recommend that your year-end tax planning include two years in tandem—the current year and the year to follow. To the extent that you can, move income and deductions into the year that will save you the most money on your taxes.

If your income and expenses run about the same every year, you'll be better off deflecting the current year's income and advancing deductible expenses by as much as you honestly can. By doing so, you postpone paying a portion of your tax bill by a full year. In the meantime, that money can be earning interest.

The saving will be even greater if your income for the current year will be higher than your income for the following year. By deflecting income and accelerating deductions, you may drop yourself into a lower bracket this year. But if next year's income looks as if it will be a lot higher than this year's, think twice. You don't want to take steps that might push you into a substantially higher bracket. If next year's income is likely to be a lot higher, you might be wise to reverse the usual year-end process. Instead of deflecting income, accelerate it; instead of accelerating deductions, postpone them.

The difference between this year and next is only a single day on the calendar, but it has the effect of 365 days. If you want to deflect income to the following year, all you have to do is take steps that will legitimately bring you payments in January that might otherwise arrive in December. You can't ask your boss to put your paycheck in his desk until January 2; that's artificial, and it won't wash. But if you sell goods or perform services, you can send your bills out late enough to make sure no one pays until January. If you are ready to cash in a profit on stocks or real estate, you can wait until early January before selling.

To accelerate deductions, pay deductible bills before year-end. Make charitable donations in December. If you make estimated income tax payments to your state, make the final payment in December instead of waiting until January; state income taxes are deductible the year you pay them. If you have a loan on your life insurance policy, pay the interest. Most life insurers will let you add the interest to the amount of your loan, but if you do that, the interest is not deductible.

If you operate a business, full-time or part-time, you should plan your purchases for late in the year. For example, let's say you plan to buy a car for business use. The year you buy it, you can write off the first $5,000 of the cost and claim a depreciation deduction on the remainder. In addition, you may qualify for an investment tax credit. These are lucrative Tax Savers, and you get them in full even if you borrow the money and don't make the purchase until December 31.

If your deductible expenses put you on the borderline between itemizing and using the standard deduction, try to pile deductible payments into either the current year or the following year. That way you'll get the benefit of itemizing one year; the other year, when your deductible expenses are low, you'll get the benefit of the standard deduction—for 1984, that was $3,400 for married couples filing jointly, $2,300 for singles, $1,700 for married people filing separately.

Will your federal withholding and quarterly estimated tax payments cover your tax bill? If it looks as if they'll fall substantially short, plan to make your fourth and final quarterly payment large enough to cover the difference, with a little to spare. That's the payment you make on January 15 of the new year.

Make sure you have carried out all the tax-saving plans that you made during the year. Then sit back and prepare to harvest your Tax Savers when you prepare your return next February.

4

The
Tax Calendar

H ere's a list of important dates for tax action. The IRS used to be lenient about deadlines, looking the other way if you were a couple of days late, but it isn't any longer. As the tax agency has added more sophisticated computers, it has adopted a strict practice of imposing penalties for tardiness of even a single day. At the very least, missing a deadline can be a nuisance. At the most it can be expensive, because penalties are imposed by the month *or any part thereof,* and interest is compounded daily. So if you're one day late, you can get socked with a full month's worth of penalty plus interest.

Don't play chicken with tax deadlines; it's simply not worth the risk. When a payment or a form is due on the fifteenth, mail it on the twelfth or thirteenth. Give yourself a cushion of a few days.

Sometimes circumstances do push you right up to the deadline. When you're mailing something to the IRS, the postmark on your envelope is the only date that counts. The IRS honors only postmarks from the U.S. Postal Service, so don't rely on a private carrier. Use stamps; the IRS is leery of metered envelopes because it knows that postage meters can be backdated. Take your envelope to the post office window and ask the clerk to hand-cancel it neatly so that the date on the canceling stamp is legible.

For some kinds of taxes—Social Security taxes for household help, for instance—the IRS may send you coupons and instruct you to make the payments at a federal depository bank of your choice. When you pay your taxes at a bank, the IRS pays attention only to the date stamped on the coupon by the bank when it receives the payment. Most banks have a cutoff time—typically noon or 2:00 P.M. If you bring in your payment after that time, it will be stamped with the date of the next business day. So ask about the cutoff time and bring in your payment early enough to beat it.

The IRS cashes checks promptly, so make sure yours is covered. If your check bounces, the IRS will slap you with one penalty for late payment and another for paying with a bad check. Many of us tend to stuff funds into our account just before making a tax payment. That's risky, because many financial institutions won't honor a check drawn on funds that have been on deposit less than a week or two or sometimes even three. Once again, the best strategy is to plan ahead.

There is one way in which time is on the taxpayer's side: When any deadline falls on a Saturday, Sunday, or legal holiday, you get until the next business day. Even a state holiday counts.

January 2

If you can afford it, make your IRA contribution for the current year now, or as soon as you can. If you earn income from self-employment, full-time or part-time, get started on your Keogh contribution, too. The sooner you invest the money, the more it will earn, with income tax deferred.

January 15

This is the deadline for the fourth and final payment on your estimated income tax for the prior year. You can skip this payment if you file your income tax return by January 31 and pay any tax due.

███████

January 31

If you paid a maid, baby-sitter, or other household employee $50 or more during the three months that ended December 31, you have to make your quarterly Social Security tax payment by today, with Form 942, Employer's Quarterly Tax Return for Household Employees.

February 1

You should have your W-2 by now; yesterday was the deadline for your employer to provide it. (If mailed, it may take a few more days.) If you moved during the past year and your employer paid your expenses, he's supposed to give you a breakdown of those payments by today. If you paid some of your moving expenses out of pocket, that portion is deductible.

Watch the mail this week for 1099 forms reporting last year's dividends, interest, and other kinds of nonemployee income, including rents, royalties, commissions, fees, and prizes. The deadline for mailing those forms to you was January 31.

February 10

Have the first of your four tax-planning sessions for the year. The details are in Chapter 3.

April 15

This is the most familiar deadline of all and the loosest. Your income tax return is due today, unless you are out of the country. You can get an automatic four-month extension by filing Form 4868 by midnight tonight, with payment of the tax you think you'll owe for the past year.

The first of four estimated income tax payments is due today. Use Form 1040-ES. Sorry, no extension is possible.

If you haven't already made your IRA contribution for last year, do it now; this is the deadline. You used to get until August 15 to make your IRA contribution, but no longer.

―――――

April 30
Another quarterly deadline for Form 942, with Social Security tax for household employees.

June 15
Pay the second quarterly installment of your estimated income tax. If you were out of the country April 15 and didn't file your income tax return for last year, this is the deadline; your two-month grace period is up.

You also should sit down about now for your second tax planning session of the year.

July 31
Another quarterly payment of Social Security tax for household help.

August 15
If you took an automatic four-month extension of the deadline for filing last year's income tax return, time's up. File it today. Include a copy of the Form 4868 you filed to get the extension.

September 15
Another quarterly installment of estimated income tax. Start working out year-end Tax Savers as part of your third tax planning session.

October 31
Quarterly payment of Social Security tax for household help.

Thanksgiving weekend
Now's the time for your fourth and final tax planning session. Start implementing year-end Tax Savers.

December 31

To crowd tax deductions into this year, pay the final installment of your state estimated income tax. Make charitable
contributions, too, and pay any bills for deductible expenses. Establish your Keogh retirement plan, although
generally you can make your Keogh contribution as late as
the day you file your tax return.

Part Two

_____

TAX SAVERS FOR EVERYONE

5

Tax Savers for Singles

*W*hen it comes to income tax, single Americans often find themselves in unfriendly territory. They are taxed at very high rates when compared to their married counterparts of equal income, and at the same time they are roundly ignored by most tax advisers. All too often, tax professionals deal only with families—husband, wife, two kids, and a mortgage.

The fact is that many singles have unique opportunities to take advantage of Tax Savers that are beyond the reach of married couples.

Tax Savers pay off best when your tax bracket is high, your responsibilities low, and your income large enough to allow you some choices. Singles, more often than married couples with families to support, qualify strongly on all three counts. Unfortunately, too few single Americans have learned how to weave these characteristics of their lives into the fabric of Tax Savers. They should. Actually, it's relatively easy to combine Tax Savers with the kind of life-style that appeals to so many single Americans.

Singles need Tax Savers almost desperately, because the law requires them to pay income tax at such high rates. The highest marginal tax rate for individuals—married or single—is 50 percent. Married couples filing a joint return do not hit that dreaded 50 percent bracket until their combined taxable income reaches $162,400, according to 1984 tax rates. If you are single, you start paying 50 percent in taxes when your taxable income exceeds $81,800.

The discrimination against singles works down to every income level. Marrieds hit the 42 percent tax bracket on $60,000 of taxable income, singles on $41,500.

Let's say your taxable income is $40,000. If you are single, you are in the 38 percent bracket, and your federal income tax will total $9,749, based on 1984 tax rates. Marrieds with the same income are in the 33 percent bracket with tax of $7,858. In other words, on the same income, you're paying 24 percent more tax than your married colleague.

On the other hand, your responsibilities are fewer. You probably have no one to support but yourself—certainly not a wife or a husband and children. You do not need to buy large amounts of life insurance or save toward college for children. You can take calculated risks without fearing that a loved one might be financially harmed if an investment or career change fails to work out. The risks are yours alone. You can move and change jobs more readily than a married person. Your time is your own, too.

And with only yourself to support, you have more discretionary income.

Many single people tend to let this advantage dribble away. Certainly this is not the case for all singles, but it is true for too many of them. The common perception is that budgeting, homeownership, retirement planning, and investing are for married couples, that singles needn't worry about such mundane things.

As a result, they often fail to plan their money dealings. They keep slipshod records, pay higher taxes, and complain that they can't seem to get ahead financially.

But they can—you can. Tax Savers will help you do it, and at the same time they will prod you into establishing a prudent investment program—without compromising your life-style.

Start by reviewing tax Form 1040, the long form. Millions of single Americans with good incomes use one of the two short forms, 1040A or 1040EZ. Perhaps because they are single, they automatically (and incorrectly) assume that they lack the necessary deductions, credits, and so forth that go with the long form. In fact, you never—absolutely *never*—save money by using either of the short forms. Once you look over the long form, you will be surprised at the number of Tax Savers that you can exploit as a single person, whether or not you itemize your deductions on Schedule A.

You can claim a political contributions credit as well as residential energy credits (even if you rent). Income Averaging on Schedule G is available if you file the long form, and so is the deduction for unreimbursed employee business expenses.

UNDERPAYMENT PENALTY

A special concern for singles is the stiff penalty assessed for underpayment of estimated taxes. This nondeductible tax penalty comes into play whenever a taxpayer—married or single—owes taxes at year-end. Those who get refunds don't have to worry.

If you owe the IRS more than $400 on your 1984 tax return, or more than $500 for 1985 or thereafter, you will automatically be subjected to this penalty—unless you take the time to fill out and attach Form 2210 to your tax return. (If the amount you owe exceeds those thresholds, you must file the long form.) On Form 2210 you must either calculate the amount of any penalty you owe or tell the IRS exactly why you don't owe any penalty. You don't owe if your withholding and estimated tax payments cover 80 percent or more of your tax bill, or if they would have been enough to pay your entire tax bill for the previous year.

For example, let's say your employer withheld $6,000 from your salary during the year, and you paid an additional $2,000 in estimated tax payments. If your tax bill comes to $10,000 or less, you'll owe no penalty, because you've already paid 80 percent of it.

Instead, let's say your tax bill comes to $20,000. Your payments fall short of 80 percent. But the year before, your

tax bill totaled $8,000 (or less). You owe no penalty, be-
cause your withholding and estimated tax payments would
have covered your entire tax bill for the previous year. Of
course, you still owe $12,000 in additional income tax, and
you'll have to pay it. But no penalty will be assessed.

For its part, the IRS says you needn't file Form 2210 if
you didn't owe any tax the year before, or if this year's withholding and payments would have covered last year's taxes.
But don't count on it. Be on the safe side; file Form 2210.

Why is this especially important for singles? Essentially
because of their high tax bracket and because so many singles, for whatever reason, tend to avoid thinking about their
taxes all year round. It is our feeling that singles probably
wind up paying this penalty more than any other group.

REFUNDS

This brings us to another problem, not unique to singles
but quite common. Once a person has suffered the indig-
nity of paying the underpayment penalty, he tends to over-
react. He will rush to his employer to adjust his W-4
withholding form so that more money is taken out each
payday. The idea is to prevent this from ever happening
again.

So the next year, instead of owing a couple of hundred
dollars, the taxpayer qualifies for a substantial refund. That
is probably the most serious tax mistake that Americans
make, year in and year out. When you get a refund, you
have lent money to the government, interest-free.

In addition, taxpayers who have a refund due tend to be
too conservative. They don't want to risk losing or delaying
their refund, so they lean in the IRS's favor on questionable
items rather than aggressively claiming every possible dollar in Tax Savers. Yet another mistaken notion is that a tax
return that claims a refund is less likely to be audited. So
for several reasons, a tax refund is not the blessing that it
appears to be.

Once a taxpayer falls into the refund trap, it's a hard
habit to break. Most carry it over to the succeeding stages of
their careers and lives.

We recommend that you avoid the underpayment of estimated tax penalty, simply because it is an unnecessary tax trap. With a minimum amount of planning you can estimate quite accurately the amount of tax you will need to have withheld each pay period. Have only that amount withheld; never have an excess amount taken from your pay.

EXPENSES

Let's get specific, and let's start with three Tax Savers connected with your job, all of which can be taken in addition to the standard deduction available to single taxpayers— $2,300 for 1984, rising annually thereafter in line with inflation.

Do you pay for any job-related expenses for which your employer does not reimburse you? Most of us do, and every penny is deductible. Let's say you drive—even around town, for short errands—and don't get reimbursed. On Form 2106, Employee Business Expenses, you can deduct that mileage, at 20.5 cents a mile. (That rate is subject to change by the IRS.) If your employer reimburses you for driving but pays you a rate of less than 20.5 cents a mile, you can, in effect, deduct the difference. Other travel expenses, even of the smallest kind, can be deducted, using the same form. You must back up these deductions with good records.

If you move from one city to another because of your work, your out-of-pocket moving expenses are deductible. File Form 3903, Moving Expense Adjustment. You can use this nice Tax Saver even to deduct the costs of moving to your first job, as long as you move at least thirty-five miles. In fact, you don't even have to have a job lined up in advance.

Let's say you graduate from college and yearn to work in Colorado. You can move there, find a job, and deduct your moving expenses, as long as you work there thirty-nine out of the fifty-two weeks immediately following your move. The job can even be a stop-gap adventure. For example, say you want to spend an easy year teaching scuba diving. You can move to Florida, California, or even Puerto Rico or the U.S. Virgin Islands, and deduct your moving expenses, as long as you work thirty-nine of the next fifty-two weeks. Later, you might quit that job, move to Chicago, and go to work in sales. Again, your moving expenses are deductible.

If your employer transfers you but does not pay all your moving expenses, you can deduct the difference, using Form 3903.

Whether in connection with a transfer or a job move of your own, you also can deduct the costs of a preliminary house-hunting trip, including meals and hotel bills while you look for a house or apartment.

Job-hunting expenses are deductible, too, but only if you are hunting for a job in the same trade or business. If you are a secretary and you go to a new climate to look for a secretarial job, you can deduct all the expenses, whether or not you find a job. Use Form 2106. It's perfectly legal to tie some leisure time into a job-hunting expedition, as long as the primary purpose of the trip is your job search. Make appointments in advance and devote at least part of every day to job-hunting. You're certainly free to stay at a resort and to spend part of each weekday around the pool—after all, you'll be exhausted from those interviews—and to make sure the trip involves a weekend. Don't be devious, but by all means enjoy yourself.

Since job-hunting expenses are deductible only if you are looking for a job in the same trade or business, you cannot deduct travel costs connected with looking for your first job. But that rule is not as narrow as it sounds. Let's say you finish college, travel to Colorado to look for a job, find one, and while you're there look for a place to live. You can legally call that a house-hunting trip and deduct it as a moving expense. Remember, moving expenses to a new job are deductible whether the job is in your old line of work or a new one.

Think of your trade or business in general terms. We know a young woman who worked as a clerk in a department store while attending college. After graduation she traveled 1,500 miles to look for a job in merchandising. Her old business was retailing, and that was the business in which she was seeking work, although at a higher level. She qualified for the job-hunting deduction.

Similarly, let's say you work as a construction laborer while studying civil engineering in college. After graduation, you can deduct the costs of looking for an engineering job with a construction company; your business has been and still is construction.

So far, we've discussed work-related expenses of three kinds—employee business expenses, job-hunting expenses, and moving expenses. All moving expenses go on Form 3903. But for employee business expenses and job-hunting expenses, you use Form 2106 only for costs having to do with travel and mileage. To deduct other expenses relating to your job, you have to itemize your deductions on Schedule A, under miscellaneous deductions. That's also the case for job-hunting expenses that you incur without out-of-town traveling.

As an employee, you may subscribe to trade or professional magazines, buy a briefcase, and join a business association. All those costs are deductible. If you are looking for a new job, your local job-hunting expenses also are deductible. That includes the cost of printing a résumé, taking a taxi to an appointment, and making long-distance calls to schedule appointments.

BUYING A HOME

Since these deductions go on Schedule A, you can't take them unless you itemize deductions. To make itemizing pay, your deductions must total more than the standard deduction for singles—$2,300 for 1984. Many singles have a hard time topping that total. But you can do it in one stroke, and at the same time make a prudent investment that will force you to save, will bless you with a lifelong variety of Tax Savers, and will probably yield an eventual profit.

Buy a home.

Single people often don't consider buying a house or condominium. They think of homeownership in connection with marriage—something for the future. But if you are single, the Tax Savers of homeownership will pay you more than they pay your married colleague, assuming your incomes are the same. Don't forget, you're in a higher tax bracket, and the higher your bracket, the more you save from every deduction.

When you buy a home, you will immediately start paying interest on the mortgage loan and real estate taxes. Both are deductible, and the two will easily total more than $2,300 a year, making it worthwhile for you to itemize your other deductions on Schedule A. Once you are using Schedule A, you also can deduct the work-related expenses that we described earlier. You can deduct your charitable contributions, your state and local income tax, your sales tax, and the interest you pay on every kind of loan, including credit cards and student loans. By taking advantage of the Tax Savers of homeownership, you will become eligible for all the other Tax Savers available through itemizing deductions.

Assuming you keep your home for a few years and do not have to sell it in a rush, you probably will make a profit when you do eventually sell. So your house is an investment, too, and a big one. The monthly payments constitute a kind of forced savings plan. As a single in a high tax bracket, you should strongly consider investments yielding profits that are largely sheltered from income tax. A house is one of the best. If you sell at a profit, you can defer tax altogether by buying another home costing as much or more. Even if you do not buy another home, you pay tax on only 40 percent of your profit, assuming you owned the home for more than one year. That's because the profit, or capital gain, on any investment held for more than one year is given favorable tax treatment; only 40 percent of the gain counts as taxable income. Under provisions of the 1984 tax law, that one-year holding period was cut to six months for property acquired after June 22, 1984.

IRAs

If you can afford it, you should start an Individual Retirement Account and contribute the $2,000 limit every year.

Your IRA contribution is deductible from your income; the interest or dividends that it earns accumulate tax-deferred. If you're in the 40 percent tax bracket, that $2,000 deduction will cut your taxes by $800, and at the same time you'll be building a nest egg for your retirement. Barring death or disability, you cannot start withdrawing your IRA savings until age fifty-nine and a half without incurring a 10 percent nondeductible penalty and paying tax on the amount withdrawn.

OTHER INVESTMENTS
An IRA introduces many young singles to the choices available to investors. It's important that you shape your other investments into Tax Savers, too. Because your tax bracket is higher than that of your married colleague making the same income, you have more incentive to consider tax-exempt municipal bonds and stocks that are more likely to yield capital gains than dividend income.

BECOMING A LANDLORD
If you like to take risks in search of substantial profits, your single years are a good time to do it; no one will be sharing your risks, so you can take them with a clear conscience.

Let's say that you already own your own home and feel more comfortable with real estate than with securities. Consider buying another house or condominium and renting it out. You get to deduct many of the expenses of buying and maintaining the home, and you also benefit from a superb Tax Saver called accelerated depreciation. That means that you deduct the entire cost of the home over eighteen years, as if you were wearing it out. In fact, most real estate will not wear out; it will gain in value. (The depreciation schedule used to be even better; you could deduct the cost over fifteen years. But even with the change to eighteen years, enacted in 1984, rental property remains a superb Tax Saver.)

A second home need not be a condo in the city or a box in the suburbs. If you like to ski, you might consider buying

47

a ski condominium; if you prefer the ocean, you might consider buying a beach cottage. You can use a vacation home as much as fourteen days a year yourself, renting it out the rest of the time, and still get all the Tax Savers conferred upon real estate investments.

WORKING FOR YOURSELF

Would you like to be your own boss? Millions of Americans yearn to start their own businesses, but they can't afford the risk or the time because of family responsibilities. As a single, your time is your own, and any risk you run can hurt no one but you. We don't recommend that you quit your job, but if you would like to turn a hobby into a business or otherwise try your hand at entrepreneurship, you are in a good position to do so as a self-supporting single.

The Tax Savers that go with self-employment are lucrative. You can deduct the costs of an office in your home and of equipment that you may now be buying with pretax dollars for your hobby. You can deduct the costs of pleasurable business trips. If you can use a car, a computer, or any other equipment in your business, you can take advantage of Tax Savers that substantially reduce their cost.

FRINGE BENEFITS

Your job probably provides fringe benefits that are Tax Savers as well. Most of these come to you automatically, but some may be optional. One of the best is a Salary Reduction Plan, sometimes called a 401(k), after the section of the tax law that describes it. A 401(k) is much like an IRA. You can have up to 25 percent or $30,000, whichever is less, automatically deducted from your salary every year and invested toward your retirement. You pay no income tax on the investment, or on the interest or dividends it earns, until you begin withdrawing it at age fifty-nine and a half or thereafter. Unlike IRAs, however, some Salary Reduction Plans let you withdraw the savings without penalty for any of three specific needs—buying a personal residence, paying large medical bills, or paying college tuition for your children. Of course, you must pay income tax on the withdrawals.

If you quit your job, you can pocket your Salary Reduction Plan savings, paying income tax spread over the next ten years, or roll them over into an IRA and continue to defer taxes. The choice is yours.

Some Salary Reduction Plans allow you to contribute an additional 10 percent of your salary. You pay income tax on that 10 percent but not on the interest or dividends it earns. And since you have paid income tax on those savings, you can withdraw them any time, for any reason.

INCOME AVERAGING

If your income increases substantially, you may benefit from a lucrative Tax Saver called Income Averaging. In effect, it lets you average your income tax over four years. You figure it on Schedule G and attach it to your long form 1040. It is a Tax Saver that you can exploit whether or not you itemize deductions on Schedule A.

To qualify, your taxable income for the past year must exceed your average taxable income for the three preceding years by at least 40 percent. Income Averaging is particularly profitable for many young people, since their salaries are likely to increase sharply as they get into their careers. To take advantage of this Tax Saver, you need your income figures for the past four years, whether or not you filed income tax returns every year. And you need to prove, if challenged by the IRS, that you provided more than half of your own support for each of those four years; and that "support" includes college costs. If you meet that test, we recommend that you at least try Income Averaging every year. If it will save you money, file Schedule G with your income tax form. If it will not, wait until next year and try again.

Many Tax Savers are written into the law specifically to ease the burden on married couples, but that's not true for singles. Single Americans face higher tax rates and have to dig out Tax Savers for themselves. But many are there for the digging, and they will benefit you more as a single than they would benefit your married colleague earning the same income. For more details on the Tax Savers outlined in this chapter, see the chapters that discuss Tax Savers for Employees, for the Self-Employed, for Investors, for Homeowners, and for the Retired.

6

Tax Savers for Young Marrieds

I f you are young and married, and both you and your spouse are working, you are due congratulations and warm appreciation from Uncle Sam. You have been vaulted into the upper tax brackets imposed on high-income taxpayers.

You need Tax Savers, and you need them quickly. In fact, you may need them now more than you will in the next stage of your life. If you and your spouse each earn $15,000 to $40,000 a year, you're in the mainstream of young people on their way to success. But the U.S. Tax Code hasn't quite gotten this new reality into focus. The tax laws were written on the old-fashioned assumption that most families would have just one breadwinner, with the wife staying home. That's the way things used to be. And the framework for today's tax brackets was calculated before the wild inflation of the 1970s, which boosted salaries (and prices) sharply, pushing all of us into higher tax brackets.

When you are married, you are almost always better off filing a joint income tax return, but that, of course, means adding your two salaries together. Once you do that, you're vaulted into the kind of high tax bracket that used to be reserved for only the very prosperous.

However, we will not devote this chapter to pity. The high income of working couples, combined with the relative freedom they enjoy, provides them plenty of opportunities to take advantage of a wide selection of Tax Savers and at the same time to lay the foundation for a prosperous future. The two go hand in hand, because many of the Tax Savers most important to childless young couples are wealth builders—investments that will enhance prosperity and ease financial burdens in future years.

That's particularly valuable if you intend to raise a family, because children—wonderful as they may be—are quite expensive. By using Tax Savers to build a solid financial base now, you can lessen your taxes while softening the financial crunches ahead.

All this takes planning, but it's not difficult, and it's certainly worthwhile. Many young couples cheat themselves by paying too little attention to taxes and by failing to dovetail their investments with their tax situations. That's costly.

Let's take John and Jennifer, a young couple recently married and just a few years into their careers. John's taxable income is $30,000, and so is that of his single colleague at the next desk. Jennifer's taxable income is $20,000. (We're not being sexist. The Census Bureau reports that women, on average, make only about two thirds as much as men. In this book we're dealing with reality, not with ought-to-be's.)

With a taxable income of $30,000, John's single colleague is in the 34 percent tax bracket, and he's paying $6,113 in income tax, based on 1984 tax rates. Together, John and Jennifer have a joint taxable income of $50,000, pushing them into the 38 percent tax bracket. Their income tax is $11,368. As John and Jennifer increase their incomes, they will move into even higher tax brackets. Just $10,000 more taxable income between them will push them another 2 percentage points into the 40 percent bracket.

As far as taxes go, marriage is a trade-off, but it's not an even one. When you are married and file a joint income tax return, you get the benefit of lower tax rates than those imposed on singles, or on married people filing separate returns, based on the same income levels. But if both of you earn income, your combined salaries push you into higher income tax brackets than your single counterparts—witness John and Jennifer. On balance, you pay more income tax than if the two of you were still single. That extra tax is the "marriage penalty."

MARRIAGE PENALTY

Let's go back to John and Jennifer. If they were single, they would be filing separate income tax returns. John's taxable income is $30,000; his tax would be $6,113. Jennifer's taxable income is $20,000; her tax would be $3,205. Combined, their taxes would add up to $9,318. But since they're married, filing a joint return, their income tax is $11,368. So their marriage penalty is $2,050.

If you got married this year or last year, you may wonder whether you are married or single for the tax year in question, or maybe a little of both. The rule is simple: Your marital status on December 31 determines your marital status for the year. If you got married on December 31, you were married all year, according to the tax law. If you were married all year but got divorced on December 30, you were single all year. An accountant friend of Strassels was well aware of this rule and well aware of the marriage penalty, too. He was engaged to marry a young woman who, like him, made a good salary. Partly to make fun of that arbitrary rule having to do with December 31, they got married at 12:05 A.M. January 1—just five minutes into the new year. By waiting until the new year, Strassels' friend and his bride avoided the marriage penalty for that previous year. Thanks to that simple stroke of timing, they cut their taxes more than enough to pay for a luxurious honeymoon, which they thoroughly enjoyed.

The marriage penalty was a hot political issue a few years ago. Strassels appeared on *The Phil Donahue Show* with a couple who were lobbying Congress, contending that they were being unfairly taxed as a result of getting married. They said their taxes would be lower if they had never married, and they were right. The couple divorced every year on December 31 so that they could file as single taxpayers. The IRS says it doesn't recognize divorces that are used strictly to determine filing status.

That brings us to the first Tax Saver for young married couples. It's called the Deduction for a Married Couple When Both Work, and it was enacted by Congress to lessen the marriage penalty—but not to eliminate it entirely. You do not have to itemize deductions on Schedule A to take advantage of it. You can even take advantage of it on the short form, 1040A, by filling out Schedule I, Part III, although we recommend that you always use the long form, 1040. Remember, you *never* pay more taxes by using the long form. You *never* pay less taxes by using the short form.

With the long form, 1040, the Deduction for a Married Couple When Both Work goes on Schedule W. It's a very simple half-page calculation. From the lesser of the couple's two incomes, you deduct 10 percent but no more than $3,000. Earned income—wages and salaries—is the only kind of income that qualifies; you cannot, for example, include interest or dividends. And you must take the deduction from net earned income—in other words, from what's left of the lesser income after other tax adjustments. (Other adjustments, most of which we will cover in this chapter, include moving expenses, IRA and Keogh retirement plan contributions, and the exclusion for disability income.)

Let's say that the lesser income between you and your spouse is her $20,000. Out of that, she contributes $2,000 to her IRA retirement account, leaving a net of $18,000. On Schedule W, you deduct 10 percent of that $18,000, or $1,800. If you're in the 38 percent bracket, that $1,800 deduction means a Tax Saver of $684. With John and Jennifer, we were dealing with *taxable* incomes of $30,000 and $20,000 respectively, after taking advantage of the Deduction for a Married Couple When Both Work. So their tax of $11,368 would have been $684 higher without this Tax Saver. They're still paying a marriage penalty, but it's not so large as it was before this Tax Saver was written into the law.

We have said before that the IRS will not call Tax Savers to your attention. The Deduction for a Married Couple

When Both Work is a perfect example. It first became available for 1982, and according to the IRS, 15 percent of the couples who could have benefited from this simple Tax Saver failed to do so. The IRS merely announced that 15 percent statistic in an obscure publication, where taxpayers were unlikely to see it. If you missed this Tax Saver—or any other—file an amended return, 1040X. You can do so for any of the previous three years.

PLANNING AHEAD

If you are both working and looking forward to having children and raising a family, you need Tax Savers that serve three needs.

1. They should cut your taxes now.
2. They should build savings.
3. They should fit your situation today while being versatile enough to fit your financial needs in the next stage of your lives.

Many young couples overlook the changes that may occur with children. They like where they live now, and they assume that they will keep on living there. They both work, and they assume that they both will continue working full-time. They have a good deal of discretionary income, and they expect to maintain their life-style.

We're not going to try to talk you into making any changes. We are only going to encourage you to consider the possibility that you may change your minds. Children tend to give couples a somewhat different perspective. The urban townhouse neighborhood that you love so much may lose some of its charm when you look into the quality of the nearby public schools. One of you may decide that full-time work outside your home doesn't leave enough time for parenting. The expense of raising a child will certainly cut into your discretionary income; if one of you cuts down to part-time work or stops working altogether, you may find your income slashed by as much as half.

So as you plan Tax Savers and put them into effect, leave yourself room for change. Think ahead and plan ahead. Most of the Tax Savers that we will recommend in this chapter are investments, and an investment, by definition, is money put aside toward future needs. Try to plan those needs and tailor your Tax Savers to fit them. If you are uncertain, pick tax-saving vehicles that can be reshaped in the future.

Let's start with savings—the money in your checking and savings accounts. We assume that you keep most of your cash in a money fund at your bank or in a money market mutual fund, so that your cash is earning a good rate of interest. While both of you are working, you have an opportunity to build up your savings. You also have a strong reason to do so, because you will almost surely need extra cash in the years ahead. You may want to save up for a down payment on a house. You also should have a cash reserve so that if one of you would prefer to stay home with a baby, you will have that choice.

The more you save, the more interest you will earn— the more income tax you will pay on that interest. But you have options.

Consider the dividend exclusion. By law, a married couple filing jointly can exclude as much as $200 in dividends they collect during the year from stocks they own. So look for a nice safe stock paying a comfortable 8 to 10 percent. The idea is to collect at least $200 worth of dividends—tax-free.

Next, take advantage of the temporary tax deferral on dividends from some public utilities. Congress wants people to invest in regulated public utilities. As an inducement, a couple filing jointly can exclude up to $1,500 of reinvested dividends from these utilities. (That significant Tax Saver expires at the end of 1985.) Additionally, when you eventually sell the stock, your profit, if any, counts as a long-term capital gain, assuming you held the stock long enough. If you bought the stock after June 22, 1984, you need hold it only six months for your gain to count as "long-term" and to qualify for the favored tax treatment. If you bought it before then, the long-term holding period is one year. Why June 22, 1984? Because that was the date Congress chose in the 1984 Tax Reform Act.

Some money market funds invest in tax-exempt securities, so that you pay no federal income tax on the interest. The yield—the interest rate—is lower than the yield on funds investing in fully taxed securities, but if your tax bracket is high enough, you'll come out ahead with the tax-exempt funds.

For example, let's say your tax bracket is 39 percent—just a shade above that of John and Jennifer. In that bracket, a tax-exempt fund yielding 5 percent nets you the same interest as a taxable fund yielding 8.2 percent. If you are in the 44 percent bracket, that 5 percent tax-exempt yield is as good as a taxable yield of 8.93 percent. Two tax-exempt money funds with good records are Calvert Tax-Free Fund (phone toll-free 800-368-2748) and T. Rowe Price Tax-Exempt Fund (phone 800-638-5660).

The same kind of formula works if you invest in bonds. In fact, it works better, because these days tax-exempt municipal bonds yield just a few percentage points below corporate or government bonds, on which the interest is taxable by the IRS. We recommend against buying individual bonds unless you are a sophisticated investor with at least $20,000 to commit to a bond portfolio. You can invest less, pay no commission, and spread your risk by investing in a no-load bond fund, while still getting a healthy yield. Moreover, you can have your interest payments automatically reinvested, so your tax-exempt savings can grow.

To illustrate the attraction of tax-exempt bonds, take two funds managed by the same company, Fidelity Investments (phone 800-343-6533). On the same day, the Fidelity High Income Fund, which invests in bonds that pay taxable income, was yielding 12.4 percent, while the Fidelity High Yield Municipals Fund, which invests in bonds that pay tax-exempt income, was yielding 9.5 percent. If your tax bracket is 30 percent or higher, the 9.5 percent yield is better. For example, if your bracket is 39 percent, 9.5 percent tax-free is the equivalent of more than 15 percent in taxable income. That's a nice yield, and it's a nice way to accumulate savings without increasing your income tax.

Bonds, like most investments, carry some risk. We describe investments and their risks more fully in Chapter 12,

Tax Savers for Investors. If you are inclined to take intelligent and manageable risks in pursuit of profits and wealth building, this is a good time of your life to do it. The more security you build now, the more choices you will have later.

Investments that yield unrealized (or uncashed) profits also yield Tax Savers. Few investors stop to think about it, but profits that build as you hold stocks, bonds, real estate, or any other kind of investment are tax-free, until you sell. For example, let's say you and your spouse buy 100 shares of stock for $1,000, and in three years the value increases to $1,500. You're $500 ahead, on paper. You owe no income tax unless you sell that stock.

When you do sell it, your profit is called a capital gain—and a capital gain can be a Tax Saver. You report capital gains and losses on Schedule D of Form 1040. (The short form is out for those who sell investments.) If you owned the investment for long enough to qualify for treatment as a long-term capital gain, only 40 percent of that gain is taxed; 60 percent of your profit is tax-free—in other words, completely sheltered from federal income tax.

If you don't qualify for long-term treatment, your profit is fully taxed.

So by putting your savings in a tax-exempt money fund and investing in tax-exempt bonds and in stocks that are likely to increase in value, you are building wealth while employing the same sophisticated Tax Savers used by people twice your age. Catch on to these Tax Savers now. If you start having children, you are unlikely to have as much discretionary income for investment.

In figuring how much money to put where, you should emphasize liquidity. In other words, don't buy bonds or stocks until you have a solid cash reserve. That amounts to two to three months' living expenses.

You can sell bonds or stocks any time, but you should avoid putting yourself in a position in which you might be forced to sell on short notice. Stocks fluctuate in price, and so, to a lesser degree, do bonds. If you sell, you want to do so when the price is up, not when it is down. The essence of investing for profit is to sell at a profitable time of your choice.

YOUR FIRST HOME

Before considering stocks and bonds, you may want to buy a house or a condominium. As a Tax Saver, a home is a terrific investment. You will surely borrow money to buy it, and the interest that you pay on the mortgage loan is deductible. So is your real estate tax. Those Tax Savers are helpful in themselves, and they open the door to others.

To itemize deductions on Schedule A, a married couple filing jointly needs deductions totaling more than $3,400. Why? Because without itemizing, you automatically get the standard deduction, which for 1984 was set at $3,400. But mortgage interest and real estate taxes will undoubtedly push you past that $3,400 barrier. And once you have passed it, you can itemize other deductions, including charitable contributions; state and local income tax; sales tax; interest on student loans, credit cards, and other debts; rent on your safe deposit box; dues and publications having to do with your work; and tax return preparation fees.

So a home provides you with a place to live and a bounty of Tax Savers as well. Assuming you plan to live there for five years or so, your home probably will yield a profit when it is sold, too.

Many young couples hesitate to buy a home because they expect to move—perhaps to the suburbs when they have children, perhaps to a different city for a better job. Those are legitimate concerns; you don't want to be forced to sell your home on short notice, when real estate prices may be sagging.

But with proper planning, a home may be a good investment now and an even better investment after you move. We're suggesting that you consider renting out the home after you move rather than selling it. Rental property provides a wonderful Tax Saver. As a landlord, you continue to deduct your mortgage interest and real estate taxes, and you also get to deduct the other costs connected with owning the property—maintenance, utilities, an agent's fee for handling the rental, and so forth. Best of all, you get to depreciate the property—a write-off that is at the heart of many tax shelters used by millionaires. You'll find details on this Tax Saver in Chapter 10, Tax Savers for Homeowners.

If you have chosen its location wisely and if you maintain it decently, a rental property probably will appreciate in value. So you will be taking tax deductions as if the property were losing its value, while in fact you will be adding to your investment wealth. That's a hard combination to beat.

A BUSINESS AT HOME

We talked earlier about providing room to accommodate possible changes in your life. A home—that most versatile of investments—also can become the place of work for one or both of a married couple. If either one of you dreams of someday operating your own business, this may be the time—while you have some extra money and extra time. We believe in starting your business on a part-time basis, so that you don't have to give up your regular job. You can immediately take advantage of the Tax Savers that accompany self-employment. When your car is used primarily for business, you can depreciate it over three years. A computer and other office equipment can be depreciated over five years. In addition, you can claim an investment tax credit for the same property. You can deduct the expenses of maintaining an office in your home. You can attend conventions and meetings having to do with your business, deduct the costs, and even tag on a vacation if you'd like. But don't be a dreamer; the Tax Savers of self-employment work best if you make money, not if you lose money.

Then, when you have a child, one of you may want to stay home, operate the business, and spend more time with your child. So a home business might make money for you now, yield immediate Tax Savers, and also provide a perfect career transition.

IRAs

An Individual Retirement Account is both a Tax Saver and a wealth builder. You can contribute up to $2,000 a year of earned income to your IRA. If your spouse works, he or she can contribute another $2,000. If only one of you works, you can set up "spousal IRAs" with a total contribution limited to $2,250 a year. You pay no income tax on your IRA contribution or on the interest or dividends it earns, until you begin withdrawing it.

That's a wonderful deal, but many young couples don't take advantage of it. They reason that their savings should go toward a down payment on a house or condominium, not toward retirement. We agree that a home comes first. But you can work toward both goals at the same time.

Let's say that you and your spouse both work, and you're saving with the idea of having a baby and buying a home in five years. Start IRAs, with both of you contributing the maximum $2,000 a year. Choose a liquid IRA investment—a money market fund or certificates of deposit that will mature within a few years. With combined contributions of $4,000 a year, you'll accumulate $26,862 in five years, assuming compound annual interest of 10 percent.

As we mentioned earlier, personal and family finances and plans change. By then you may have saved enough money so you can buy a home without tapping your IRA nest egg. But if need be, you can get to it. You can withdraw any amount that you need. You pay income tax on that withdrawal for the year in which you withdraw it, and you pay a nondeductible penalty of 10 percent to the IRS. In addition, you may be subject to a penalty from the IRA holder, such as your bank or savings institution.

To be sure, you would rather avoid those penalties and taxes, but in five years you will have saved roughly $10,000 in income tax, assuming a 40 percent tax bracket, thanks to the Tax Saver aspect of your IRAs. You may be able to time your withdrawal so that it falls within a year of lower taxable income—perhaps a year in which one of you was between jobs or took time off from work. That will keep your tax bracket down. On balance, you have saved on income tax, despite the penalty. And the remainder of your IRA account will continue building wealth toward retirement on a tax-deferred basis.

PENSIONS

Many firms offer their employees a pension plan. Inquire as to the length of time you must stay with the company before your pension rights are vested—are due you no matter what happens in the future. Keep that time frame in mind when considering career moves or time off to have a family.

Other firms offer IRA plans. Still others are using pension plans that save on taxes but are more versatile. These plans go by various names, including Salary Deferral, Deferred Compensation, or 401(k); that's the section of the U.S. Tax Code that brought this new type of plan into existence.

When you elect to participate in your employer's 401(k) plan, you tell the payroll department to set aside a certain amount of your salary, up to 25 percent or $30,000, whichever is less. That amount is automatically invested in a pension fund; you never see the money. Income tax is deferred on your contribution and on the interest or dividends it earns.

Many companies add to your contribution. For example, your employer might chip in one dollar for every two dollars that you have withheld from your salary. Most 401(k) plans are terrific.

If you leave your employer, you are permitted to withdraw your 401(k) savings, and you have this choice: You can pay income tax on the withdrawal, spread over the next ten years, or you can roll your 401(k) money over into an IRA account, tax-free. Moreover, many 401(k) plans allow withdrawals even while you remain on the job for any of three purposes—buying a personal residence, paying large medical bills, or paying college tuition for your children. For details, check with the pension department of your company.

JOB EXPENSES

Your job may provide other Tax Savers. You can deduct job-related expenses for which your employer did not reimburse you. Typically, these include professional publications, mileage, taxi fares, and the like.

Moving expenses also are deductible if you are moving in connection with your job or to take a new job. You must work at the new location at least thirty-nine of the next fifty-two weeks. Although this deduction benefits you and your spouse, only one of you need have a job-related reason for the move, and only one of you has to meet the thirty-nine-week working requirement. Job-hunting expenses are deductible, too—in town or out of town—if you are looking for a new job in your field. Although you can deduct moving expenses to take a new job in a new field, you can deduct job-hunting expenses only while looking for work in your present field. That's one of many vagaries of the tax law.

INCOME AVERAGING

Most people whose income is considerably higher now than in past years can benefit from Income Averaging, a nifty Tax Saver available only to long-form filers. It lets you partially average your taxable income for the past four years. Young couples often mistakenly ignore Income Averaging, assuming that they do not qualify because they have not been filing joint income tax returns.

In fact, you don't have to have filed any kind of income tax returns for past years. The form, Schedule G, asks you to list your income for the past four years, but it says nothing about old tax returns.

To qualify, both you and your spouse must have provided at least half of your combined support for the past four years. You don't have to meet that support test if both of you were twenty-five or older during the past tax year and if neither of you was a full-time student during any of the three years before that.

Let's assume that you got married two years ago. On Schedule G, you and your spouse will list your combined incomes, as singles, for the first two years of the four and your joint income for the last two years. Then work through the formula on the form. You may reap a substantial Tax Saver.

CATCHING UP

Marriage prompts many young people to pull their financial lives together. Strassels was contacted by a musician, twenty-seven years old, who was about to get married. He had never filed an income tax return; much of his income had been in cash, which is difficult for the IRS to trace. He wanted to come clean, and he was right to do so. He was also lucky. Once he figured in his expenses, he found that he didn't owe any tax for any year. In a case like that, the taxpayer isn't penalized; the IRS imposes penalties only for unpaid taxes.

If either you or your spouse needs a copy of a past tax return, you can get it by filling out Form 4506 and mailing it in with a check for five dollars. You have to fill out a separate form—and pay a separate five bucks—for every past return that you need. Then you send the form to the IRS service center where your old return was filed. Be patient. The process can take as long as three months. For the addresses of IRS service centers, see Chapter 22.

Whether you are just pulling things together or have already started paying taxes and accumulating savings, the years of early marriage often provide a sudden and compelling need for Tax Savers. Two incomes mean high taxes. By working Tax Savers into plans for your future, you can lessen the bite today and brighten the outlook for tomorrow.

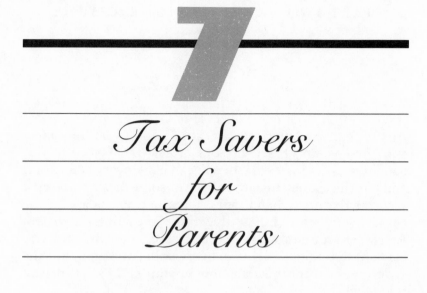

Tax Savers for Parents

*A*s parents, most of us try to transfer our personal values to our children. In practice, that philosophy can build work habits for children and Tax Savers for parents at the same time.

Our federal income tax is called progressive because it imposes lower rates on lower incomes and progressively higher rates on higher incomes. That's made to order for parents and children who are willing to plan and work as a unit in order to achieve their mutual goals. The foundation for the Tax Saver most beneficial to parents is simple: Transfer your highly taxed income from you to your child. The assumption is that your child is in a very low tax bracket.

But be careful. The techniques and strategies for transferring wealth to a child were narrowed considerably in 1984, first by the Supreme Court and then by Congress. You can only go so far. For example, you can't tell your employer to make out your paycheck for one month to your son or daughter. You earned it, it's yours, and you'll have to report it on your tax return. In other words, you can't assign away income that is properly yours. Still, there are Tax Savers you can use quite effectively.

TAX-FREE INCOME

Any unmarried American can earn $3,300 a year free of federal income tax, based on 1984 rules. So if your son or daughter earns $3,300, he or she can bank every penny of it and put the money toward college or some other purpose. If you, on the other hand, put $3,300 of your salary in the bank toward your child's education, you will have to earn $4,455, assuming you are in the 35 percent tax bracket. Uncle Sam will take 35 cents of every dollar you earn. But the government won't take a penny of your child's earnings at this level.

Taking this one step further, let's say that you collect 10 percent interest on your savings. Again, you'll pay 35 percent to the government. Generally your son or daughter will pay nothing, as long as his or her salary and interest income don't reach that magical $3,300.

The rules for tax-free income break down this way: Anyone can receive as much as $3,300 free from income tax. However, no more than $999 of that amount can be unearned—for example, dividends or interest. Your child can collect $999 from interest on his savings account, and earn $2,300 in wages, and pocket the entire amount free from income tax. He hasn't broken either the $1,000 barrier for unearned income or the combined $3,300 barrier for total income.

So your child can earn wages free of income tax, bank or invest those wages, and earn interest or dividends free of income tax. The dollar your child earns is more valuable than a dollar you earn—a lot more valuable. He gets to keep the whole dollar. You get to keep only 70 cents if you're in the 30 percent tax bracket, 60 cents if you're in the 40 percent bracket, 50 cents if you're in the top bracket of 50 percent.

Nor does the difference stop if your child's income exceeds that tax-free allowance of $3,300 a year. Let's say your child's income reaches $4,300, including no more than $1,000 in unearned income. His tax is $113. If you had earned that additional $1,000, you'd have to pay $350 of it in income tax, assuming your bracket is 35 percent.

Or perhaps your child takes a year off between high school and college and earns $12,000. His tax is $1,300. If you or your spouse took an extra job and earned $12,000, you would be pushed into a higher tax bracket—let's say from the 35 percent bracket to the 40 percent bracket. So you would pay Uncle Sam $4,800 of that $12,000. (We're assuming that you and your spouse file a joint tax return. If you file a separate return rather than a joint return, the tax bite would be even worse.)

Income that your child earns provides a better Tax Saver than income he receives from interest or dividends. Since your child lives with you, he or she almost surely is better off using the standard deduction of $2,300 rather than itemizing deductions on Schedule A. But once your child's unearned income—that is, income from investments, trusts, and the like—tops $1,000, he has to itemize deductions on Schedule A. He won't have many, but he should by all means scrape up every legal itemized deduction he can—church contributions, sales tax from the tables, perhaps state income tax paid—but it's unlikely that his itemized deductions will total as much as $2,300. Of course, your child's tax bracket is still lower than yours, so his income tax still won't be even close to what yours would be on the same income.

On its face, it seems quite unfair that a child with $1,000 in interest would have to file the long form 1040, plus itemize deductions on Schedule A. Actually, it's not. The reason for it is that the standard deduction is built into the tax tables used to calculate the tax bill. Your child will get the $2,300 standard deduction simply by using the tables.

EMPLOYING YOUR CHILD

If you or your spouse runs a business, full-time or part-time, you can magnify the benefits of this Tax Saver by hiring your child. Let's say you hire your daughter to address envelopes, a job that you used to do yourself. She works a few hours every week, and for the year you pay her $3,000. She banks it toward college. You may think you've done her a favor—after all, you used to address those envelopes yourself, so you created a job for her and paid her $3,000 that used to go into the family account. But, in fact, you've done yourself a favor. In a business, wages paid to employees are a deductible business expense. So by hiring and paying your daughter, you've lowered the family's taxable income by $3,000. If you're in the 35 percent bracket, that's a savings of $1,050. At the same time, your daughter has earned $3,000, and her tax on that is zero. It can all be put aside toward college. Moreover, she did productive work—good experience for her, less work for you.

To the IRS, there is nothing suspicious about a taxpayer who hires his or her children, as long as the work is appropriate to the age. You don't need to worry about child labor laws; it's perfectly legal to hire your eight-year-old. At that age a child might empty trash, work a copying machine, stamp and stuff envelopes. You have to pay your child a reasonable wage. Don't try hiring a six-year-old as a high-salaried executive. In other words, don't set up a phony arrangement. You don't have to; the Tax Saver is beneficial as it stands.

In fact, if your business is a sole proprietorship rather than a corporation, you get an additional benefit from hiring your children: You don't have to pay Social Security tax on your children's wages. A "sole proprietorship" means the kind of business that you report on Schedule C, Profit (or Loss) from Business or Profession. If your business is incorporated, you'll have to pay Social Security tax on the wages of your children, just as you do on the wages of any employee.

One question frequently asked is if you should take $2,000 of your child's salary and place it into an IRA. That way the interest or dividends on the IRA will accumulate tax-deferred until withdrawal. And if the child needs the cash for college or other expenses (say a house down payment) at a later date, it will be available even though there is a 10 percent premature withdrawal penalty and the amount withdrawn has to be included in taxable income in the year of the withdrawal.

Our answer is a resounding no. Don't put the money into an IRA for your son or daughter. You don't need or even want the tax deferral on this income. Remember, your child is in a low tax bracket. It makes no sense to use the IRA Tax Saver if your child owes no taxes anyway.

ONE CHILD, TWO EXEMPTIONS

To avoid pitfalls, you have to understand how we figured that $3,300 level of tax-free income. If you look at the Tax Table that comes with your income tax forms and instructions every year, you'll see that a single person doesn't start paying tax until taxable income exceeds $2,300. That $2,300 is the so-called standard deduction for singles. It is $3,400 for married couples filing jointly, $1,700 for married couples filing separately. In addition, every taxpayer gets his or her own personal exemption of $1,000. So $2,300 of standard deduction plus $1,000 of personal exemption equals $3,300 of tax-free income.

Starting in 1985, both the standard deduction and the personal exemption will rise every year in line with an inflation index. Tax brackets also will be "indexed."

That personal exemption is one of the few automatic Tax Savers for parents. Your child gets the exemption for himself—and you get it, too. It hardly pays the costs of supporting a child; if you're in the 35 percent tax bracket, a $1,000 exemption will reduce your tax bill by $350. You can claim your child's exemption every year until the year of his nineteenth birthday, and even beyond that as long as your child is a full-time student for some part of at least five calendar months within a year.

That five-month rule sounds peculiar, but it's very practical. It was designed to grant parents the dependency exemption for the year their child graduates from college. Many colleges wind up the school year in May, the fifth month of the year. So if your child graduates in May—even the first of May—you may claim the exemption for that year. Of course, if your child goes on to graduate school, you can keep on claiming the tax break; there is no age limit. Vocational school qualifies, too, but night school and correspondence school do not.

If you have not already done so, get your child a Social Security number. Just call the nearest Social Security office for the procedure and forms. When your child goes to work —for you or for someone else—he will have to provide his employer with his own Social Security number. When he opens a bank account or otherwise saves or invests, again make sure he lists his own Social Security number. From employers, banks, and others, the IRS gets reports of how much income was paid to whom. The IRS keeps track of us—and our income—by Social Security number. It's important that your child's income goes into the IRS computers as his income, not yours.

When your child gets a job, he'll routinely have to fill out Form W-4, which determines how much federal income tax will be withheld from his paychecks. If his income will be below the barrier—$3,300 or less for 1984—he should check the line stating that he expects no tax obligation. That way he'll have no federal income tax withheld.

But even if your child's income stays below that threshold, we recommend that he or she file an income tax return. Assuming the income is from wages and perhaps some savings interest, the job is simple. Filing a tax return doesn't necessarily mean paying tax; the bottom line will be a zero. But the hour or two spent on that return could save you and your child a potential headache. Remember, the IRS gets reports on any and all wages, interest, and dividends paid to your child. Unless your child files a tax return, the IRS won't know that his total income is below the taxable level. So the IRS is likely to knock on your door (by mail) and ask your child why he didn't report that income. With a tax return on file—or rather, in the computer—the numbers reported by employers and banks will match up against the numbers on your child's tax return.

Make sure your child keeps copies of those old tax returns. (Most likely, you'll keep them for him.) Then, when he starts earning a year-round salary, he might be able to take advantage of the Income Averaging Tax Saver. The figures from the old tax returns will help in filling out the Income Averaging form and will also be useful evidence should the IRS challenge an Income Averaging claim.

SAVING FOR COLLEGE

Let's assume your child works hard and over the years saves $10,000 toward college. Together, you and your child have reaped a big Tax Saver and have used it to build money for education. Terrific. Unfortunately, $10,000 will not be nearly enough to cover college costs. Even if your children are still toddlers, you must know that you will have to come up with a good deal of money for their education, beyond the amounts that they earn and save themselves.

You have several choices. You can use them individually, or in combination with each other.

1. If your income is large enough, you can simply pay for your children's college needs out of your pocket. But few of us have incomes sufficiently large; a year of college can cost $12,000 or more, and the prices for tuition, room, and board will loom still higher in the years ahead. Keep in mind that you pay for your children's college costs with after-tax dollars. For you to shell out $12,000, none of which is tax-deductible, you need to earn $16,200, assuming a 35 percent tax bracket.

2. You can borrow some or all of the money, perhaps pledging your house or some securities as collateral, and then repay it gradually, paying interest on the debt and deducting that interest on your tax return.

3. You can have your child take out the loan under various student loan and repayment programs. The debt is his, and so will the interest deductions be.

4. You can plan ahead, using Tax Savers and putting money aside so the cost of your children's education will be paid gradually and will cost you less in total.

We prefer this last option. Once again, the ideal strategy involves putting money in your child's name—and your child's low tax bracket—to take it out of your name and your high tax bracket.

The simplest approach is to save in your child's name,

so the interest or dividends are his, not yours. But first, you have to make an important decision. Once you put money in your child's name, you have given him the money. It is his, and you can't take it back. If he reaches adulthood and chooses to spend it on a sports car rather than on a college education, you can't legally stop him. Under the law, a gift is a gift. You must decide whether to take that risk. We'll tell you about one Tax Saver plan if your answer is yes, and another if your answer is no.

SCHOLARSHIPS

The best Tax Saver of all bypasses this issue altogether. Scholarships and fellowships are terrific Tax Savers and in many cases are tax-free. Just ask the sponsor. Most are awarded on the basis of need, some on merit, and a surprising number are given according to the whim of the donor. About a billion dollars' worth of scholarships and fellowships go unclaimed every year. It's worth looking into, whether or not your child is a great scholar.

GIFTS

A gift to your child has no immediate effect on anyone's taxes, unless it is an exceptionally large gift. Your child is not a charity, so your gift is not deductible on your tax return. A gift doesn't count as taxable income to the recipient, so your child pays no income tax on it. You, the donor, can give as much as $10,000 a year to any individual, whether to your child or to a stranger. If you are married, you and your spouse can, together, give $20,000 to any individual every year. If you give more than that in a single year, you must file a gift tax return. Even then, you won't have to pay any tax (unless your gifts over the years exceed $400,000). But when you die, the amount of your estate that is exempt from federal estate tax will be reduced by the amount of your gifts exceeding that annual $10,000 (or $20,000) limit. There's a very important exception to the annual gift ceiling. By law, you can give limitless amounts to cover tuition and medical bills.

As a practical matter, few of us worry about gifts exceeding $10,000. Most parents have trouble scraping up $1,000 a year to put aside toward a child's education. But whatever the amount, the important thing is to put that money where it will earn substantial interest or dividends, in your child's name and your child's tax bracket. If you start a savings account in your own name, planning to pay your children's tuition with it, you will have to save more, because every dollar of interest or dividends will be taxed in your higher tax bracket.

Here are four conservative, high-yield investments worth considering for your child's college fund:

Savings certificates

Buy savings certificates that will mature periodically during each of your child's college years. You get a better yield on certificates than on straight savings because you tie up your money long-term.

Zero-coupon bonds

These bonds pay no annual interest. Instead, they are sold at a steep discount. For example, you would pay about $333 for a zero-coupon bond that will mature in ten years at $1,000, assuming a yield of 12¼ percent. Every year, the bond's owner has to report imputed interest on his tax return—in other words, interest that is, in effect, accumulating. But since your child's income is low, he'll have to pay little, if any, tax on that imputed interest. Once again, pick bonds that will mature when your child needs the money for tuition, and make sure you file a tax return for your child every year. A parent can sign the tax return for his child, but to take advantage of this Tax Saver a return has to be filed, every year, even if no tax is due.

U.S. savings bonds

The yield on these bonds used to be far below what was generally available from other investments, but it is now competitive. U.S. savings bonds are sold at a discount; for example, you pay $25 for a bond that will mature in seven years at $50. With a U.S. savings bond, you have a choice:

You can report the interest all at once when the bond matures, or you can report it annually—once again, imputed interest. With the bond in the name of a child whose income is too low to be taxed, you're better off reporting the interest annually. Once again, make sure you file a tax return for your child every year.

Stocks

Any investment in stocks is somewhat speculative, but if your child's income is high enough to be taxable, you may want to take advantage of two Tax Savers designed to encourage investment in stocks. For any investor, the first $100 of dividends is exempt from federal income tax. In addition, through 1985 the first $750 in dividends from public utility stocks is exempt if reinvested in stock of the same utility. Most utilities offer plans under which dividends are automatically reinvested, with no brokerage charge. Through these reinvestment plans, a number of utilities even sell their stock at a 3 to 5 percent discount. Utility stocks pay a high dividend yield and most of them are less subject to the ups and downs of the market than are most stocks.

LOANS TO CHILDREN

Many parents prefer to lend their children money, and until mid-1984 a handy Tax Saver allowed you to lend large amounts to your children, charging no interest. Your child could then use the borrowed money for college, or even invest it in his name, so the interest or dividends it earned would be taxable to him, in his low bracket, rather than to you.

But as part of the 1984 Tax Reform Act, Congress sharply limited this Tax Saver. Now you can lend your child up to only $10,000, using the tax-saving arrangement described above. For loan amounts above $10,000, you, the lender, have to pay income tax on the loan interest—even if you don't receive any interest: The IRS figures a logical market interest rate (it's 10 percent for 1984), assumes your child paid you that amount of interest, and adds it to your taxable income.

As a result, the largest amount you can lend to each of your children under tax-saving arrangements is $10,000. You can exceed that limit, however, with a more elaborate arrangement called a Clifford Trust. You put a certain amount of money or property into the trust, with your child as beneficiary. The trust pays the income to the child, so it is taxable to him. After a certain number of years—a minimum of ten, under the law governing Clifford Trusts—the assets revert to you.

You need a lawyer to set up a Clifford Trust, and for most parents a gift or an interest-free loan up to $10,000 is simpler and just as effective. But if you own a business with capital assets such as an office building or factory machinery, you can shape a Clifford Trust into a superb Tax Saver. Let's say your business owns and occupies a small office building. Transfer that building to the Clifford Trust. You then pay rent on the building to the trust. You deduct the rent as a business expense, and the trust pays that rent to your child—in his low tax bracket. After ten or twelve years, the trust dissolves, and the building reverts to you.

COLLEGE HOUSING

Since providing for a child's college years is of great concern to most parents, you should consider the expense in two distinct parts—tuition and housing.

To cover housing needs and possibly to make some money for yourself at the same time, consider purchasing a townhouse or condo in the town where the school is located. You will be able to rent the place to your child and roommates, declare the rental income, and claim all the corresponding deductions associated with rental property. This way, you can cut down on the increases in housing prices at college towns and at the same time take advantage of the superb Tax Savers yielded by rental property.

When school is over and your son or daughter graduates, you have the option of selling or keeping the property for still further rental. Not a bad deal.

CHILD CARE

Another Tax Saver is available to you when your children are still young. If you and your spouse both work and pay someone to care for your child, you can take advantage of the Child and Dependent Care Credit, a nifty Tax Saver enacted by Congress to ease the costs connected with child care. This is a simple Tax Saver and a lucrative one: It can cut your tax bill by as much as $480 to $720 a year for one child, $960 to $1,440 for two or more. It can even help defray the bill for summer camp.

To qualify, both you and your spouse must work or be actively looking for work or attend school. Part-time jobs qualify, but volunteer jobs don't. You must be working for pay or looking for a paying job.

With few exceptions, you and your spouse must file a joint income tax return. You claim the credit on Form 2441, Credit for Child and Dependent Care Expenses. You can even claim this credit on the short form, 1040A.

The formula works this way: If your adjusted gross income is $10,000 or less, your credit is 30 percent of your child-care expenses. That percentage declines by one percentage point for each $2,000 increase in adjusted gross income. With adjusted gross income above $28,000, you get a credit of 20 percent of your child-care expenses; the percentage does not decline any further. But no matter how low or high your income or your child-care expenses, your credit is based on no more than $2,400 worth of expenses a year for one child, $4,800 a year for two or more. That's the ceiling. The children must be under fifteen, unless they are disabled or otherwise need special care.

The IRS doesn't care whether your children are cared for by a neighbor, a day-care center, your mother-in-law, or a summer camp. Nor does it care whether your child is cared for at home or away. But things are more complicated if you hire someone to come into your home, because then you have to pay Social Security tax on that person's wages, even if the sitter is your mother. It doesn't take much in wages to incur the obligation. If you pay someone $50 or more a quarter—that's fifty bucks spread over three months—you must pay Social Security on those wages. And unless you deduct the employee's share of the Social Security tax from his or her wages, you'll have to pay both shares—for 1985, a total of 14.1 percent.

Most parents don't stop to think about it, but raising children makes you a small-time philanthropist. Every time you drive kids to Girl Scouts or Little League, bake cookies for the PTA, or drive to church to teach Sunday School, you are contributing to a tax-exempt charity. You can deduct those expenses. These may be the tiniest of Tax Savers, but they add up. Keep receipts and make notes on your calendar. Parents often feel as if we're doing a lot for our children and their organizations. It's time we got a little in return.

Tax Savers
for
Employees

*A*ll of us gripe about work. Employees particularly gripe about the tax breaks they don't
get because they're not among the superrich or the high-
rolling entrepreneurs.

Instead of griping, employees should cash in the numerous Tax Savers that are uniquely available to them—Tax
Savers that can greatly enhance the value of any salary.

To be sure, employees do not qualify for many of the
Tax Savers that benefit the self-employed, but employees
qualify for their own distinctive and lucrative Tax Savers.
Take advantage of them.

Some of the best employee Tax Savers are put on your
plate and served to you, with no effort or thought on your
part. These are the fringe benefits that employees normally
take for granted, failing to realize that fringes increase
the compensation of the typical American employee by
roughly 15 percent and failing to appreciate their additional
value as Tax Savers. By using available fringe benefits to
your best advantage, you can increase your worth even
more.

In addition, other employee Tax Savers are there for the
taking—if you understand them and care to work them
into your plans. Let's start with those.

TRAVEL SUBSIDIES

If there is anything that employees as a group envy most about the self-employed, it is their ability to write off plush vacation trips as business expenses—or, more realistically (and more legally), to tack a vacation onto a deductible business trip. Good news, employees; you can do the same thing. In fact, you can have an easier time of it than self-employed people.

"Writing off" a trip doesn't mean that someone else pays for it. It simply means that the costs associated with the trip are deductible from your taxable income. Since you are an employee traveling on business, your employer will either directly pay your way or reimburse you. He pays for your airplane tickets, your hotel bills, your meals, and other expenses. When an expense-account business trip happens to take you to a pleasant spot, why not work in a vacation? It's perfectly legal. Your employer has to pay for your round-trip transportation anyway; it doesn't matter that the return leg follows a vacation. Of course, you'll have to pay for the side trip and the costs for your family or anyone else who goes along purely for fun. If the place is nearby—or if you have time enough—you might drive to your business meeting. You'll get reimbursed by the mile, and any companions will travel free.

Here's another plus: During the business portion of the trip, your employer will pay your hotel bill. Most hotels charge just a few dollars more for a second adult in a room, and many don't charge at all for children in the same room. For a traveling family with one member on an expense account, some of the best and most luxurious accommodations are offered by the growing number of "suites only" hotels. For the regular room rate—reimbursed by your employer—you get a suite of rooms, so the family isn't cramped.

This is a perfectly legal way to enhance the benefits of your expense account. Why do we call it a Tax Saver? Because it is worth even more than the dollars you save by not having to pay your own travel costs. After all, you normally pay for vacations and other pleasures in after-tax dollars. Depending on your tax bracket, you might have to earn $3,000 to take a $2,000 vacation, with the other $1,000 going to Uncle Sam in income tax. But not if your employer pays the tab. Those dollars are not earned dollars, and neither you nor your employer has to pay tax on them.

Fine, you say, but my business trips are always to Minneapolis in January and Miami in July. You'd like to reverse those destinations, and still find a Tax Saver along the way. We can arrange it—Strassels and Mead, your friendly travel advisers.

Once again, it's a case of mixing business with pleasure. This time, your business trip is to look for another job. As long as you are exploring job opportunities in your present trade or business, your expenses—including travel—are deductible. You don't actually have to change jobs. But you must build the trip around job-hunting. One job interview during a two-week excursion won't pass, although your expenses that day will. Three or four interviews spaced through the two weeks probably would, assuming you could show—if you are audited—that you scheduled appointments ahead of time and otherwise acted in a businesslike way.

You can't deduct job-hunting expenses if you are looking for your first job or if you have been unemployed for more than about six months. Nor can you take a deduction if you are changing careers; the jobs you interview for must be in the "same trade or business," as the IRS stiffly expresses it. That's a good reason to state your occupation, at the top of your income-tax form, in broad terms. Call yourself a writer not a newspaper reporter, a businessman not a financial analyst, an educator not a math teacher. These job descriptions are perfectly honest, and yet they provide elbow room that might make the difference between a job-hunting trip that is deductible and one that is not.

When you prepare your income tax return, you have to divide job-hunting expenses into two places. Expenses you incur while on your home turf tend to be pretty small, covering such items as lunches, résumés, phone calls, and taxi trips. Lump those under miscellaneous deductions on Schedule A, Itemized Deductions, and write in "job-hunting expenses." If they come to $400 or more, attach an itemized list.

For job-hunting expenses out of town, use Form 2106, Employee Business Expenses.

The same form down at the bottom has space for educational expenses related to your current job. We know a teacher who spent a summer in Egypt, learning all she could about the country and enjoying it thoroughly. She carefully brought home films, slides, and other materials, and she used the material extensively in her teaching. That qualified her to deduct most of the costs of the trip, because the money she spent helped her in her job. She even deducted her passport fee—perfectly legitimate.

The rules for educational deductions are sticky. A legal secretary can deduct tuition for legal courses because they would help her become a better legal secretary. But if she enrolls in law school, with the aim of becoming a lawyer, her tuition is not deductible, because you can't deduct educational costs designed to prepare you for a new career. So if you want to attend school with the thought of moving up, avoid enrolling in a degree program as long as you can.

If you are paying your tuition with tax-free money from a scholarship or a veterans' program, your educational deduction is severely limited. Since that income isn't being taxed anyway, you can't deduct what would otherwise be deductible educational expenses from your taxable income.

EMPLOYEE EXPENSES

Form 2106 is a catchall for a number of employee Tax Savers, because it gives you an opportunity to list—and deduct —money you spent in connection with work that was not reimbursed by your employer. And you can use Form 2106 whether or not you itemize other deductions—medical expenses, charitable contributions, state and local taxes, and interest—on Schedule A.

Form 2106 provides Tax Savers beyond these. How often have you traveled on business and chafed because your expense account didn't cover all your expenses? Most traveling executives consider that a routine burden; they invariably spend money out of pocket. The costs are deductible; just list them on Form 2106. Your out-of-pocket expenses have to be reasonable, but you can be pretty self-indulgent. Let's say your employer limits you to $20 for dinner, and you spend $30; the additional ten bucks is deductible on Form 2106. So is the difference between first-class and coach air fare if your employer pays only for coach. To substantiate these deductions, keep good records.

Some jobs require you to take temporary assignments away from home—not simple business trips but periods of several weeks or months at a different location, where you have to set up temporary housekeeping. Those living and travel costs are deductible on Form 2106, as long as the assignment is clearly temporary. If you maintain a household back home, the IRS will be satisfied.

You probably spend personal money in connection with your job even without traveling. For example, you might drive a couple of hundred miles a year on minor business errands. That's deductible, at 20.5 cents a mile. (That amount is subject to change.) If your employer reimburses you by the mile but pays less than 20.5 cents, you can deduct the difference.

In recent years the IRS has tightened up Form 2106, limiting it almost entirely to automobile and travel expenses and the costs of education related directly to your business or profession. But the law didn't change; you still can deduct any reasonable work-related expense that wasn't reimbursed by your employer. If it won't fit on Form 2106, list it—or, in most cases, lump it—under miscellaneous deductions on Schedule A. If you buy a desk set for your office at work, deduct the cost. If you buy a briefcase, deduct that, too. Deduct professional and business dues. If you are a sales representative, deduct subscriptions to *The Wall Street Journal* and *Business Week*, for example, and the cost of books that relate to your work. But don't try to deduct the cost of your local daily newspaper or of *Sports Illustrated*. (It helps you converse with your customers? Sorry, that's too indirect.)

When you buy lunch for a customer, that's clearly de-

———

ductible as an employee business expense. When you buy lunch for someone in connection with looking for a new job in your present trade or business, that's clearly deductible as a job-hunting expense. But what about buying lunch for someone in your office? The rule under employee business expenses is clear: You can deduct the cost of lunch (or flowers or any other reasonable expense) for those who rank below you, but not for your peers or superiors. As a job-hunting expense, however, you probably could deduct the cost of buying lunch for your boss if you use the occasion to ask him for a promotion.

MOVING COSTS

If you move your household to take a new job or a transfer, your moving costs are deductible, including some of your travel and living expenses while you look for a new home. The move can even be a short one; you qualify if the new job location would have added as much as thirty-five miles to your commuting distance. Like so many employee Tax Savers, this one requires a special form—3903, Moving Expense Adjustment. You can use this Tax Saver whether or not you itemize deductions on Schedule A.

All that is pretty logical, as tax rules go, but logic founders on the aggravating rules having to do with the costs of commuting and buying business clothes. Both costs are clearly related to your job—after all, you make your living by being an employee—but neither is deductible except in very narrow circumstances. You can deduct commuting costs only if you have to carry tools back and forth in your car or truck. (A briefcase is not a tool.) You can deduct clothing costs only for work-related uniforms.

A few years ago, a woman tried to strike a blow for all those millions of working Americans who spend hundreds of dollars every year for suits, dressy shoes, and other such clothing that they rarely wear outside the work place. This heroic woman worked in a fashionable clothing boutique, and she was required to dress the part. She couldn't afford that kind of clothing, and she didn't even like it; her tastes were more conservative. She wore those expensive outfits only to work, and she deducted their cost from her taxable income. To her, they were uniforms.

But not to the IRS. She appealed to the U.S. Tax Court and won, but it was a hollow victory. The IRS appealed to a still higher court and emerged the winner. The woman may not have liked the clothing, the appeals court ruled, but these outfits were general-purpose clothes, not uniforms. We might summarize the rule this way: steel-toed safety shoes, yes; high heels, no; an airline pilot's uniform, yes; plain overalls for a dirty job, no.

Another unkind provision: Let's say you bring a lot of work home from the office, so you set up an office in your home where you do the work, keep files, and so forth. You may even use your home computer for business chores. Nevertheless, those costs are not deductible unless your employer requires you to maintain that home office. The same restriction applies to your home computer, courtesy of the 1984 tax law: You get no deductions unless your employer requires you to have one. The home-office Tax Savers are only for self-employed people. If you use your home office and computer for a self-employed moonlighting venture, they qualify.

DAY CARE

Working parents qualify for a Tax Saver lobbied through Congress by the women's movement. It provides a tax credit that, in effect, repays you for part of the money you spend on day care.

Want to send your children to camp and get a Tax Saver along with the peace and quiet? If your child is under fifteen, you can do it with Form 2441, Credit for Child and Dependent Care Expenses. Many working parents aren't aware that summer camp qualifies; they tend to think of day care in narrow terms. In fact, any kind of reasonable expense qualifies as long as you spend the money to take care of a dependent so that you and your spouse can work.

And the dependent need not be a child. He or she can be an elderly parent or anyone else who can't care for himself or herself and for whom you provide more than half the

support. It doesn't matter whether or not that person qualifies as an exemption on page 1 of your tax return. But with
the exception of children under fifteen, the person has to be
cared for in your home—no summer camps for the elderly.

There's more to this wonderful Tax Saver. Although it's
designed primarily for working parents, one spouse can attend school instead of working. If you're separated or unmarried, you still can qualify; after all, the child or other
dependent needs care when you're away at work or school,
and that's what the credit is designed for. You can even use
this Tax Saver if your spouse is laid up and needs care. Did
your spouse need a day nurse for a week while you work?
That qualifies.

This is a tax credit—better than a tax deduction, because every dollar of credit is a full dollar off your tax bill.
The lower your income, the more this Tax Saver pays you.
If your adjusted gross income is $10,000 or less, your credit
is 30 percent of your day-care expenses. That percentage
declines gradually as your income rises, dropping to 20 percent when your income reaches $28,000 or more. You apply
the percentage to the first $2,400 of expenses for one depen-
dent or $4,800 for two or more. So depending on your in-
come level, that credit ranges from $480 to $720 with one
dependent, $960 to $1,440 with two or more.

FRINGE BENEFITS

Fringe benefits make terrific Tax Savers. In fact, some can
be considered double Tax Savers. There are two types of
fringe benefits. For the first, you get the benefit but must
include the value in your income for tax purposes; for the
second, you get the benefit completely tax-free.

For example, let's say your employer provides you with
$50,000 in group life insurance as a fringe benefit. The com-
pany pays $150 a year for the coverage. You don't pay any
income tax even though your family would get the insurance money at your death. If you tried to buy comparable
insurance on your own, you might pay a $250 annual pre-
mium. If you are in a 40 percent tax bracket, you would
have to earn $416, because your tax on $416 comes to $166.

Furthermore, many fringe benefits are of such extraordinarily high quality that you could not buy them on your own. You are covered by your employer's group life insurance policy regardless of any ailments you may have; as an individual, you would have to take a physical examination before the same insurance company would sell you a policy. The group health insurance policies offered by many employers provide superbly broad coverage, often beyond the limits of policies for sale to individuals.

Fringe benefits are almost too good to be true. They protect you and your family against the financial ravages of illness, death, and retirement. If you are fortunate enough, they may also provide you with a car, a club membership, day care for your children, education, free or discounted goods or services from your employer, financial counseling, legal help. And every one of these bountiful benefits carries the additional sweetener of being a Tax Saver.

To be sure, employees do pay income tax on some fringes. For example, let's say you win a sales contest and are awarded a $2,000 vacation for you and your family. That $2,000 will show up on your W-2 form; you'll have to pay income tax on it. If you're in the 40 percent bracket, the tax will be $800. Still, you're getting a Tax Saver as well as an award. Compare your costs with those of another family that took the same vacation, and paid for it out of pocket. We'll say they're in the 40 percent bracket, too. To come up with $2,000 for their vacation, they have to earn $3,300—$2,000 for the vacation, $1,300 for income tax.

A company car is among the lushest of fringes. Authorities figure that it costs the average family 35 cents to 40 cents a mile to maintain a car. Since most of us drive a car 10,000 miles or so each year, that's roughly $4,000 every year. And once again, that doesn't take into consideration the income tax you would have to pay on the earnings that you use to buy the car.

Many fringe benefits are beyond your control, but some can be parlayed so they provide even greater value. Many companies pay all or part of an employee's educational expenses and let the employee take whatever courses he or she wants. If you pay for your own education while working, you can deduct the costs only if the courses apply to your present job. But if your employer foots the bill, the IRS imposes no such limitation. So a legal secretary can train to be a lawyer or a draftsman can study to be an engineer, and the employer graciously pays the tuition. If you are looking for a job while hoping in the future to prepare yourself for a better occupation, ask potential employers about their educational benefits. They're your ladder upward.

The group insurance that employers provide is much cheaper than individual policies, simply through the economies of scale. Many companies that provide free group life insurance let employees buy additional coverage, at much less cost than an individual policy.

Company pension plans traditionally provide one of the three legs on which prudent Americans build their retirement security; the other two are Social Security and personal investments. Pension plans are among the most bountiful of Tax Saver fringes, because you pay no income tax on the contribution your employer makes in your behalf every year, and you pay no income tax on the interest or dividends it earns.

To take full advantage of company pension plans, you have to know their terms. Typically, employees become vested—meaning entitled to benefits at age sixty-five—after ten years of service. Under some plans, fewer years of service are required. Once you know just when you will become fully or partially vested and how much greater your pension will be for additional years of service, you can work that into any decision to change jobs. For example, if you're due to become vested in six months, you might wait that long before switching to another job. Also, find out if your pension is transferable to another employer.

When you do leave a job, stop by the personnel office and find out precisely how, and when, to claim your pension. Most of us work for several firms during our lifetimes, and if you plan things right, you might earn a pension from every one of them. If you left the XYZ Company at age forty, don't expect the pension department to look you up when you reach sixty-five. Apply for your pension; you're the one who will benefit.

Nowadays, the traditional company pension plan is just one of two or three Tax Saver pension programs available to employees. Any working American can contribute up to $2,000 a year to an Individual Retirement Account. If your spouse works, your family can sock away $4,000. If your spouse does not work, the two of you can make a combined annual contribution of $2,250 into spousal IRAs. IRA contributions are deductible from your income, and—like other pension plans—you pay no income tax on the earnings until you withdraw them. Barring death or disability, you can't start withdrawing your IRA money until you are fifty-nine and a half years old. You can choose where to invest your IRA; we discuss this wonderful Tax Saver thoroughly in Chapter 13.

SALARY REDUCTION PLANS

Many companies today offer their employees a tax-deferred capital accumulation program that may be even more enticing than an IRA. Sometimes it's called a Salary Reduction Plan or a 401(k) plan, after the section of the Internal Revenue Code that describes it.

Under a 401(k) plan, you sign up with your employer to have a portion of your pretax salary deducted and invested in a 401(k) plan. The legal limit is 25 percent of your salary or $30,000, whichever is less. To encourage retirement planning by their employees, many firms partially match the employee's contribution. For example, for every dollar you authorize to be deducted from your salary, your employer might add 50 cents. All of that goes into a fund toward your own retirement, and you pay no income tax on any of the contribution or on the interest or dividends it earns, until you withdraw it.

Under a 401(k) plan, the withdrawal rules aren't as strict as they are for an IRA. Let's say you build up $40,000 in your 401(k) account and then leave that company. You can cash in your 401(k) money and pay income tax on it spread out over the next ten years. If you prefer to keep that money working toward retirement, you can switch it into what is called an IRA rollover account, avoiding taxes until withdrawal.

Even if you stay with the company but meet with a hardship, you may be allowed to withdraw money from your 401(k) account. The IRS has defined "hardship" as buying a personal residence, paying unusually large medical bills, or paying college tuition for your children. If the occasion arises, check with your company's plan administrator.

Let's say you are taking full advantage of both the IRA and your company's 401(k) plan and would like to save still more toward retirement. With the government's blessing, many companies will deduct another 10 percent of your salary and put these funds in the pension plan. Although this 10 percent isn't deductible, the interest or dividends this sum subsequently earns accumulate tax-deferred. And since it's your money, and you've already paid tax on it, you can withdraw whatever you've contributed when some big expense arises—for example, college tuition or purchase of a second or vacation home.

The bounty of employee Tax Savers runs counter to conventional wisdom that Tax Savers are unavailable to employees. Too many employees just shrug their shoulders and dig into their pockets on April 15.

For any employee, fringe benefits provide a solid foundation, both in Tax Savers and as props for family security. If you plan things carefully, you can make your fringes worth more, and at the same time you can take advantage of other employee Tax Savers. They can improve your fortunes while you work, help pay for your vacations, insure you against loss, and provide a comfortable retirement.

9

Tax Savers for the Self-Employed

M illions of Americans work for themselves, and millions more would like to. The Tax Savers connected with self-employment are bountiful. No other arrangement offers so many opportunities to reduce your taxes. If you run a profitable business, full-time or part-time, you can choose from a selection of Tax Savers as tempting as the choices at a candy store.

THE MYTHS
First of all we want to kill two myths that tend to mislead many budding entrepreneurs.

Myth 1: Even a home business that loses money can be profitable, because Tax Savers pay you back for your losses.

That's not true. Tax Savers can ease the pain of business losses. For a few years, you can deduct business losses against your other income, thereby lessening your tax burden. But you can't do that indefinitely. For the long haul, nothing—not even Tax Savers—can turn losses into profits.

We recommend that you go into business to make

money. Tax Savers will help make your business profitable and will help you keep those profits so that you won't have to turn them over to Uncle Sam.

> *Myth 2: Most Americans can't afford the*
> *risk of going to work for themselves.*

People who voice that myth assume that to start a business, you have to quit your regular job, but that's nonsense. Your business can be a tiny moonlighting enterprise. You may turn a personal hobby into a fledgling business operation. To the IRS, a business is a business. The Tax Savers for self-employment are the same whether you work on your enterprise full-time or part-time. Many entrepreneurs start their businesses in their spare time; that's certainly safer than cutting yourself off from a regular paycheck. In fact, employees who run their own businesses on the side get to double up on Tax Savers. They get the Tax Savers available to employees, which we discuss in Chapter 8. At the same time, they get the Tax Savers of self-employment.

In fact, once you go to work for yourself, you can compound your Tax Savers in several ways. All at the same time, you can hang on to your old job, be a sole proprietor, and have your own corporation. Each one of those arrangements offers unique Tax Savers, and by fitting the pieces together you can benefit from all of them. In this chapter, we'll show you how.

Throughout this book, we emphasize the importance of planning your Tax Savers. That's especially important when you work for yourself. Most of the Tax Savers you reap from self-employment are not the kind that you stumble across in April as you fill out your income tax form. You must plan them, just as you plan other aspects of your business and your personal finances. Tax Savers will help pay every dollar of your business expenses. If you buy a car or a computer for your business, Tax Savers will pay a surprisingly large portion of the price.

Any business has to weigh dollars coming in against dollars going out. Unless you work Tax Savers into that formula, you'll be working with misleading calculations. More important, you'll be cheating yourself. Frequently,

Tax Savers make the difference between a "go" and a "no-go" business decision.

That's no accident. Our economy runs on the wheels of profitable businesses, large and small. Over the years, Congress has sweetened the U.S. Tax Code with numerous Tax Savers designed to help make business profitable and to encourage people to start their own businesses. The tax cuts enacted in 1981 at the urging of President Reagan sweetened business Tax Savers even more. Congress cut back on a few provisions in 1984, but not drastically. As you read this chapter, you will be surprised at the generosity of the Tax Savers available to business.

THE HOBBY AS BUSINESS

In business? Can that be you? Indeed it can. If it isn't you, perhaps it should be. It may be time for you to turn your hobby into a profitable business. If you are an amateur photographer, find a way to sell your pictures, or to offer your services for weddings, bar mitzvahs, or school functions. If you are a collector of stamps or coins or baseball cards, become a professional trader. If friends come to you for advice on home decor or investing or auto repair, set yourself up as a consultant or a part-time mechanic. You don't have to quit your job or hire a secretary or even rent an office. You can moonlight at home, and it may not take much more time than you now devote to the same interest. But now you'll earn money, and you will benefit by converting previously nondeductible personal expenses into valuable Tax Savers.

Before we get into the details and tell you about the choices you need to make, let's look at the difference in cost between buying something for your hobby and buying the same item for your business. It doesn't matter whether we're talking about a camera or a batch of Portuguese stamps or a home computer. For the sake of our example, let's say you buy items costing $1,000 in total. We'll say your tax bracket is 40 percent. Okay. If you spend that $1,000 for personal use—for your hobby—you'll have to earn $1,666—$1,000 for the item you're buying plus $666

■■■■■

in income tax. That's because in your bracket, you have to earn $1,666 for every $1,000 you spend on anything.

Now let's say you have set yourself up in business. You may have just started the business yesterday, simply by telling your spouse that, darn it, you're going to try to make a little money on that hobby of yours, opening a separate bank account, and placing an ad in the newspaper. Now go out and buy that $1,000 worth of items. Now they are deductible, so the cost to you comes to only $600—$400 less! Like magic! You're deducting the cost as a legitimate business expense.

Here are some other things that you can now do that you could not do before. These sound like dreams, but they are perfectly legitimate. You don't have to cut corners, and we don't recommend that you try to. The law is generously sprinkled with Tax Savers.

1. You can deduct the cost of business trips, and you can plan business trips that are lots of fun. If you collect baseball cards, go to collectors' shows, maybe a couple of ballgames to see who's hot. If you take nature photographs, spend a week in the desert—we recommend January or February—or time in the mountains or at the beach in the summer, and build up a portfolio for sale. If you are a consultant, attend seminars or conventions. If you and your spouse operate a business together, take a weekend at a resort for a business conference.

2. You can take advantage of generous depreciation formulas and tax credits on a car, a computer, or other equipment that you use in your business.

3. You can put aside a large portion of your business profits toward retirement and pay no income tax on that pension contribution or on the interest or dividends it earns, until you withdraw it. Sounds like an IRA, doesn't it? Actually it's even better than an IRA, because you can put aside lots more money, saving more on taxes and yielding more for your retirement years.

Now let's get down to specifics and to telling you just how to work each Tax Saver into your plans. The most important choice you have to make is whether to work as a sole proprietor or to incorporate. Both have advantages; in fact, many entrepreneurs combine the two. We'll spell out the differences so you can weigh the benefits and drawbacks. We know them firsthand. Strassels has incorporated his business. Mead works as a sole proprietor.

SOLE PROPRIETORSHIP

If your business is a relatively small operation, we recommend that you work as a sole proprietor. The paperwork is a lot simpler, and the Tax Savers dovetail neatly with your personal finances.

To become a sole proprietor, you simply decide to do it. By all means check with your local government about any requirements for licensing or zoning; these depend on the nature of your business and where you live. But as far as the federal government is concerned, you don't have to do a thing. You don't have to register or fill out any federal forms. The IRS requires every business to have an identification number; for a sole proprietor, it's simply your Social Security number.

In fact, a sole proprietor doesn't even have to fill out a separate business tax return. You figure your business income and expenses on Schedule C, Profit (or Loss) from Business or Profession. You then put the bottom-line figure—your net profit or loss—on the first page of Form 1040.

The instant you make the decision to go into business, every expense related to your business becomes deductible. To be specific, we mean every expense that is "ordinary and necessary and reasonable," in the IRS's words. If you are a photographer, your photography magazines are now deductible. If you are an auto mechanic, that new set of wrenches becomes deductible. If you are a writer, nearly every magazine that you buy is now deductible; you can even depreciate your home library.

To satisfy the IRS—to take full advantage of all the Tax Savers that go with self-employment without risking disaster at an audit—you must keep precise records and operate in a businesslike manner. That doesn't mean that you have to buy a new suit or even shine your shoes. Let's confess:

Mead is typing this chapter while sitting at home in old corduroys and a sweater with a cat on his lap. He deducted the cost of the typing paper, the pencils, and everything else on his desk. He works in a converted bedroom and takes advantage of all the Tax Savers that go with an office in the home. He depreciated the cost of his desk and typewriter long ago. Later this year he may buy a word processor; thanks to Tax Savers, the government will pay almost half the cost. His old car is pushing 98,000 miles. This year or next he'll replace it. Thanks to Tax Savers, he can buy a Cadillac at the cost of a Chevy—or a Chevy for what a Chevy cost years ago.

None of these deductions is phony or devious, but they do have to be backed up with records and with evidence that the purpose of the business is profit. Beginning in 1985, failure to keep proper records can subject you to an expensive negligence penalty, in addition to costing you the unverified deductions. The government is blind to the merit of your work and the hours you put in. It doesn't care whether you produce great works of art or tawdry schlock or whether your work is enjoyable or miserable. For you to take advantage of the Tax Savers that go with self-employment, your goal must be profit. This is the one and only requirement.

If you make a profit, that's easy to prove; the bottom line is your evidence. But many businesses lose money from time to time, particularly during their early years of operation. Tax Savers cushion that blow; your business losses are deductible from your other income. The IRS has a simple test you must pass in order to deduct those business losses: Your business must show a net profit in at least two of any five consecutive years.

Oddly enough, the amount of profit doesn't much matter. If you show a profit of $100 for each of two years and losses of several thousand dollars for the other three years, you have still passed the test. Given that kind of elbow room, it's wise to plan your business cash flow so you can meet the two-of-five test. For example, if the current year is certain to wind up in the red, stock up on business supplies and equipment before the year is out. Even if you borrow the money to pay for your purchases, you may claim the deduction the year you buy them. At the same time, defer business income into the next year if you can. In other words, concentrate expenses, losses, and other deductions into the unprofitable year and push income into the following year so that it may show a profit, no matter how small.

As long as you are not backdating or otherwise falsifying records—in other words, as long as your books are honest—it is perfectly legal to regulate your cash flow to help hold down your taxes. To the IRS, that sort of thing is routine; every business has done it since our tax system began.

Let's say that despite your best efforts, your business loses money year after year. You're on the brink of flunking the two-in-five rule and becoming what the IRS calls "an activity not engaged in for profit"—in other words, a hobby. If your tax return is audited, all your business deductions could be wiped out. But all is not lost. Even the two-of-five rule can be overcome if you plan wisely. To overcome it, you will have to persuade the IRS that the goal of your business was profit. The IRS will be skeptical, even cynical; lots of people try to deduct their hobby expenses. To prepare for the possibility of such an event, you have to set up your business in the right way to begin with and conduct it in the right way year after year.

So from the first day that you go into business, be businesslike. If you are a photographer, try to sell your work, and keep records that demonstrate the sincerity of your sales effort. If it's appropriate, advertise. Give your business a name and get a separate telephone listing. Join trade or professional associations and attend their conventions. Set up a commercial checking account. Don't mix your business money with your household money. When you write a letter seeking to sell your services, keep a copy; when you make a phone call soliciting business, make a note of it in your daily log. When the IRS challenges someone who has been claiming at-home business losses year after year, the agency usually wins. But in hundreds of cases, taxpayers have come out on top. We've examined many of those cases. In virtually every one, the successful taxpayer has been meticulously businesslike.

▬▬▬

Anyway, a businesslike approach is beneficial whether your business loses money or—we hope—makes money. We talked about managing your cash flow; that is best done if you are on top of your income and expenses. The law does not require you to open a business checking account or get business stationery or use a separate telephone listing. Without knowing the nature of your business or your prospects for profit or loss, we can't tell you exactly what steps to take. If you are audited, separate check registers make a clear and persuasive distinction between business expenses and personal expenses. Besides, if an auditor wants to go over the checkbook register for your business, you're better off giving him those check stubs only. If he wants to look at your personal checkbook register, you're better off giving him those stubs only. If you use your personal bank account for your business, you'll have no choice but to give him a look at every check stub.

Similarly, if you have separate telephone listings, the IRS isn't likely to question your deductions for business telephone expenses; the bills for your business telephone will be clearly separate from those for your personal phone.

Whatever your business, you have to keep detailed records of your expenses and your income. That's not hard. Mead has a simple system—an open file folder for receipts, a small ledger book for income, and a pocket diary to note expenses and mileage. Your business may require a more sophisticated system. You may want to ask an accountant to help you set up a bookkeeping system—one that you understand and can handle yourself.

CARS AND COMPUTERS

Perhaps the sweetest Tax Savers of all are the generous write-offs allowed for a car, a computer, and other equipment you use in your business. These Tax Savers work best if you buy new equipment, but they pay very nicely even if you simply start using your old family car—or anything else—partly for business.

In 1984, Congress imposed limits on these generous write-offs. But the new law does not cripple these Tax Savers; far from it. The changes apply to cars and other business equipment purchased after June 18, 1984. Anything you bought on or before that date continues to benefit from the old rules, which were more generous.

With a car, old or new, you have a choice. Option One: You can keep track of the actual miles you drive for business and deduct 20.5 cents per mile. (That's the existing allowance. It may rise or fall in subsequent years.) Option Two: You can depreciate the car and deduct your actual automobile expenses—gasoline, oil, maintenance and repairs, insurance, tags, inspection fees. If you use the car for business and personal use, once again you must keep track of your business miles. For example, if you drive your car 60 percent for business and 40 percent for personal use, you deduct 60 percent of your actual auto expenses and depreciate 60 percent of its value. Every time you use the car for business, jot down the date, where you went, the business purpose, and the number of miles you drove. Keep a pad in the car so you can keep track day by day.

Unless your car is quite old, you're generally better off with the second option. Under Option One, the government's mileage allowance of 20.5 cents is too low, in the opinion of many authorities. Besides, Option Two lets you depreciate the car over three years—in other words, deduct its cost in three chunks, as if you were going to throw it away after using it three years.

In addition, you may also get an investment tax credit— in effect, a bonus Tax Saver for newly acquired business equipment.

Whichever option you choose, you have to keep records of your mileage and expenses. At the end of the year you can work the formula both ways and see which one saves you more on your tax bill.

To start, let's assume you're buying a new car for your business. Under Option Two, you deduct the operating expenses for the year and choose among three formulas for depreciation and investment tax credit. Whichever formula you use—and all three are generous—you're subject to two limitations if you bought the car after June 18, 1984.

1. Although your investment tax credit remains at 6 percent, it cannot exceed $1,000.

2. Your depreciation deductions cannot exceed $4,000 the first year, or $6,000 in any subsequent year.

Congress imposed these limitations to discourage purchase of expensive foreign cars for business use. Contrary to news reports, the law does not bar write-offs of luxury cars. But under the change, the Tax Savers pay off most handsomely for cars costing $16,000 or less.

We'll assume that you buy a new car after June 18, 1984. You pay $12,000 for it, and you use the car entirely for business. Here are your three choices:

Choice 1

Take a 6 percent investment tax credit. That's $720 off the top of your tax bill for the year in which you buy the car. Reduce your Basis (cost) by one half of the tax credit—in this case, $360. So your depreciation Basis is $11,640. Deduct that $11,640 over three years as a business expense, using this formula:

	Deduction	Tax Saving, assuming 40 percent tax bracket
Year of purchase 25%	$ 2,910	$1,164 + $720 tax credit. Total $1,884
Second year 38%	$ 4,423	$1,769
Third year 37%	$ 4,307	$1,723
Total 100%	$11,640	$5,376

The government has paid nearly half the cost of your car, not to mention your deductions for operating expenses.

If, instead, you had bought a high-priced car—say, one costing $35,000—your investment tax credit would bump against the $1,000 ceiling, and your annual depreciation would bump against the ceilings of $4,000 the first year and $6,000 for subsequent years. As a result, it would take seven years to write off the entire cost.

Getting back to our $12,000 car, here are your other choices.

Choice 2

Reduce the investment tax credit by two percentage points—to 4 percent—or $480. Depreciate the entire cost of the car, using the same formula:

	Deduction	Tax Saving, assuming 40 percent tax bracket
Year of purchase 25%	$ 3,000	$1,200 + $480 tax credit. Total $1,680
Second year 38%	$ 4,560	$1,824
Third year 37%	$ 4,440	$1,776
Total 100%	$12,000	$5,280

Although the totals come out within $100 of each other, you're probably a little better off with Choice 1 because the larger tax credit concentrates more of the Tax Saver in the first year.

Choice 3

Congress shaved this formula in 1984, but it nevertheless usually works out best of all. The year you buy the car, deduct the first $5,000 of the price. (Starting in 1988, deduct the first $7,500. Starting in 1990, deduct the first $10,000.)

On what's left—the purchase price minus $5,000—apply Choice 1 or Choice 2; your decision. We'll work it out here under Choice 1.

	Deduction	Tax Saving, assuming 40 percent tax bracket
Year of purchase	flat $5,000	$2,000 + 420 tax credit.
For *Depreciation*, your Basis is $6,790. (That's $12,000 minus $5,000 minus half of the tax credit, or $210.) $6,790 × 25%	$ 1,698	$ 679
		Total $3,099
Second year 38%	$ 2,580	$1,032
Third year 37%	$ 2,512	$1,005
Total 100%	$11,790	$5,136

Again the total Tax Saver comes out close. But you get much more of it the first year. In most cases, Choice 3 is best.

We've been assuming that you use your new car entirely for business. Actually, the IRS does not object to what it calls incidental use for personal trips. For example, if you drive to the grocery store twice a week, don't worry. That's incidental, and you can still take the Tax Savers on the basis of 100 percent business use.

If you use the car partly for business and partly for personal use, you must keep track of the mileage in a diary, noting the purpose and mileage of every business errand and keeping track of the total mileage. Then figure the ratio. In the 1984 tax law, Congress sharply curbed the Tax

Savers for cars used 50 percent or less for business. If your driving ratio comes out more than half for business use—even just 51 percent—then you can apply that percentage to the amounts computed under Choice 1, Choice 2, or Choice 3. One bonus: Under Choice 3, you get that delicious $5,000 deduction the first year no matter what. So in our example of 51 percent business use, your business "cost" of the car would be $6,120—a $12,000 car, used 51 percent for business. And you would deduct the entire $5,000 the first year. In addition, you can deduct 51 percent of all your auto expenses for the year—gasoline, repairs, insurance, tags, inspections.

If the business use of your car comes to 50 percent or less, your Tax Savers are not nearly as generous, although they're not bad. You lose the investment tax credit entirely. Instead of depreciating the car over three years, you must depreciate it over five years, in equal amounts. For example, let's say your $12,000 car is used 40 percent for business, 60 percent for personal use. Forty percent of $12,000 is $4,800. That's the amount you get to depreciate, in five annual installments of $960 each. In addition, you can deduct 40 percent of all your auto expenses. You'll want to compare the result with what you'd get for simply deducting 20.5 cents for every business mile you drive.

If you buy a computer or any other piece of equipment, and use it more than half the time for business, you have the same choices for combining depreciation with a tax credit, including Choice 3's flat $5,000 depreciation deduction for the year of purchase. But computers and other kinds of business equipment have to be depreciated over five years rather than three years. Here are the depreciation percentages for each year. Otherwise, the formulas work exactly the same as with a car:

Year of purchase	15%
Second year	22%
Third year	21%
Fourth year	21%
Fifth year	21%

If the business portion of the cost of your computer comes to $5,000 or less, you won't need those percentages. You'll simply deduct the entire cost the first year, using the flat $5,000 deduction allowed under Choice 3.

As with a car, if your business use of a home computer or any other equipment comes out to 50 percent or less, you lose the investment tax credit and your depreciation must be spread out—in this case, over twelve years of equal installments. To get any deduction, you have to log every use of the computer, business and personal, so you can work out the ratio, based on time. Without a log, you can't claim the deduction.

Although Congress limited the dollar amount of the investment tax credit and annual depreciation for cars, it placed no such limitation on the purchase of computers or other business equipment.

Whether you're buying a car, a computer, or anything else, make sure you pay for it (with cash or borrowed money) and put it in service before the end of the year. It isn't enough to order something in December, or even to order it and pay for it in December. To qualify for depreciation that year, it must be put *in service* before year-end. As with a car, the use of a computer or any other kind of equipment can be divided between personal and business use.

A different formula, just as attractive, is available for depreciating real estate. For example, let's say you buy a small office building for your business, using part of it and renting out the rest. You do not get an investment tax credit for real estate, but you get to depreciate the building over fifteen years if you bought it before March 15, 1984, or over eighteen years if you bought it after that date. Either way, that's quite a Tax Saver, especially when you consider that most real estate does not depreciate in value; it appreciates. For details on investing in real estate, see Chapter 12, Tax Savers for Investors.

Let's say you bought a business car, a computer, or office furniture a year or two ago but were unaware of the depreciation deduction and the tax credit and failed to take advantage of them. Good news: You can reach back and amend those old tax returns as long as they are no more than three years old. One exception: You can't use an amended return to claim that flat $5,000 first-year depreciation deduction. For details, see Chapter 17, Cash In Your Old Tax Returns.

OFFICE AT HOME

If your business is in your home, you may be able to deduct a portion of your housing expenses. Figure the portion in one of two ways: the ratio of business rooms to total rooms (not counting bathrooms) or the ratio of business square feet to total square feet. Let's say your office occupies one tenth of the total square feet of your house. That means you can deduct one tenth of your utility costs and cleaning costs, and you can depreciate one tenth of the cost of your house. It doesn't matter how many hours you work at home; a moonlighting business that keeps you busy only a few hours a week qualifies just as much as a full-time enterprise. Your home office does not have to be a separate room.

Office-at-home deductions are divided into two categories, with differing rules. To qualify for the depreciation deduction, the space must be used entirely for business. To be sure, you can pay bills on the same desk once a week; that's incidental use. But under the rules covering depreciation, an office in the home cannot be divided between business and personal use. And even if the space *is* used entirely for business, you can take the depreciation deduction only against business profits. That particular Tax Saver can be used to take your home-business net down to zero, but no further.

That is not true, however, for other expenses connected with your home office. If you use the space half for business and half for personal use, you deduct 50 percent of the appropriate expenses—utilities, cleaning, and so forth. And those expenses can be used to push your business into the red, as long as you meet the other criteria governing business losses.

A tip: Strange as it may seem, it's not wise to qualify for the home-office depreciation deduction for the year in which you sell your house, assuming you are selling the house at a profit and buying another home. That kind of housing deal enables you to defer the capital gains tax on the profit. But if you claim a home-office depreciation deduction for, say, one tenth of the house, you'll be barred from deferring tax on one tenth of your profit. Even if you have claimed depreciation year after year, don't claim it for that final year, and make sure you don't qualify for it. Even if it's a bother, use the space for personal use at least part of that year. That is a tax maneuver, but it is not a dodge. It is perfectly legal.

KEOGH RETIREMENT ACCOUNTS

The more profit your business earns, the better the Tax Savers will be. As a sole proprietor, you can shelter a great deal of your profits from taxes by investing in a Keogh retirement account. Until recent years, the Keogh Tax Saver for sole proprietors wasn't as generous as the kind of pension Tax Saver you could establish by incorporating. But Congress evened the two. Now the Keogh Tax Saver allows you to contribute 20 percent of your business net profits or $30,000, whichever is less, into pension funds of your choice. Your contributions are deductible, and the dividends or interest that they earn accumulate tax-free until you withdraw the money in retirement. To contribute the full 20 percent, you have to divide your Keogh contribution into two kinds of accounts—a technical distinction, but an important one. Any Keogh custodian—a bank, a savings institution, or a mutual fund, for example—can tell you how to do that. The most flexible kind of Keogh account is called a profit-sharing plan; put as much of your Keogh contribution as possible into a profit-sharing plan. Put the remainder into the other kind of Keogh account, which is called a money-purchase plan. From a profit-sharing Keogh, you can begin withdrawing money at age fifty-nine and a half, even if you are still working. From a money-purchase Keogh, you cannot withdraw money until you retire, no matter how late in life you work.

Many self-employed people assume they have to choose between a Keogh and an IRA, but they do not. Any working American can have an IRA. If you are self-employed, full-time or part-time, you can have both a Keogh and an IRA, taking advantage of both Tax Savers while building a retirement nest egg.

HIRING YOUR FAMILY

Most small businesses need part-time help, at least occasionally. For a sole proprietor, there is no better deal than hiring your spouse and children. You must pay them the going wage for whatever work they do. Thanks to a quirk in the law, you do not have to pay Social Security tax on their wages, as you would with any other employee. If your spouse does not work elsewhere and you are planning together toward retirement, by all means put him or her to work, at least enough to earn $2,000 a year. Put that $2,000 into an IRA. That way you have a double Tax Saver: a deduction for your business and a tax-sheltered investment for your spouse.

Your children can help your business—and earn money for themselves—even when they are quite young. The IRS once challenged a couple who operated a trailer park and paid their children to pick up trash, operate the laundry machines, and do other odd jobs. After all, the IRS huffed, these kids were seven, nine, and twelve years old. The youngest was earning $20 a week, the eldest $40. A federal court reviewed the case and ruled that the parents were within their rights in hiring their children; in fact, the judge said that the salaries were too low.

Pay your spouse and children by check, as you would any other employee. You might encourage the children to save their money toward college; they'll earn interest on their savings, and their tax bracket probably is lower than yours. Be sure they file income tax returns.

AVOIDING ERRORS

As a sole proprietor, you figure your business profits or losses on Schedule C, Profit (or Loss) from Business or Profession. If you earn a profit of $400 or more, you have to pay Social Security tax; calculate that on Schedule SE. To depreciate a car, a computer, or any other equipment, use Form 4562, Depreciation and Amortization. To take an investment credit, use Form 3468, Computation of Investment Credit. These forms are one page each and are not terribly complicated. Nevertheless, we suggest that you consult a tax professional.

As a group, sole proprietors make more mistakes on their taxes than anyone else. Their rate of compliance, according to the IRS, is below 60 percent, as compared to better than 90 percent for wage earners in the highest brackets. For some reason, in the past the IRS has audited only 4 percent of the tax returns filed by sole proprietors reporting $50,000 or more in income, but the IRS audited 6 percent of the tax returns filed by wage earners in the same income group. However, the agency has upgraded its computers and is cracking down on small businesses that don't fully pay withholding and Social Security for employees on time. Of course, if you have no employees, you can take care of those payments as part of your quarterly estimated income tax.

INCORPORATING

Incorporating is more complicated than operating as a sole proprietorship, but it has its advantages. A corporation is a separate citizen and taxpayer.

Unlike a sole proprietorship, a corporation can, in effect, pay lots of your family expenses with pretax dollars. A corporation can pay the life and health insurance premiums of its employees. In drafting the bylaws of your corporation, you can state that the corporation also must pay any medical and dental bills not covered by health insurance. These fringe benefits are deductible to the corporation and do not count as taxable income to employees. But if you plan to hire employees, look out; benefits must be the same for all. You can't pay all of your own family's medical expenses while limiting an employee's health benefits to insurance premiums only.

For a car, a computer, and other equipment, a corporation gets the same depreciation allowances and tax credits as does a sole proprietor. But remember, your corporation is a separate taxpayer. If it winds up the year in the red, you cannot deduct its business losses on your individual income tax return.

Corporations are justly famous for the flexibility they allow. Let's say your corporation is having a bad year. You need a new car for business use, but if you buy it, the Tax Savers won't do your corporation any good; it's in the red, with no profits to take the deductions or tax credits against. As an individual, you have income from other sources and would like to pay less income tax. Solution: Buy the car in your own name and lease it to your corporation, at the going rate. Take the depreciation and tax credit on your personal income tax return. If you don't want to pay tax on the rental income, put the rent in a Clifford Trust for the benefit of your children. We explain that maneuver in Chapter 7, Tax Savers for Parents.

Arrangements of this kind require careful planning. As the president of your corporation, you are free to establish a fiscal year—in other words, to pick any New Year's Day you want for your corporation. Let's say you decide to start your fiscal year January 15. On January 14, you pay yourself your entire salary for the previous twelve months. As an individual, you received that salary in January; you won't have to report it as income for fifteen months, until April 15 of the following year. But as a corporation you paid out that money just before the end of your fiscal year; it's an immediate deduction.

ACCUMULATING PROFITS
Lots of advisers urge entrepreneurs to set up what is called a Subchapter S Corporation. We disagree. A Subchapter S has

one advantage only: Losses as well as profits can be passed through to you as the owner, so you get to deduct them. But we urge you to go into business for profit, not loss. If your business will lose money for a few years, stick with a sole proprietorship.

A regular corporation, unlike a Subchapter S Corporation, can accumulate money and invest it. The corporate tax rate is 15 percent on the first $25,000 of profit, 18 percent on the second $25,000, 30 percent on the third $25,000, 40 percent on the fourth $25,000, and 46 percent on net profits above $100,000.

The corporation is yours, so you get to decide how much of its income is retained as profit and how much is paid to you (and perhaps to your spouse and children) as salary. After paying yourself enough for a comfortable living, you can make that decision on the basis of tax rates. If your personal tax bracket is high, leave the money in the corporation and let it pay tax at the lower corporate rate. Some year when your personal income is low, pay yourself a bonus from the corporate treasury. On the other hand, if you want to avoid paying corporate income tax, simply pay all the profits to yourself as salary, leaving the corporation with a profit of zero.

A corporation that provides services can accumulate as much as $150,000; a nonservice business, such as a manufacturer, can accumulate $250,000. Those limits don't apply if the money is being saved toward a new building or some other form of expansion. If your corporation accumulates money, you need not let that money lie idle. You can invest it with complete freedom. You can buy stocks, bonds, real estate, or anything else.

Corporate stocks are a particularly good investment for your corporation, because a corporation pays tax on only 15 percent of dividend income. If you owned the stock yourself, you would pay income tax on all the dividend income, less the $100 exclusion. Of course, when you later draw that money from the corporation as salary, you will have to pay income tax on it. But you can time your withdrawals according to the rhythms of your tax bracket.

Most of us remark from time to time about the lavish

spending habits of big business. Firms send employees to leisurely conventions at lush vacation spots; they reward salespeople with luxury cruises; their employees travel for seemingly trivial reasons and entertain at expensive restaurants. None of this would be possible without Tax Savers— the multitude of deductions and credits that ease the way for American business. It's hard to believe, but when you start your own business, you instantly become entitled to use every one of those generous Tax Savers. They are available whether you set yourself up as a sole proprietor or as a corporation. To take full advantage of them, all you have to do is make a profit. With careful planning, Tax Savers will help you achieve that goal.

Tax Savers
for
Homeowners

*M*ore than forty-five years ago, Congress made it the official policy of our government to encourage Americans to own their homes. It did so by providing homeowners with very generous Tax Savers—so generous they are difficult to ignore. That policy has not changed; indeed, the Tax Savers available if you own your home have been expanded over the years. Additional Tax Savers—just as lucrative—have been enacted to sweeten the investment potential of buying a second home and renting it out. Homeownership is one of America's most generous and popular Tax Savers, and unless your circumstances are unusual, it is one you should work into your plans.

In this chapter, we'll tell you how to plan and use the Tax Savers that come with owning your own home, whether it is a house, a townhouse, a co-op, or a condo. These Tax Savers are expansive; they can easily save you thousands of dollars every year. We'll tell you how to protect your profits and compound your Tax Savers as you move from one home to another. Finally, we'll introduce you to the Tax Savers that come with owning a second home, including a new and phenomenally generous one that you get if that second home qualifies as an investment property.

We'll start, as most families do, with what the IRS calls your principal residence—the home you live in.

ITEMIZED DEDUCTIONS

For most Americans, homeownership provides not only its own Tax Savers but also the foundation for other Tax Savers as well. The interest you pay on your mortgage loan and the real estate taxes you pay to your locality are deductible from your taxable income on Schedule A, Itemized Deductions. These are substantial deductions—usually large enough, all by themselves, to make it worthwhile for you to itemize all of your other Schedule A tax deductions—charity, tax and interest payments, medical expenses, and miscellaneous items.

If you do not itemize deductions, you get to use the so-called standard deduction, or "zero bracket amount," which for 1984 was pegged at $2,300 if you are single, $3,400 if you are married and filing a joint return, $1,700 if you are married and filing a separate return. That's not small change, particularly since the deduction for medical costs has been all but eliminated for most of us. (Medical expenses are deductible *only* to the extent they are unreimbursed by insurance and exceed 5 percent of your adjusted gross income.)

Let's say you buy a home at the beginning of the year for $100,000. You put $20,000 down and borrow $80,000 at 12 percent interest. The first year, you'll be paying more than $9,500 in interest on that loan. Every penny of that interest is deductible. Congratulations! You have joined the indebted ranks of American homeowners who take advantage of Tax Savers. On top of that, your real estate taxes might run anywhere from a few hundred dollars to a couple of thousand or more. Every penny of that is deductible, too.

Without these homeownership Tax Savers, it's hard for prudent people of moderate income to pile up enough deductions to make itemizing worthwhile.

We say "prudent" because every income tax deduction reflects money you have spent, right out of your pocket. Much as we like Tax Savers, we don't recommend that you

———

throw money around just to increase your deductions. Deductible expenses should have a sound purpose of their own, so the deduction is a sweetener rather than an end in itself. Keep these guidelines in mind:

If you are in the 30 percent tax bracket, every dollar in tax deductions cuts your income tax bill by 30 cents. In other words, the dollar you spend costs you not a dollar but 70 cents.

If you are in the 40 percent tax bracket, every dollar in tax deductions cuts your income tax bill by 40 cents; the dollar you spend costs you only 60 cents.

If you are in the 50 percent tax bracket, every dollar in tax deductions cuts your income tax bill by 50 cents; the dollar you spend costs you only 50 cents.

Those are nice sweeteners. The higher your income, the sweeter they get. Still, you wouldn't want to borrow money and pay interest just to get the tax deduction (interest on most kinds of loans is deductible). But if you can put borrowed money to good use, the tax deduction is a lovely sweetener. And what better use than buying a personal residence?

Let's tick off some of the advantages of owning your home:

1. It's yours. Owning a home gives most Americans a wonderful warm feeling. That psychological lift can be just as important as the economic advantages.

2. You are combining a very large and very sound investment with an absolute necessity. After all, you have to live somewhere, so you'll have to spend money either to rent or to buy a home. With today's homes costing anywhere from $60,000 to $600,000, the commitment to buy is a commitment to invest a very large sum of money gradually. You have to choose real estate wisely, but picking a well-built home in a good neighborhood is easier than picking a good stock off the back page of the newspaper. With some exceptions, housing is a less volatile investment than most. And over the long haul, housing prices have increased impressively. So if you buy wisely and keep your home for a number of years, you can expect to sell at a profit. In the

meantime you get a place to live. It's a reasonable deal, even before we start talking about Tax Savers.

In homeownership, the Tax Savers pile up, one on top of the other, from the day you buy your first home through the day you sell your last one. (Most of us own several homes in our lifetimes.) To realize the full benefit of these Tax Savers you have to understand them, plan for them, and use each one at the right time. Since these Tax Savers are so closely intertwined with the normal progression of adult life, let's go through these events, one by one, just as you are likely to experience them. We'll tell you how to take advantage of every Tax Saver along the way. There are lots of them.

TAPPING RETIREMENT SAVINGS

Many people have trouble coming up with a down payment for their first home. One little-known Tax Saver may help. A growing number of companies offer their employees Salary Reduction Plans, called 401(k) plans, after the section of the tax law that created them. A 401(k) is much like an IRA (Individual Retirement Account). In both, you can save without paying income tax on your contributions or on the interest or dividends earned until you withdraw money. But unlike an IRA, a 401(k) plan permits withdrawals before retirement without penalty for any of three situations defined by the IRS as "hardships"—buying a personal residence, paying unusually large medical bills, or paying college tuition for your children. So if your employer offers a 401(k) plan, use it to the hilt. It's a Tax Saver toward retirement and a Tax Saver source of money toward a down payment.

SETTLEMENT COSTS

When you buy your first home, pay attention to the settlement sheet—the piece of paper that lists all the mysterious expenses connected with the real estate deal. Hidden in those figures are some valuable Tax Savers. If you don't recognize them, ask your lawyer or your mortgage lender to point them out to you.

———

Here's what to look for:

1. Points, also known as loan origination fees or loan processing fees. A point is 1 percent of the amount you're borrowing. For example, you might take an $80,000 mortgage at 12 percent, plus two points. Two percent of $80,000 is $1,600. At settlement, you pay that $1,600 in cash. It's extra money out of your pocket, but it's not necessarily deductible. Here's the rule: Points are *not* deductible if your mortgage is backed by the Federal Housing Administration or the Veterans Administration—in real estate shorthand, if it's an FHA or VA mortgage. Points *are* deductible as interest on Schedule A if your mortgage is "conventional," meaning that it's not backed by the FHA or VA.

2. Interest on your mortgage, from the date of purchase to, typically, the first of the following month. That, too, you pay in cash, as part of settlement. It's deductible no matter what kind of mortgage you have.

We can't emphasize enough that you have to take advantage of these settlement-sheet Tax Savers on your own. Typically, you pay them as part of overall "settlement costs" or "closing costs"; you won't even have a separate check stub for your points or for that partial month of interest. And they probably will not be mentioned in later statements from your mortgage lender. You must pick those numbers off the settlement sheet for yourself. Here's our recommendation: Make two copies of the settlement sheet. On one, circle the points and the partial month's worth of interest and put that copy in your tax file for the current year. Put the other copy in an important new file marked "House." When you sell—even if it's twenty or thirty years later—that old settlement sheet will yield additional Tax Savers. We'll get to that in its place, as we continue your homeowning chronology.

APPRECIATION

You're a homeowner now. Let's hope that the value of your new home will increase over the years. That in itself is a neat Tax Saver. This appreciation in value is yours, tax-free, until you decide to sell. If you buy at $75,000, and over the years your home increases in value to $200,000, you still have to pay not one dime in income tax. The IRS does not get involved until you sell.

INTEREST AND PROPERTY TAX

Every month you will send your mortgage lender a check. That monthly payment will include principal toward repayment of your mortgage debt, interest on the loan, a month's share of your annual premium for homeowner's insurance, a month's share of your annual real estate tax, and, in some cases, a month's premium for mortgage insurance. At the end of the year, your lender will send you an annual statement, listing how much you paid for each of these items.

Two of those items are Tax Savers: the interest and real estate tax, both of which are deductible. Make sure the monthly breakdowns add up to the figures on your annual statement. Sorry, but you can't prepay interest or real estate tax to get an extra month's worth of those deductions. Your deductions are limited to one year's worth of interest and one year's worth of real estate taxes, period. On the other hand, if you make your December mortgage payment late in the month and your check doesn't get cashed or credited until early January, that payment is nevertheless deductible for the December year. That's when it was due, and that's when you paid it.

Lest we make our tax system sound too logical, consider this example, which illustrates how sticky the IRS can be. One homeowner dutifully forked over his monthly mortgage payments, added up what he paid in interest and real estate tax, and claimed both deductions on his income tax form. It's all quite proper so far. Unfortunately, his lender had not passed on to the county his monthly payments for real estate tax until after the first of the tax year. The IRS normally wouldn't catch that kind of a glitch, but this time it did (on a fluke)—and it disallowed that part of the taxpayer's deduction for the unpaid taxes. After all, said the IRS, no real estate tax was paid to the locality during that year. The homeowner appealed, but the courts upheld the IRS.

The following year, of course, that taxpayer got to deduct two years' worth of real estate tax payments, but you can bet he wasn't satisfied. That's a rare occurrence, but it illustrates the importance of comparing your itemized monthly payments with the itemized totals listed on your annual statement. Don't forget, you're dealing here with Tax Savers that are worth thousands of dollars to you, every year.

You list those Tax Savers on Schedule A, Itemized Deductions. The blocks on the form are clearly marked; these aren't the kinds of Tax Savers that require an accountant's skill. You'll see two lines for home mortgage interest expense. If to buy your house you borrowed from a savings institution, bank, or mortgage banker, list your interest payment. If you borrowed from the seller—not unusual in this era of so-called creative financing—list that interest payment separately, and also list the name and address of the person you borrowed from. You may have both kinds of mortgages—for example, a first mortgage from a savings institution and a second mortgage from the seller. If so, break down your interest payments accordingly.

If you have not itemized your deductions before, you'll immediately notice other deductions that you can now take, thanks to the homeowners' Tax Savers. You can deduct your state and local income tax and sales tax; those deductions become Tax Savers worth hundreds of dollars to you. You can deduct interest from other loans, including interest on credit cards and charge accounts. You can deduct every penny you contributed to charity, including the value of old clothing and other goods you may have given to a worthy cause. You can deduct dues to unions and professional organizations, fees for preparing your tax return, the cost of financial publications—for example, *Money* magazine, *The Wall Street Journal,* and this book.

Your home has literally opened the door to a cornucopia of Tax Savers. And these wonderful homeowners' Tax Savers are not tricky or controversial in any way. They are the Tax Savers most commonly used in America, the ones that produce the largest overall savings for taxpayers—or losses to the U.S. Treasury, depending on your viewpoint. They are so clear, pat, and straightforward that the IRS rarely audits them.

To plan your finances and Tax Savers for future years, you'll want to anticipate your annual deductions for mortgage interest and real estate tax. If you have a flat-rate mortgage—one with an unchanging interest rate—your lender can give you an amortization schedule that shows you, month by month, how much your interest payments will be. The amount of interest gradually declines, because as you repay principal, the amount of your loan gradually shrinks; you pay interest only on the amount that you still owe.

If your mortgage has a variable or adjusted interest rate, you can't be sure exactly how much you'll pay in interest in future years. Many such mortgages allow the rate of interest to rise only by certain amounts; the lender should be able to tell you the range of possibility.

Sometimes, a better mortgage deal may come along while you're still repaying your old mortgage. Rates may decline, or one lender may come forward with an attractive deal that wasn't available when you bought your house. To take advantage of such a change, it may be worthwhile for you to take out a new mortgage and pay off your old one. That's called refinancing your house. Before you do it, read your old mortgage; it may impose a penalty for prepayment. Any such penalty is deductible; it counts as additional interest. So in deciding whether to refinance, figure the impact of the prepayment penalty, minus the amount of tax you'll save through the deduction.

OFFICE AT HOME

If you run a business out of your home, you can take advantage of the home-office Tax Saver. The business can be full-time or part-time—moonlighting enterprises fully qualify—and your office need not be a separate room. Let's say your office amounts to one eighth of your house, in square feet. You can deduct as business expenses one eighth of your utility costs and other overall home expenses. In addition, you can depreciate one eighth of the value of your house, provided your office space is used exclusively for business.

YOUR COST BASIS

All these are year-by-year Tax Savers. Most of them are pretty easy to remember; after all, you're writing a mortgage check every month, getting a year-end statement from the lender, and filing an annual income tax return. Now we want to introduce you to a homeowners' Tax Saver that is very important but not nearly so obvious. It's a long-range Tax Saver, and one you have to keep track of yourself. It's called Basis.

Basis means the total amount of money you spend to buy your house and improve it. When you eventually sell, you have to report any profit to the IRS; your profit is your sale price minus your cost, or Basis. So the higher your Basis, the smaller your profit—and the less you might have to pay in capital gains tax. (To be sure, that capital gains tax may be deferred. We'll discuss that further along in this chapter. But it is still important to keep track of your Basis and to raise it as much as you honestly can.)

Earlier in this chapter, we recommended that when you buy your first house, you start a new file simply labeled House. That file serves primarily to trace your growing Basis. Start it with the purchase contract, which tells what you paid for the house, and the settlement sheet. We told you how to deduct certain items off the settlement sheet. Every settlement cost (or closing cost—the terms are synonymous) that is not deductible in the year of purchase can be added to your Basis. Typically, that includes such items as your lawyer's fee, a county recording tax, and a state transfer tax. So when you sell your home, that old settlement sheet will help you figure your Basis—and help you prove it if the IRS insists.

From that day on, stuff your House file with receipts and notes having to do with improvements of any kind. Frankly, few homeowners do a good enough job of this. Of those who don't, few realize how much they have spent over the years to improve their homes. The cost of any improvement can be added to your Basis. Remember those two key words—"any" and "improvement." Most of us think that home improvements have to be big ones—a deck, an additional bathroom, a swimming pool. Those are important and costly, and you certainly want detailed financial information about them in your House file. But most homeowners spend a lot of money on small improvements, too.

If you plant trees, that's an improvement; stick a receipt in your House file. If you weather-strip a drafty house, that's an improvement. So is a can of paint for a room that was unfinished when you bought your home. It's an improvement to insulate, to add shrubbery, to fence the yard.

An improvement need not be visible, and it need not be essential. But it must be something that was not there before.

Maintenance expenses don't qualify. If you replace an old furnace or a leaky roof, that's not an improvement. If you paper a room that previously was painted, that's not an improvement, even though it may be a step up on the decorating ladder. But if you air-condition a house that was not air-conditioned before, that is an improvement. If you resurface your driveway, that's not an improvement; if you widen your driveway, it is. If you add a skylight or a chimney or smoke alarms or storm windows and doors, you have improved your home, and every penny that you spent —for both materials and paid labor—can be added to your Basis. (Don't try to put a value on your own labor and add that on. To the IRS, your labor doesn't count.)

So keep track of your Basis—a running total—simply by sticking receipts and notes in your House file. Here's a backup: When you do your income taxes every year, look for check stubs and receipts having to do with home improvements. If those expenses aren't already documented in your House file, put them in at that time. Keep a running tally of your Basis by going through your file once a year. You'll be surprised how many thousands of dollars you spend over the years to improve a home—expenditures that you would largely forget if you did not keep track of them as you went along.

ENERGY CREDITS

Every improvement eventually becomes a Tax Saver. Some are Tax Savers twice, and energy savers, too. To encourage energy conservation, the government allows you a tax credit if you spend money for certain items that reduce your home's energy consumption. This Residential Energy Credit, as it's called, can be applied only for homes completed before April 20, 1977, and you have to make the energy-saving expenditures by the end of 1985, when this Tax Saver will expire unless Congress renews it. It covers these items and no others: storm windows and doors, insulation, caulking and weather-stripping, replacement furnace burners, devices that increase heating efficiency by modifying flue openings, furnace ignition systems that replace gas pilot lights, thermostats with timers that cut back the heat or cooling at certain times of day or night, and meters that tell you how much you're spending on energy.

For every dollar you spend on any of those items, you get a tax credit of 15 percent. The limit, for the entire time you live in that home, is $2,000 in expenses. Fifteen percent of $2,000 is $300; that's the maximum credit you can take. You can use it all in one year or spread it over any number of years. You can take it whether you own the home or rent it. If you move, you can take advantage of the energy credit on your new home—and whoever bought or rented your old home can take advantage of it there.

Three hundred dollars may not sound like much, but note that it's a tax credit, which is worth at least twice as much as a deduction, depending on your tax bracket. A deduction cuts the amount of your income subject to tax. A credit is a dollar-for-dollar subtraction from your tax bill. Besides, you're adding to your Basis and reducing your energy costs. So the Residential Energy Credit is a unique bargain—a small Tax Saver but one with gold plating.

A related Tax Saver is even more generous—and almost has to be, because the improvements it covers tend to be expensive. This one is called the Renewable Energy Source credit. It provides a tax credit of 40 percent on expenditures up to $10,000 for solar, wind-powered, or geothermal energy savers installed in your home. The most common of these is a solar-powered water heater—although one enthusiastic member of Congress installed a windmill in his yard to generate electricity. With a 40 percent credit, the government will, in effect, pay 40 cents of every dollar you spend on such equipment. This Tax Saver too will expire at the end of 1985 unless Congress extends it.

SELLING EXPENSES

When you sell your home, you get a second settlement sheet—this time, as the seller. Again, it includes expenses that you can use as Tax Savers. Let's say you go to settlement on the twentieth of the month. Knowing that the settlement is scheduled, your lender may tell you not to make your regular house payment for that final, partial month; he'll suggest that it be taken care of at settlement. If that's the case, you will pay twenty days' worth of interest and real estate taxes at settlement—actually, it will just be deducted from the amount you get for the house. Those payments will appear on your settlement sheet. Pick them off, just as you did when you bought your house; they're deductible. On the other hand, if you made a full, regular house payment for that final month, you should be repaid at settlement for the final ten days' worth of interest and real estate taxes. You'll have to adjust your interest and real estate tax totals for the year to reflect that repayment.

In addition, the seller often is charged an additional week or two of interest to cover the period required for the checks to clear. That may not seem fair—after all, you, as the seller, didn't even write a check. Nevertheless, lenders routinely impose that extra interest, and they rarely include it on the settlement sheet. Ask your lender or settlement attorney to give you that figure; it's deductible.

Sometimes it's difficult to arrange all the details of a sale so that the date of settlement fits the date the new owner wants to move in. You may move out a few weeks or

———

even a few months early, depending upon when your new home is ready. The new owner may want to move in a month or so before the date of settlement. That puts you in a position to rent the house to the buyer for a month or two during that transition period—and to use yet another Tax Saver. This one is simple: Any rent money you collect that was simply incidental to the sale is not taxable. You simply pocket it. Do not report it on your tax return in any way.

Hang on to your settlement sheet. For the year the sale took place, you must file with your income tax return IRS Form 2119, Sale or Exchange of Principal Residence. Here's what you have to list on that form:

1. Your Basis. You determine that by adding up the purchase price, the nondeductible closing costs from your original settlement sheet, and all your improvements.

2. The sale price and the date of sale.

You then subtract the Basis from the sale price. That yields a profit figure, but you get to reduce it with these two adjustments:

—Costs of the sale. That means everything on your seller's settlement sheet that was not deductible— seller's points, lawyer's fees, real estate commissions. Include, too, the costs of any ads you ran to sell the house and other miscellaneous expenses connected with the sale.

—Costs of preparing your house for sale, commonly called fixing-up expenses. Typically, these include a fresh coat of paint, carpet cleaning, and minor repairs.

If you lose money on the sale of a home—in other words, if you sell it for less than your Basis—you get no tax break at all. You can't deduct that loss in any way.

ROLLING OVER YOUR PROFIT

Even after all the adjustments, you'll probably show a substantial profit—which brings us to another extremely generous Tax Saver. This one actually requires you to defer tax on the profit you make selling your home. To show you how it works, let's run through this hypothetical example:

You bought your house for	$100,000
Nondeductible closing costs at purchase added another	3,000
Over the years, your home improvements totaled	22,500
So your Basis was	$125,500
You sold your house for	$175,000
So your profit was	49,500
Less your costs of sale	10,500
And less your costs of preparing the house for sale	1,000
So your net profit was	$ 38,000

If you owned your house for more than a year, that $38,000 profit is a long-term capital gain. If you bought the house after June 22, 1984, it qualifies for long-term treatment after only six months. Only 40 percent of a long-term capital gain is taxed. Even so, you surely don't want to pay tax on $15,200.

You don't have to—if you buy a more expensive home and move in within two years of the date you sold your old one. That Tax Saver is a unique provision in the law that is offered only when you sell one home and buy another. Both homes have to be your principal residences—you must move from one home to the other.

If the new house costs as much as or more than you realized from the old one—in our example, $175,000—you pay no capital gains tax at all. If it costs less, you pay capital gains tax only on the difference. For example, let's say your new house cost $160,000. You would report $15,000—in long-term capital gain. Only 40 percent of a long-term capital gain is taxed.

Most people trade up to a more expensive house, partly

because this Tax Saver encourages them to do so. In our example, you wound up with a $38,000 profit on your old house. Let's say you bought a new house for $200,000. That deferred profit of $38,000 reduces your Basis in the new house by that same amount; that's the rule. So in figuring the Basis in your new house, you start not with $200,000, but with $162,000. If you sell that house, your profit will be magnified by that lower Basis. But again, you can defer tax on the profit by buying another home. It is not unusual for a family to move as often as six or eight or even ten times, buying a more expensive home each time, and thus deferring tax on profit after profit.

(Caution: If you run a business out of your home and take annual deductions for your home office, consider skipping the depreciation deduction for the year in which you sell the house. Otherwise you'll have to pay capital gains tax on a portion of your profit. For example, if your home office takes up one eighth of your house and you are depreciating one eighth of your house costs, you'll have to pay capital gains tax on one eighth of the profit when you sell. But if you don't claim home-office depreciation deductions for that single year—the year of the sale—you can defer the entire profit on the house. So that final year, use your home office for something other than business, at least a little, so it will no longer qualify for depreciation.)

Many people assume that in order to take advantage of this Tax Saver, they have to plow the proceeds from the old house into the new one, but that's not true. You may prefer to invest the money from the old house in the stock market or simply spend it, while borrowing fully to buy the new house. The choice is yours. To defer the tax, you have to buy another home and pay as much as you got for the old home. The IRS doesn't care whether or not you use the same dollars.

Another misconception has to do with the two-year time period. You can buy the new house within two years after selling the old one—or within two years before the sale. Again, the choice is yours. You might buy a vacation home and decide a year or a year and a half later to move into it year-round. As long as you sell your old home soon enough to fit within the two-year limit, you qualify for the deferment.

Oddly enough, if you sell one home and buy another within that two-year period, the IRS won't let you pay tax on your profit even if you want to. The tax deferment isn't a choice; it's a requirement.

Every time you sell a home—at a loss, at a profit, or at break-even—you must file Form 2119 as part of your federal income tax return. In your House file, keep copies of every Form 2119. Without those forms, you can't keep track of your Basis, since one house sale affects the Basis for the next house. Besides, you need to keep track of how much tax you're deferring. Those deferments are your stake in continuing to own your home, and you need to know the amount of that stake.

POCKETING HOUSE PROFITS

At age fifty-five, you get another choice—and another Tax Saver. Once in your life, at any age from fifty-five up, you can sell a home and pocket up to $125,000 in profits without paying any tax, whether or not you buy another home. If you're married, only one spouse has to be fifty-five; the other can be younger. If you sell at a profit of less than $125,000, you do not get to carry over the balance and use it in another house sale. This Tax Saver can be used just once. If you sell at a profit of more than $125,000 and buy a more expensive home, you can combine two Tax Savers. Let's say that at the age of fifty-five you sell your home at a profit of $150,000 and buy a more expensive home. You can avoid tax on $125,000 of the profit because of your age and defer tax on the other $25,000 because you're trading up. By deferring tax on only $25,000 rather than $150,000, you don't reduce your Basis on the new house nearly so much—a safeguard that will restrain your capital gains tax in case you wind up selling that new house without buying another.

So the Tax Savers connected with owning your home

provide benefit after benefit throughout your adult life. When you are young, your first home opens the door to itemizing deductions and allows you to build a valuable asset with the help of numerous Tax Savers, including appreciation. When you move, other Tax Savers come into play, allowing you to defer capital gains tax on your housing profits. When you reach fifty-five, yet another Tax Saver becomes available, permitting you to pocket a substantial amount of profit, tax-free. No matter how knowledgeable and sophisticated you may become, or how much money you may have to invest, you will have a hard time finding anything that matches homeownership for combining a basic need with generous Tax Savers.

A SECOND HOME

A second home, rented out to others, provides a bedrock investment for many Americans. It is an investment close to home, that you can manage yourself. A home is something solid that you can look at and feel; it is familiar, and if you own your own home in the same community, it is part of a real estate market that you are familiar with.

In addition to all that, a rental home can provide a bonanza of Tax Savers. The biggest and best of them was substantially sweetened as part of the Reagan tax law enacted in 1981. That Tax Saver is called accelerated depreciation. Congress abridged it slightly, in 1984, but not by much.

As a result of the two changes, rental property operates under three different depreciation formulas. The one you use depends upon when you *bought* the property, not when you started *renting* it out. For example, if you bought a house in 1970, lived in it until this year, and then began renting it out, you must use the depreciation rules that were in effect in 1970.

Here are the three formulas:

1. If you bought the property before January 1, 1981, you have to use the old system, under which depreciation had to be spread over twenty-five to forty years. The year-by-year formula wasn't fixed by law. You must

map out your own depreciation formula when you begin renting out the property, and you must be prepared to defend it against IRS challenge.

2. If you bought the property between January 1, 1981, and March 15, 1984, you get the best Tax Saver of all—accelerated depreciation, spread over fifteen years. The formula is fixed by law: You get to deduct 12 percent of the cost the first year, 10 percent the second, 9 percent the third, 8 percent the fourth, 7 percent the fifth, 6 percent each of the next four years, and 5 percent each of the final six years.

3. If you bought the property after March 15, 1984, you get a formula nearly as good but spread over eighteen years rather than fifteen.

When you stop to think about it, fifteen or eighteen years is almost too good to be true. After all, you don't expect that home to depreciate in value. You expect it to appreciate; that's why you bought it. Assuming you are a sensible investor and landlord, you'll maintain the property so that it won't deteriorate. And since this home is an investment rather than your principal residence, every penny you spend on maintenance is deductible, from fixing the roof to cutting the grass.

Nevertheless, the tax law gives you a fixed formula under which you can depreciate the home, providing you with thousands of dollars a year in tax savings. And you also get to deduct the interest on the mortgage loan and the annual real estate taxes, plus all costs having to do with the business of being a landlord. That includes the cost of hiring a professional manager if you decide you don't want to deal personally with your tenants.

For example, let's say you bought a condominium for $80,000 in January 1984, when the fifteen-year formula was in effect. We're choosing a condominium rather than a house because it provides a simpler example. You are allowed to depreciate only the value of a building; land isn't depreciable. With a house, your real estate tax bill will show you what portion of the value is attributable to the land and what portion to the building—or, as it's usually called, the improvements. When you buy a condominium, you don't buy land. So in our example the entire $80,000 is depreciable.

We'll say you put down $20,000 and borrow $60,000, at 12 percent for thirty years. You rent out the condo for $400 a month. Here's your hypothetical balance sheet for the first year:

Income	
Rent	$ 4,800
Expenses	
Mortgage principal and interest	$ 7,400
Real estate tax	1,000
Maintenance	1,000
Manager's fee	600
Total	$10,000

So you're $5,200 in the hole, right? Let's work in the Tax Savers.

Here are your deductible expenses:

Mortgage interest	$ 7,200
Real estate tax	1,000
Maintenance	1,000
Manager's fee	600
Depreciation	9,600
Total deductions	$19,400

If you are in the 35 percent tax bracket, $19,400 in deductions means that you save $6,790 on your income tax, because you deduct that $19,400 from your taxable income. So now the equation looks this way:

Income	
Rent	$ 4,800
Tax Savers	$ 6,790
Total	$11,590
Less expenses	$10,000
Profit	$ 1,590

That's much better, and it doesn't take into account the appreciation in the value of your property—the reason you bought it in the first place. You've even paid back the first $200 of your loan. Let's assume that the market value of the house rises by 10 percent a year. That adds another $8,000 to the positive side of the equation. And when you sell, you benefit from yet another Tax Saver, because your profit counts as a long-term capital gain; you pay income tax on only 40 percent of that profit if you owned the rental property for more than a year. If you are unfortunate enough to sell at a loss, you can use that loss to offset other income, at least to a limited extent.

Since more than half of your income from the rental home is in the form of Tax Savers, you won't get it right away; you'll simply owe less tax the following April. But you needn't postpone those benefits. Calculate them in advance and reduce your quarterly estimated income tax payments accordingly, or ask your employer for a new Form W-4 so that the amount that's withheld from your paycheck can be reduced.

Without that depreciation Tax Saver, investing in a rental home would be a close call. Only people with substantial incomes could afford it, because you would have what's called a negative cash flow. That means you'd be spending more every year than you took in. Even with that big boost from depreciation, some owners suffer a negative cash flow, particularly on vacation properties that can be rented out for only a few months a year. We can't teach you everything you need to know to become an intelligent real estate investor, but we can acquaint you with the Tax Savers, which provide the incentive to consider investing in rental property. That generous depreciation formula is the big incentive, the big Tax Saver. It has spurred the growth of real estate tax shelters, which you might want to consider if you would prefer to be a distant partner in a real estate investment.

ENJOYING YOUR RENTAL PROPERTY

What if you buy a ski condo or a beach house, and you want to use it part of the year yourself and rent it out the rest of the time? To preserve the Tax Savers that we've just described, a second home must be primarily a rental property. The rules are strict: You cannot use it more than fourteen days, or 10 percent of the days it's rented out, whichever is greater. (That doesn't count days you spend fixing up the place.) And your balance sheet must indicate that you bought the home primarily as an investment and are renting it profitably. All your tenants—even relatives and close friends—have to pay an honest amount of rent, based on the market.

If you use your second home more than fourteen days or 10 percent of the rental days, you lose a great deal of the tax advantages. The formula is complicated—depending on how many days you use it and how many days you rent it. Altogether, counting interest and depreciation and all the other real estate Tax Savers, you can't deduct more than you receive in rent. Look back at our calculations on pages 129 and 130, and see how your balance sheet would suffer if you could deduct only $4,800. That's a fraction of the deductions you can get on a real rental property.

Of course, there's nothing wrong with buying a second home purely for enjoyment. You still get to deduct the interest and real estate taxes. And as a final gesture in the wonderful world of homeownership Tax Savers, you're allowed to rent out your second home for as much as two weeks a year without paying any income tax on that rental income.

Tax Savers
for
the Divorced

$\mathcal{D}$ ivorce can be painful in many ways; at the very least it can impair the economic health of one or both partners. We've seen divorce destroy otherwise financially strong people. A careless or angry divorce proceeding can increase the taxes of both, benefiting only one party: the Internal Revenue Service. On the other hand, a carefully crafted divorce settlement can employ Tax Savers that help both the man and the woman at a critical and vulnerable time in their lives.

Your divorce settlement—whether agreed upon by both parties or mandated by a court—will affect your finances and taxes for the rest of your lives, so it's critically important that you fit Tax Savers into your settlement. From the standpoint of taxes, a settlement that looks equitable may in fact heavily favor one partner to the disadvantage of the other. The partner who is getting the better of the deal is unlikely to agree to any change once the settlement is in place. So it's vitally important that you nail down an equitable agreement in the first place, with tax considerations firmly in mind.

If you have read other chapters in this book, you know that we believe in self-help taxpaying. In other words, we think you'll save more on your taxes if you pick your own

Tax Savers and fit them into your life. In divorce, however, we recommend that both partners employ tax professionals. Put your tax pro in touch with your divorce lawyer and work closely with both of them so you understand what's going on. Your costs for tax advice are deductible. Other legal expenses connected with your divorce are not.

For most people, it is difficult to separate anger and emotion from divorce negotiations. The tax rules affecting divorce are detailed, precise, and, frankly, a little peculiar. If one party understands them and the other doesn't, the knowledgeable one can take advantage of the other. A knowledgeable and vindictive spouse can use Tax Savers that help his or her own finances while severely wounding the finances of the other.

The 1984 tax reform law considerably modified some of the rules having to do with divorce. If you were divorced before provisions of the new law become effective, you're still bound by the old law, even for future tax years. In this chapter, we'll give both versions—the rules under the old law, and the rules under the 1984 act. You may find that the changes work in your favor. If so, you and your former spouse can modify your divorce settlement and, in effect, switch from the provisions of the old law to the provisions of the new law. To find out whether that would be a worthwhile move in your case, consult your attorney. You'll certainly find it to your advantage to understand the provisions as they affect you.

You must understand the tax rules, and you probably need professional help. We feel that your goal should be a mutually beneficial settlement. If your partner will not negotiate, you'll need knowledge and counsel to protect yourself against an unfair settlement.

Often, spouses who are separating cannot or will not sit down and negotiate calmly. Emotions run too high. In that situation, let your lawyers do the negotiating. Encourage yours to strike a mutually beneficial agreement if the other side is willing. In divorce, a lawyer can act as a buffer as well as a legal and tax adviser. Make sure your lawyer understands your finances thoroughly, including the tax implications of every aspect of your divorce agreement. Some

Tax Savers are negotiable; they can go to either spouse, depending upon the agreement. So make sure your lawyer knows what Tax Savers are at stake. In case of disagreement, they can be used as valuable bargaining chips.

JOINT RETURNS

We hope that you and your spouse worked together on family finances and taxes during your married years and that you both were thoroughly familiar with every year's tax return. If not—if your spouse handled the family financial affairs, and you merely signed joint tax returns—look out. We recommend that you get copies of those returns for the past three years and take them to the tax professional whom you hire to advise you in connection with the divorce. He can tell you whether the tax returns look sound, and if they do not, he can advise you on what to do.

Why? Because you are surprisingly vulnerable. If you filed jointly, you both signed the tax returns. According to the IRS, you are just as liable for any tax deficiency, penalty, and interest as your spouse is, even if he or she made all the money, wrote all the checks, and figured and paid all the taxes. Nor does your liability end with divorce. Generally, the IRS audits returns as far back as three years. If you filed a joint return, you can be called in for audit and stuck with any and all tax deficiencies.

Of course, the IRS will be just as eager to go after your ex-spouse as after you, but the agency will not play referee between the two of you. It will want answers to its audit questions, and if the answers don't verify the numbers on the return, it will demand money. It will not care which spouse pays. For example, let's say you earned the money and you paid the family taxes for the year under examination. Surely, you hope, your ex-spouse should pay the few hundred in additional taxes that the IRS is demanding. After all, at the time you paid all the bills. Tell that to an IRS auditor, and he will yawn. It's his job to collect. It's your job to work out a deal with your former spouse.

If your former spouse has cut out and can't be found, you can be sure the IRS will demand that you pay all money due—again, no matter who figured the taxes and who paid them. It does not matter if you have remarried. Your past obligation remains. There's nothing you can do about it.

That sounds pretty rough, and it is. We can offer only one tiny way out—so tiny that few people can wriggle through. It's called the innocent spouse rule.

If the IRS rules that you and your former spouse owe back taxes, you can plead innocent spouse and escape obligation only if you can persuade the IRS of three things:

1. You were unaware of the error on the joint tax return, whether it was unreported income, excessive deductions or credits, or an unrealistic basis, or cost, for property sold during the year. (Under the old law, only unreported income qualified. The broader definition, enacted as part of the 1984 Tax Reform Act, gives an innocent spouse more elbow room. What's more, you can apply the new rule not only for this year and future years but also for past years in case a previously filed return is audited.)
2. You had no reason to suspect the error.
3. You did not benefit from the error.

TIMING
The timing of your divorce affects your income taxes. To the IRS, your marital status for the year depends on a single date—December 31. If you were married that day, you were married all year. If you were single that day, you were single all year. The IRS doesn't care whether you and your spouse were living together on that date. Only the legal status of your marriage counts. If by December 31 you had received a final decree of divorce or a final decree of separate maintenance, both of you were legally single for the year. If not, you were married; temporary decrees don't count.

Your marital status makes a big difference, because it affects your filing status, which in turn determines your tax rates. Married couples filing jointly pay lower rates—in other words, lower percentages of their taxable income. Working up from the lowest rates to the highest, here are the four steps of filing status:

> Married filing joint return.
> Head of household.
> Single.
> Married filing separate return.

(We're skipping a fifth status—for widows or widowers with children—because it doesn't fit this discussion.)

To the extent that you can time your divorce, you can pick your filing status for that year. The date of your divorce can become a Tax Saver. It can be a Tax Saver for both of you, so by all means work out the most practical arrangement with your spouse, through lawyers if necessary. No matter how much anger and hurt may be involved, neither of you should want to donate money to the IRS just to spite the other.

Among the four filing statuses, the one you definitely do not want is married filing separately. The rates for married filing separately are half again as high as the rates for singles, which in turn are higher than for married filing jointly. So if you were still legally married on December 31, arrange to file a joint tax return.

If you didn't have much income but your spouse did, we can guess what you're thinking. The law says if one of you files a separate return, both must. So why not file separately? That will force your spouse to file a separate return, too. Your tax will be low, and his will be high. You'll be better off, and you'll stick it to your spouse.

We disagree. File a joint return, stipulating in advance that you get to share in the tax saving. That way both of you will wind up ahead.

If you are separating or divorcing, chances are you won't trust your partner's promise to send you your share of a refund check from a joint return. We've heard of too many cases in which someone forges a signature to cash the check. Don't resort to that. If you're uncomfortable with trusting your spouse to send you the money, work it out so that the tax refund goes through your attorneys.

For the sake of example, let's assume that your spouse worked, and you didn't. The taxable income—all his—came to $32,000. If you file a joint return, the tax will be

$5,672, based on 1984 tax rates. If you file separate returns, his tax will be $8,898; yours will be zero. The difference is $3,226. Why not file a joint return, agreeing in advance that he pays the entire tax bill and in addition gives you half of that $3,226 tax savings?

If, as in that example, your family income was top-heavy on one side, both of you will be better off postponing the final decree until after December 31 and filing a joint tax return. To prove that, let's look at the tax your spouse would have to pay if your divorce or separation became final before December 31. He would then file as a single taxpayer, and his tax on $32,000 of taxable income would come to $7,197. That's $1,525 more than the tax on the same income for a couple filing jointly. Again, why not set the final date after December 31 and file a joint tax return, agreeing in advance that he will pay the entire tax bill and, in addition, will split that $1,525 tax savings with you?

Things work out differently, however, if both you and your spouse make good and substantially equal incomes. By filing jointly, you get lower rates. But by adding your two incomes together, you're propelled into higher brackets— so much higher that you may be better off getting a final divorce before December 31 and filing as single taxpayers.

For example, let's say each of you has a taxable income of $25,000. If you file jointly, your tax on $50,000 would be $12,014. But if both of you are single, your tax on $25,000 of income would be $4,828 each, for a total of $9,658. So if you stay married through December 31, you'll pay an additional tax of $2,356. That's the so-called marriage penalty; it hits couples who both make good incomes, not those whose income is earned almost entirely by one partner.

Remember that the worst filing status of all, except in unusual cases, is married filing separately. Let's say you and your spouse are still legally married on December 31, but you cannot get together on a joint tax return. Under certain circumstances, you may be able to file as a single taxpayer or as a head of household, assuming there are children involved in the marriage. The 1984 tax law made these rules a little less strict than they used to be.

You can file as a single taxpayer (1) if you paid more

than half the cost of keeping up your home during the year, and (2) if your spouse didn't live in your home during the last six months of the year (under the old law, you had to live apart for the entire year), and (3) if your child lived with you at least half the year, and you supported the child and can claim him as a dependent. If your child lived in your home for the entire year, you can do even better; you qualify for head of household status, which carries slightly lower tax rates.

Given time, marital tempers often cool. Let's say you and your spouse were in the throes of a nasty divorce, couldn't get together on a joint tax return, and filed separate returns. Up until three years later, you can file an amended return, choosing joint filing status and claiming a refund. If you filed jointly the first time, however, you cannot switch the other way, to separate returns. Those rules may sound inconsistent. They are.

Once a divorce or separation is final, a parent with custody of a child can claim head of household filing status. If you and your spouse have two children and each takes custody of one, both of you can claim head of household filing status. It's a small Tax Saver; on $25,000 of taxable income, the tax for singles is $4,828; for a head of household it's $4,432.

SENSIBLE SETTLEMENTS

It is ironic that so much about divorce calls for agreement between two people who are at odds with each other. But it's true. If you want to include Tax Savers in your divorce settlement, you and your spouse will have to agree not only on filing status but also on a number of other important details.

Federal income tax laws provide a great many choices. If you and your spouse can make these choices rationally, according to your mutual financial interests, you will both wind up ahead. Surprisingly, you and your spouse can choose which one of you will get the dependency exemption for each child (set at $1,000 for 1984)—and it need not be the same parent who gets custody of the child.

For example, let's say Nora and Tim got divorced in 1984 or earlier. Nora, with a taxable income of $20,000, was awarded custody of both their children. Tim's taxable income is $40,000. Each dependency exemption reduces taxable income by $1,000. Nora can claim head of household status; her tax bracket is 25 percent. So the $2,000 in exemptions would reduce her taxes by $500. Tim has to file as a single taxpayer, and his bracket is 40 percent. So $2,000 in exemptions would reduce his taxes by $800.

Although the children live with Nora, the couple had the right to agree on a divorce settlement granting Tim the dependency exemptions, assuming he satisfied the tax rule requiring him to provide at least $600 a year toward the support of each child. Tim obviously would have wanted to do so. If Nora is wise, she would have agreed, while insisting that Tim give her an additional $650 a year in child support. Why $650? Start with the $500 in tax reductions that she's giving up. Add to that half of the remaining $300—the difference between his tax savings and hers. Nora and Tim are splitting the tax savings. The only loser in such a setup is the IRS.

To strike a deal like that, a couple had to agree ahead of time and stipulate in their divorce settlement that he (in our example) gets the dependency exemptions. Without such an agreement, the exemptions usually go to the partner who gets custody of the children. The divorce settlement could also stipulate which parent will get any tax deductions resulting from medical expenses for the children.

For divorce settlements reached in 1985 or later, the new tax law imposes a stiffer requirement. If you claim the dependency exemption even though your ex-spouse has custody of the child, you have to get a written declaration signed by your ex-spouse, promising that he or she won't claim the same exemption—and you have to attach that declaration to your tax return. Moreover, you'll have to attach a signed declaration to your tax return every year the arrangement continues.

For divorces that took effect before 1985, a different system must be used. Let's say your ex-spouse takes the dependency exemptions but you wind up supporting the children. You can nevertheless claim the exemptions, but you must be prepared to prove that you provided at least $1,200 a year for the support of each child. If you can prove that, and your ex-spouse cannot prove that he or she provided more support for the children than you did, you will be entitled to the exemptions.

If you remarry, money chipped in by your new spouse counts as if you made the contribution. Your ex-spouse, of course, gets the same benefit from any money spent by his or her new spouse to support your children.

Remember, the IRS will not serve as referee between you and your ex-spouse. If the agency audits your ex's tax return, it will probably audit yours, too, because it is accustomed to finding divorced parents claiming the same Tax Savers. If both of you claim the dependency exemption for the same child, or if both of you claim head of household status in connection with caring for the same child, the IRS will not weigh the evidence and pick a winner. Instead, it will probably pick two losers, disallowing the Tax Savers for both of you. To hang on to your exemption or your head of household filing status, you'll then have to persuade the IRS that you're entitled to it. So you're much better off striking an agreement with your ex-spouse in advance.

CHILD CARE

If you wind up with custody of a child under the age of fifteen and have to pay someone to care for the child so you can work, look for work, or attend school full-time, you are entitled to a nice Tax Saver called the Credit for Child and Dependent Care Expenses. With the long form, 1040, you figure this credit on Form 2441. If you happen to use the short form, 1040A, you figure this credit on Schedule 1; it's one of a handful of Tax Savers that can be taken on the short form as well as the long. And if you paid for the day care and had custody of the child for most of the year, you can claim the credit even though your ex-spouse may be providing most of the child's support and claiming the dependency exemption.

The lower your income, the greater percentage of your child-care costs can be claimed as a credit. The percentage ranges from 30 percent if your adjusted gross income is $10,000 or less to 20 percent if your adjusted gross income is $28,000 or more. The maximum amount subject to the appropriate percentage is $2,400 for one child, $4,800 for two or more. It doesn't matter whom you pay to care for your child, or where your child is cared for—your home, the home of a neighbor, a day-care center, even a summer camp. However, if you hire someone to care for your child at your home, you will have to pay Social Security tax on that employee's wages.

ALIMONY AND CHILD SUPPORT

In a divorce settlement, money that one spouse pays to another can be in any—or all—of three forms, each with different tax implications. The three are alimony, child support, and property settlement. Once again, the two partners can choose which form they want, within certain boundaries, as part of their divorce settlement. The 1984 tax bill made important changes in some of these rules.

Alimony payments can be deducted by the spouse who pays them and must be reported as income on the tax form of the spouse who receives them.

Child support payments are not deductible by the person who pays, nor do they count as income to the recipient.

A property settlement doesn't count as a deduction or as income, unless the settlement involves sale of a house, a business, or some other property. If it does, and you make a profit on the sale, you have to pay capital gains tax on the profit.

Under the old tax law, you had to figure any profit and pay capital gains tax, whether or not you sold the property. In other words, let's say you had paid $50,000 for your house and had spent $25,000 over the years improving it. Your Basis was $75,000. You got divorced, and as part of your divorce agreement you gave the house to your ex-spouse. By that time, the house was worth $125,000. Under the old law, you had to report a capital gain of $50,000—the

$125,000 market value minus your $75,000 Basis. So even though you hadn't pocketed a penny of profit, you had to pay tax on $50,000 of long-term capital gain.

A lot of people considered that rule unfair, so Congress changed it, effective on the date the 1984 tax bill became law—July 18, 1984. Couples can choose to use the new provision retroactive to January 1, 1984. Under the new provision, you pay no tax on property that goes to your ex-spouse as a property settlement. But your ex-spouse gets not only the property but also your Basis. In our example, your ex-spouse would get the house and you would pay no capital gains tax on the transfer. But if your ex-spouse subsequently sold the house, she would have to figure her profit—and her capital gains tax—based on your Basis, or cost, of $75,000.

The choice between alimony and child support is a trade-off.

Let's say that Tim and Nora are working out a divorce settlement. Tim, remember, has taxable income of $40,000, while Nora's taxable income is $20,000. Nora gets custody of their two children. Tim and Nora agree that he will pay Nora $15,000 a year for eleven years. They can call the $15,000 alimony or child support or a mixture of the two.

Tim would like to count it all as alimony. That way he gets a deduction of $15,000—a big Tax Saver for him.

Nora, however, would have to report that $15,000 as alimony income and pay tax on it. So she'd rather count the $15,000 as child support.

Once again, both Tim and Nora will be better off if they make their choice based on the tax effect and split the tax savings. In our example, they'll benefit by counting most of the $15,000 as alimony. Why? Because Tim is in a higher tax bracket. As a result, the deduction cuts his taxes more than the extra income increases Nora's taxes. They should work out an agreement giving him the deduction and giving her higher payments so that she, too, comes out ahead.

We mentioned earlier that if one spouse understands the tax laws and the other does not, the knowledgeable one can profit at the other's expense. See what we mean? Unless Tim and Nora stipulate otherwise in their divorce agreement, all the payments will count as alimony. So far so good, but what if Nora didn't realize that she'd get stuck with an additional $15,000 of taxable income? She needs to know that so she can bargain with Tim to get a big share of his tax savings. That way she too winds up winning.

Your alimony agreement has to be nailed down under a court decree of divorce or separate maintenance. Voluntary payments don't count. In other words, if you and your spouse separate and you voluntarily start mailing a check every month while negotiating divorce terms, don't expect to deduct it on your tax form.

Moreover, to count as alimony, payments must be periodic. "Periodic" can mean once a week, once a month, or once a year, but a single lump-sum payment cannot count as alimony—and thus cannot be deducted.

State divorce laws prevail, but federal tax laws do define alimony, since it is a deductible expense for one partner and an item of taxable income for the other. You can't live with the person to whom you're paying alimony, and the two of you can't file a joint tax return. If you and your former spouse agree on flat payments—say, $400 a month—your divorce agreement has to call for the payments to last at least ten years for divorces that became final in 1984 or before, or, under the new tax law, at least six years for divorces that become final in 1985 or later. Otherwise, the IRS considers those payments nondeductible installments on a property settlement.

Under the old law covering divorces that became final before 1985, an escape hatch was available if the two of you wanted the payments to count as alimony but didn't want them to continue as long as ten years. You could agree on an alimony formula rather than on flat payments. For example, you might agree on an alimony settlement of one third of your salary for eight years.

The new law shortens the period to six years but requires that alimony payments cannot vary by more than $10,000 from year to year. The new law also requires that all alimony must be paid in cash; property, such as jewelry, stock, or a car, cannot be used as a substitute.

To straighten out the difference between alimony (deductible) and child support (nondeductible), the new 1984 tax law imposes these additional rules covering divorces made final in 1985 or later:

1. If you want the payments to count as alimony, your divorce decree must stipulate that the payments will cease when the recipient dies.

2. If you claim a tax deduction for paying alimony to your ex-spouse, you have to give the IRS your ex-spouse's name and Social Security number; otherwise you'll be hit with a $50 penalty. That's so the IRS can make sure your ex-spouse reports that alimony as income and pays tax on it.

3. If your divorce decree calls for alimony payments to decrease by some set amount when a child reaches adulthood, that set amount will count from the very beginning as child support, not alimony.

AMENDING THE DIVORCE DECREE

If you and your spouse are hardly speaking, you may think we're suggesting the impossible by recommending that you agree on a cold, rational, dollar-and-cents divorce agreement. But the Tax Savers are there, and you should take advantage of them. If you do not—or if you did not—the door is not closed. A divorced couple can ask a court to amend their divorce decree, working in the Tax Savers that we have outlined. In some cases, an amended decree can be made retroactive. Federal tax law, in a burst of leniency, allows those retroactive amendments to affect tax liabilities retroactively. Things may not be as bad as you feared.

12

Tax Savers for Investors

$\mathscr{E}$ very dollar you save is an investment, and practically every investment you make can be shaped into a Tax Saver. A dollar earned in a savings account is treated differently from a dollar earned from dividends or from appreciation in the value of your house or from rent paid to you by a tenant. To make any investment really pay, you need to consider its immediate as well as its long-term effect on your taxes plus its return on your invested dollar.

Many Americans shy away from investments because they consider them too complicated to understand. Others invest in enterprises that they truly do not understand. The former are neglecting opportunities, and the latter are risking their financial futures. In many cases, the seeming complexity of an investment results from its effect on your federal income tax. If you understand your own tax situation, you can intelligently choose investment Tax Savers that fit your needs, your aspirations, and your degree of interest in financial affairs.

That last factor is important. The boom in complex tax shelters has led many Americans to believe that they are stuck with high tax rates on their own modest investments, while richer and more sophisticated investors pocket huge profits, free of tax. To be sure, many tax shelters cater only to big investors and provide breathtaking deductions. But these tax shelters tend to be risky. The investor often is locked in to the investment, unable to sell. Frankly, the tax rules that benefit investors in these shelters can be put to work for you in simpler investments that carry less risk, are closer to home, and can be more readily sold.

In evaluating any investment, the paramount consideration is *your* goal. Some investments yield high income; others yield no income at all but build value; still others combine the two, yielding income while offering the prospect of appreciation in value. The advice of friends may be helpful, but keep in mind that your friends' goals may differ from yours, and the investment that is just right for them may be wrong for you. You can find investments that will meet your own goals; there is no lack of variety. And whatever your goal, Tax Savers can be built into every investment.

In many cases, the Tax Savers were built in by Congress. As a matter of economic policy, Congress wants all of us to invest our money, and it coaxes us to do so with very generous tax incentives. We call these incentives Tax Savers.

OWNING YOUR HOME

The most basic investment Tax Saver, and perhaps the most important, is your home. Homeownership builds value, provides generous tax deductions, and enables many Americans to itemize their tax deductions for the first time, thus giving them the opportunity to take advantage of other Tax Saver deductions. In Chapter 10, we discuss Tax Savers for Homeowners in detail.

Owning your home is an early and important investment goal. So is saving toward retirement—a distant goal but one that is best pursued when you are relatively young. Just as the tax laws provide generous deductions to encourage you to buy a home, they provide unique and substantial Tax Savers to help you build a retirement nest egg. Some of these are bestowed through your job, in the form of pension

━━━━━━━

and profit-sharing plans. Others are provided through the Individual Retirement Account, or IRA, and its even more generous sister plan for the self-employed, the Keogh account. Because retirement is such an important investment goal, and because the Tax Savers for retirement are structured so uniquely, we discuss them on their own in the next chapter.

COORDINATING YOUR
INVESTMENTS

No investment—and no Tax Saver—stands by itself. You can tailor your other investments and their Tax Savers to dovetail with the investment and Tax Saver features of your home and your IRA. Let's start with a strategy that diversifies your investments while exploiting the quite different Tax Savers of an IRA and of common stocks or real estate bought outside an IRA.

The IRA Tax Saver allows you to contribute up to $2,000 of your earnings every year, paying no income tax on the contributions or on the interest or dividends that they earn until you withdraw them. Once you begin withdrawals, usually in retirement, every dollar that you withdraw is taxable as ordinary income.

Outside an IRA, the capital gains Tax Saver allows you to pocket, free of tax, 60 percent of the profit you make on the sale of any property you have owned for more than one year—or for more than six months if you bought the property after June 22, 1984. In other words, only 40 percent of your profit is taxed. "Property" can mean any capital asset—stocks, bonds, real estate, gold coins, rare stamps, Persian rugs, old baseball cards. In tax and investment jargon, your profit is called a capital gain. If you owned the property for more than one year—six months if you bought it after June 22, 1984—it's a long-term capital gain, and only 40 percent of it is taxed. If you owned the property for a shorter period, it's a short-term capital gain, and all of it— all of your profit—is taxed as ordinary income. (Congress changed the holding period from one year to six months as part of the 1984 tax law and at the same time stipulated that the holding period reverts to one year in 1988.)

Congress did not enact the IRA and the capital gains Tax Savers together. They were enacted decades apart and with entirely different purposes in mind. But today they co-exist in the Tax Code, and they provide a superb example of how one Tax Saver can be used to mesh with another, thus enhancing the benefits that you receive from both.

Let's say that you already own your home (with a mortgage, of course), and in addition you can afford to salt away $4,000 a year. Your goals:

1. Build a nest egg; you don't need steady income from your savings.
2. Accumulate a comfortable retirement fund.
3. Establish a savings account that you might tap at an earlier age, perhaps to buy a second home or to cover you during a change in careers.
4. Diversify your investments so your risk is spread around.

Those are goals that most of us share. Coincidentally —and happily—the IRA and capital gains Tax Savers are tailor-made to meet them.

To diversify, you probably would be wise to split your savings between conservative investments that yield a healthy percentage of interest or dividends, and stocks or real estate that appear likely to increase in value over the years. The split is simple: With your IRA contribution, buy bank certificates, money funds, bonds or utility stocks. Your $2,000 contribution will yield substantial interest or dividends. Outside an IRA, you'd have to pay tax on that yield. Inside an IRA, the interest or dividends accumulate and compound free of income tax.

With the other $2,000, buy common stocks of profitable, growing companies that use their profits for research and expansion instead of paying them out in dividends. As these stocks appreciate in value, you pay no income tax on that gain. So while your IRA nest egg is compounding free of tax, so is the nest egg outside your IRA. Why no tax? Because you pay tax on a capital gain only when you sell. As long as you hold the property, your gains are not taxed.

To keep this example simple, we'll say that you paid $10 a share for your stock, and we'll consider your $2,000 investment for one year only. Further, we'll estimate that in twenty years each share of stock will be worth $114, reflecting an annual return of 12 percent, compounded. So your $2,000 stock investment will be worth $22,800. We'll say that your IRA investment achieves precisely the same return. It too will be worth $22,800. You have built up two nest eggs, worth $45,600 in total, on initial investments of $4,000, and you haven't paid a penny in income tax along the way.

Now, however, you want to sell your stocks—perhaps to start a business, make a down payment on a vacation home, take a sabbatical. We mention those goals at random to whet your appetite, because the purpose of investments and investment Tax Savers, remember, is to meet your own individual goals.

If you sell that $22,800 worth of stock, you'll have a long-term capital gain of $20,800. Only 40 percent of that gain—$8,320—is taxable. If your tax bracket is 33 percent, you'll pay $2,746 in income tax on that gain. The rest is yours to spend.

That's a real Tax Saver, but you might do even better by checking the calendar. Remember, advance tax planning is the key to virtually every investment Tax Saver.

We'll say that it's September when you and your spouse decide that you'll need that money and want to sell that stock. But you won't really need the money until the following March. You can sell the stock now, take advantage of the capital gains Tax Saver, and pay $2,746 income tax next April, when you file your income tax return.

But look at your marginal tax bracket and look at the calendar. By selling the stock all in one year, you boost your taxable income by $8,320—enough to push you into a higher tax bracket. And by selling it this year, you obligate yourself to pay that tax next April.

You don't need the money until next March. You have planned ahead. And you have choices—choices that will yield substantial Tax Savers on top of the capital gains Tax Saver.

Choice 1
Sell half (or another carefully calculated portion) of the stock now and the remaining half in January. The capital gain will boost your taxable income by $4,160 for this year and by $4,160 for next year. That may keep your tax bracket at 33 percent, rather than boost it to 38 percent. If so, you'll save $416 in tax. Even better, you won't have to pay the tax on the final half of that sale for another year.

Choice 2
Sell all the stock in January. Your taxable gain won't be any less, but you won't have to report it for another fifteen months—until April 15 of the following year. Of course, you may have to pay the tax gradually over the next year as part of your estimated income tax.

What's the better choice? That depends on your circumstances. Your marginal tax bracket is an important factor. If your bracket will be lower next year, by all means defer the sale until next year. For example, let's say that you plan to buy a vacation home next year. You'll use the proceeds from the stock sale for a down payment and borrow the rest. Your gross income, we'll say, will be about the same next year as this year. But next year you'll have far greater deductions, because of the mortgage interest and property taxes on your new vacation home. So your tax bracket will be lower next year. That factor weighs in on the side of postponing the stock sale until January.

MARGINAL TAX BRACKET
Before we go any further, let's define what we mean by your "marginal tax bracket." It does *not* mean the percentage of your income that you pay in income tax. It means the percentage that you pay on the *last dollar* of your taxable income. Just look at the Tax Rate Schedules, which are in-

cluded in the instruction book that you get with your income tax forms. Let's say that you are married and filing jointly, and your taxable income is $38,000. Your income tax—we're simply lifting this from the Tax Rate Schedule for 1984—is $6,274, plus 33 percent of your taxable income over $35,200. That 33 percent is your marginal tax bracket. By looking one step up and one step down on the schedule, you'll see that your marginal bracket would decline to 28 percent if your taxable income declined to $35,200 or lower, and that your marginal bracket would climb to 38 percent if your taxable income topped $45,800. In timing your capital gains—indeed, in timing any income—the effect on your marginal tax bracket is of paramount importance. Beginning in 1985, tax brackets will be indexed in line with inflation.

TIMING YOUR LOSSES

To carry our example further—and to introduce you to another Tax Saver—let's say that in addition to the stock that has grown in value from $2,000 to $22,800, you have a stock that has lost $3,000 in value. You bought it, we'll say, last July. It's now September, so you've owned it for less than six months. You want to sell both stocks—the one that you've profited on so handsomely over twenty years, and the one that's cost you so dearly over two months. Remember, once again, that you don't need the money until next March. Should you sell both stocks now? One now and one next year? Both next year?

This year—in fact, within a couple of months—sell the stock that has declined in value. Next year, sell the stock that has appreciated in value. The reason is rooted in a happenstance of tax law.

If you sell the stock that has declined in value before you have owned it for six months, your loss will be a short-term capital loss. Up to $3,000 in short-term capital losses can be deducted in full against your ordinary income (such as wages, interest, and dividends) for the year. So if you're in the 33 percent bracket, that $3,000 short-term capital loss will cut your income tax by $999. In other words, Uncle Sam will cover about one third of your loss.

But if you have a long-term capital gain the same year, you must use the short-term loss to offset the gain. For you, that would be wasteful. Your capital gain is long-term, so only 40 percent of it will be subject to tax. But if you sell both stocks this year, your $3,000 loss will cancel out the first $3,000 of your gain. You'll lose that $3,000 deduction against ordinary income. Instead of cutting your tax bill by $999, that short-term loss will cut your tax bill by only $396. To get the best of both worlds, all you need to do is take the short-term loss this year and take the long-term gain next year. In figuring taxes, the calendar is what counts: You can sell the stock at a loss in December and sell the other stock at a gain in January. You'll still get the full benefit of the $3,000 loss on this year's income while postponing the long-term gain until next year.

Indeed, the interaction between capital gains and capital losses, long-term and short-term, can be a Tax Saver or a Tax Soaker, depending on when you sell and how your gains and losses in a year balance out. Any time you purchase an investment, make a note on your calendar to review it five months later. When it comes up for review, decide whether you would be wise to sell it while it still holds short-term status—in other words, before you have owned it for more than six months. Make the same kind of review every fall as part of your year-end tax planning. Schedule your sales to take best advantage of your gains and losses, to keep your tax bracket down, and to postpone your capital gains tax obligation for a year, when feasible. Get a copy of Schedule D—the tax form on which you report your capital gains and losses. Pencil in your alternatives, work out the figures, and time your sales so every one of them becomes a Tax Saver.

Sophisticated investors often take losses on one security, strictly for the tax benefit, and immediately invest the proceeds in another security. In bond trading, this is called a bond swap. In order to claim the tax benefit of an investment loss, you cannot buy exactly the same security—the same bond or stock that you just sold—unless you wait at least thirty-one days. But that's not much of an obstacle. It's easy to find a bond, a stock, or a mutual fund very similar to the one you just sold and just as good.

This kind of transaction can be particularly valuable when you have cashed in a big capital gain. Let's say you and your family own a beach house. You sell it at a profit of $100,000—not an unusual profit, assuming you owned the property for a number of years. Forty percent of that $100,000 is taxable, so you would have to pay income tax on $40,000—enough to push you up several brackets.

But perhaps you have been hanging on to a portfolio of bonds that you bought fifteen years ago, before rising interest rates pushed down the market value of bonds. Sell those bonds. For the sake of this example, we'll say that you bought the bonds for $60,000 and sell them for $40,000. That's a long-term capital loss of $20,000. On your tax return, that $20,000 loss will offset $20,000 of your long-term capital gain on the beach house. Instead of a gain of $100,000 your gain will be only $80,000, of which 40 percent—$32,000—is taxable. You've reduced your taxable income by $8,000. Assuming your tax bracket is 38 percent, that's a saving of $3,040. And you can invest the $40,000 that you got for the bonds in other bonds, paying the same yield.

T-BILLS

U.S. Treasury bills are not generally considered Tax Savers, but in fact they provide an opportunity to collect interest in one year while deferring tax on that interest until the following year. Treasury bills are short-term investments; you can buy T-bills that mature in thirteen weeks, twenty-six weeks, or one year. Let's say you buy a $10,000 Treasury bill yielding 10 percent and maturing in one year. You'll pay only $9,000 for it. The missing $1,000 is your discount. In effect, it is your interest, paid to you in advance. A year later, the Treasury bill matures and you get $10,000. Your yield is $1,000 in interest, and it's taxable for the year the bill matures, not for the year in which you bought it. Another plus for T-bills and other Treasuries is that the interest is exempt from state and local taxes.

DIVIDENDS

To take full advantage of the capital gains Tax Saver, we talked about investing in stocks that reinvest their profits rather than pay their profits to shareholders in the form of dividends. In fact, many firms do both: They pay dividends, and at the same time the value of their stock increases. So we don't mean to recommend that you avoid dividends. Neither does Congress, which has written two nice dividend Tax Savers into the law.

Every year, the first $100 of dividends that you receive is exempt from income tax. If you are married and filing a joint income tax return, you and your spouse can exempt the first $200 of dividend income.

UTILITY DIVIDENDS

The second dividend Tax Saver is more generous, but it can be used with only one kind of stock and one kind of plan. Fortunately, that stock and that plan make a solid, conservative investment.

If you buy qualified stock in a public utility (ask your broker) and have the dividends automatically reinvested in additional shares of the company's stock, you get the first $750 of annual dividends free of tax. If you're married filing a joint tax return, the exclusion doubles, to $1,500. That's a big tax shelter. Most utilities offer reinvestment plans, and many of them sell stock through such plans at a discount of 3 percent or 5 percent from market value. *(An important warning: This Tax Saver is scheduled to expire at the end of 1985.)*

Utilities are considered safe stocks. The companies are regulated monopolies, providing electrical and natural gas service to localities. Even if a utility is mismanaged, it's very unlikely to go out of business; a utility provides a vital service, and state regulators make sure that the companies stay solvent. In addition, utilities pay relatively high dividends.

Even so, some utility stocks are safer investments than others. Some are in financial trouble because of difficulties with nuclear power plants. A full-service broker such as Merrill Lynch or Dean Witter can recommend safe utility stocks that offer dividend reinvestment plans. If you prefer to do your own stock research and use a discount broker to save on commissions, here's a partial list of utilities that offer discount dividend reinvestment plans.

Baltimore Gas & Electric
Commonwealth Energy
Eastern Utilities
Florida Power & Light
Hawaiian Electric
Illinois Power
Iowa Resources
Kansas Power & Light
Louisville Gas & Electric

Minnesota Power & Light
Montana Dakota Utilities
New England Electric
System
Oklahoma Gas & Electric
Public Service of Colorado
Southern California
Edison
Texas Utilities

When we compiled this list in 1984, all these utilities were considered safe, solid investments. But stock ratings change. Before you buy, go to the reference room of your public library, ask for the Value Line Investment Survey, and check the current ratings of the utility stocks you're considering. Value Line has an excellent record, and you can tell at a glance how well each firm is rated.

SELECTING INVESTMENTS

We've talked about investing your IRA for a high yield—interest or dividends—and investing your "outside" money for capital gains. That leaves you with the job of picking the right investments. We doubt the ability of anyone to forecast the course of the stock market day by day or even year by year, but if you are a long-term investor, it's helpful to see how various investments have fared over the decades. The studies are voluminous, and all of them conclude that common stocks have provided far and away the greatest gains, followed in order by real estate, bonds, and U.S. Treasury bills.

But stock prices are also the most volatile. For example, here are recent year-by-year highs of the Dow-Jones Industrial Average, a barometer of blue-chip stocks:

1974	892
1975	882
1976	1,015
1977	1,000
1978	908
1979	898
1980	1,000
1981	1,024
1982	1,071
1983	1,287

Many investors don't have the stomach to ride those big waves. Besides, some investors believe that the stock market will never again provide the returns that it used to. Certainly, you should buy stocks only if you will be able to sell them at your own convenience, when the price is right. A forced sale may coincide with a trough in prices, and that will cost you money.

We recommend mutual funds for most investors. A mutual fund is managed by a full-time professional. Your portfolio is diversified among scores of stocks. You can pick a mutual fund with an objective in line with your own objectives. Schabacker Investment Management (8943 Shady Grove Court, Gaithersburg, Maryland 20877) tracks the statistical performance of mutual funds and divides them according to their respective objectives. Through August 1984, here are the performances of five mutual funds that have excelled, with their respective objectives. "Performance" means appreciation in value, with dividends or interest reinvested.

Fund	Objective	Performance
Fidelity Magellan (phone 800-225-6190)	Long-term growth	up 1,685% over past 10 years up 319% over past 5 years down 3% over past year
20th Century Select (phone 816-531-5575)	Long-term growth	up 1,083% for 10 years up 201% for 5 years down 6% for 1 year
Quasar Associates (phone 800-221-5672)	Growth	up 1,165% for 10 years up 163% for 5 years down 8% for 1 year
Vanguard Windsor (phone 800-523-7024)	Growth with income	up 654% for 10 years up 136% for 5 years up 13% for 1 year
Fidelity Equity Income (phone 800-225-6190)	High-yield stocks and/or bonds	up 667% for 10 years up 154% for 5 years up 4% for 1 year

MUNICIPAL BONDS

If you want your investments to yield income—money that you can spend—then join the parade of tax-conscious investors in state and municipal bonds. "Munies" pay interest twice a year, and the interest is exempt from federal income tax. If you buy bonds issued by your own state or by Puerto Rico, the interest will be exempt from state and local income tax, too.

Because their interest is tax-exempt, municipal bonds pay lower rates of interest than do Treasury bonds and corporate bonds, on which the interest is fully taxed by the IRS. But the difference in yield, or interest rate, is so narrow that if your marginal tax bracket is 30 percent or higher, you're better off with a municipal bond than with a bond paying taxable interest. The higher your tax bracket, the greater the advantage of municipals over any investment that yields taxable interest. Here's a simple chart that will let you compare for yourself, using your own tax bracket:

Tax-free yield	EQUIVALENT TAXABLE YIELD		
	30% bracket	40% bracket	50% bracket
8%	11.4%	13.3%	16%
9%	12.9%	15 %	18%
10%	14.3%	16.7%	20%
11%	15.7%	18.3%	22%
12%	17.1%	20 %	24%

In buying any bond, you are literally lending money to the issuer. The issuer agrees to pay you interest at a fixed rate for a certain number of years. The bond then "matures," and you get back the exact amount that you paid for the bond—or, to put it another way, the issuer pays you back the money you lent him.

Although the bond's interest rate, maturity date, and maturity value are fixed, these so-called fixed-income investments carry some risk. For one thing, a bond issuer could go broke and default. That's very unusual, but it happened not long ago to the Washington Public Power System. That was the notorious WHOOPS default, which cost many investors a good deal of their money. WHOOPS issued bonds to finance construction of five nuclear power plants in the Pacific Northwest. Costs soared and demand for electricity failed to grow as projected, so construction was halted on several of the plants. Since the plants were not producing revenue, no money was available to pay interest to bondholders. WHOOPS bondholders are still waiting to find out whether they will get any return on their investment, and if so, how much.

The more common risk results from changes in prevailing interest rates. For example, let's say you buy a municipal bond yielding 9 percent interest and maturing in six years. At the time you buy, 9 percent is the going rate. But say interest rates rise next year to 11 percent. Your money will be tied up at less than the going interest rate. You can sell your bond, but if you do so, you will get less for it than you paid. Why? Because the investor who buys it will pay just enough so that the yield he receives will be today's going rate—11 percent. On the other hand, if interest rates decline—say, to 8 percent—the value of your bond will increase.

You can buy bonds individually through a broker, but we caution against it unless you know the market and have $20,000 or so to invest. For small investors, brokers "mark up" bonds by 4 or 5 percent when they sell them, and mark them down by 4 or 5 percent when they buy them. You never know exactly how much the broker is pocketing. Besides, municipal bonds rarely are offered in denominations of less than $5,000, so you need a lot of money to get even a little diversification.

You have two alternatives, both of them convenient and worthwhile. Through a broker, you can buy shares in a municipal bond trust—a portfolio of twenty or so bonds, all chosen by professionals and all maturing about the same time—typically in ten to thirty years. If you live in a state that imposes a high rate of income tax, ask your broker about municipal bond trusts that invest entirely in bonds issued by your state. That way your Tax Saver spares you state income tax as well as federal income tax.

You can achieve even greater safety and diversification through a mutual fund that invests in tax-exempt bonds. Your shares in a mutual fund never mature, because the fund continually buys and sells bonds. As a result, its portfolio reflects the going interest rate not just for the present, but also for various past years. When interest rates are at their peak, your shares in a tax-exempt fund will probably not be paying quite as high an interest rate as you could get on an individual bond. But when interest rates are at their trough, your fund's yield will probably be higher than the going rate. In addition, the fund's managers will try to sell bonds at a profit, generating capital gains. You can sell back, or redeem, your shares any time at their current value. In late August of 1984, these two municipal bond funds were yielding tax-exempt interest of 9.8 and 9.7 percent, respectively: Fidelity High Yield Municipals (phone 800-225-6190) and Vanguard Municipal High Yield (phone 800-523-7910).

One note of caution: If you receive Social Security income plus income from municipal bonds, you may have to pay a small amount of income tax. Some refer to this relatively new tax as a levy on Social Security income, while others call it a tax on municipal bond income. In fact, the terminology doesn't matter. We work through the precise formula for this tax in Chapter 14, Tax Savers for Senior Citizens.

ANNUITIES

Annuities, which are sold by insurance companies, vary greatly. They are not bad as Tax Savers, but usually they are not so good as investments. When you buy an annuity, you either pay a lump sum—say, $5,000—or make regular monthly contributions. Your contributions are not deductible, but the interest or dividends that they earn accumulate free of tax. The annuity becomes payable at a predetermined date; most people who buy annuities schedule them to start paying when they retire. You can then withdraw your money all at once or take fixed monthly payments for the rest of your life. Each payment is considered partly a return of your initial investment and partly a return of the interest or dividends it has earned; you pay income tax only on the latter portion.

With an annuity, the longer you live, the more you

profit, because the insurance company will pay you until you die. If you are married, you can choose to have the payments continue until both you and your spouse are dead. In that case, of course, your monthly payments will be smaller.

That's all good. The trouble is that annuities tend to impose high fees, and the net yield on your savings often is very low—so low that even with the tax advantage of annuities, you could do better by choosing a mutual fund. Moreover, an annuity is not without risk. Baldwin-United, one of the biggest annuity firms, declared bankruptcy in late 1983 because too many of its investments went sour. Baldwin-United's annuity investors probably will get their money back but not until it has been tied up for several years.

As with mutual funds, you can choose annuities that invest in money market funds, fixed-income securities such as bonds, or common stocks. According to Lipper Analytical Services, Inc., an investment advisory firm, fixed-income and stock annuity funds managed by Compass registered the best gains for the twelve months through January 1984.

TAX SHELTERS

Whether you invest in one or not, tax shelters yield advantages for every taxpayer. According to the director of the Internal Revenue Service's Los Angeles office, as quoted in *The Wall Street Journal,* the IRS is so busy auditing the returns of tax-shelter investors that it has little time or manpower left over for other tax returns. So if you are not claiming tax-shelter write-offs on your tax return, your risk of being audited is relatively low.

Tax shelters are groups of investors who, through a sponsor, finance ventures in real estate, oil and gas drilling, and a few other projects, including movie distribution. Let's say that you buy into a shelter that is erecting a shopping center. You may put up as little as $2,500, although $5,000 is a more typical minimum. You and the other partners then share the Tax Savers that accompany real estate investments. The first year, for example, it is quite normal to get two dollars' worth of deductions for every dollar you invested. Ratios of three to one and four to one are not out of the question. In other words, you might invest $5,000, and on a three-to-one shelter get to deduct $15,000 from your regular income. If your tax bracket is 50 percent—the highest bracket—$15,000 in deductions saves you $7,500 in taxes. That's $2,500 more than you invested, and you still own a share of the property. If all goes well, that shopping center eventually will be sold at a profit, and you'll share (and be taxed) on those profits.

But all does not always go well. A few years ago a number of Hollywood celebrities were socked with huge tax bills because a shelter in which they had invested failed to pass muster with the IRS. More recently, a popular oil and gas tax shelter disappointed its investors—not because the IRS disapproved of it but because it failed to make money. After the first few years of wonderful deductions, even the best tax shelters start generating tax obligations for the partners. This drives many investors to find yet another tax shelter so they can avoid tax on the earnings from the first shelter. Unfortunately, some tax-shelter investments never pan out. And although you can tell in advance what your deductions will be the first few years, it's very difficult to assess the more distant future of a tax-shelter investment.

To protect investors—and to curb the drain on the Treasury—Congress now requires tax-shelter promoters to register their offerings with the Treasury Department and to furnish lists of investors upon request. That rule may keep dishonest promoters from latching onto your money, but even a registered shelter may turn out to be a poor investment.

Moreover, a tax shelter is hard to analyze. Both of us have painstakingly read detailed prospectuses for various shelters. A prospectus describes the project in detail but usually doesn't give you much insight into whether it will be profitable.

We prefer tax shelters that the investor can understand. Our favorite is rental property—for example, a house or a small office building. When you buy a house, condominium, or office building and rent it out, you reap a bonanza of Tax Savers—the same Tax Savers, in fact, that are at the foundation of many tax-shelter partnerships.

You get to deduct all your mortgage interest, real estate taxes, maintenance and repair bills, utilities, and, if you hire someone to manage the property for you, management fees. Most important, you get the advantage of a Tax Saver almost too good to be true: Although the property is likely to increase in value, you get to depreciate it as if it were losing its value. Property purchased after March 15, 1984, can be depreciated over eighteen years, and property purchased between January 1, 1981, and March 15, 1984, can be depreciated even more rapidly—over fifteen years. Those are very short periods, considering the life of most real estate. In fact, this so-called accelerated depreciation spawned many real estate tax shelters; it's that good a Tax Saver. For property purchased before January 1, 1981, you had to use the old straight-line depreciation formulas, spreading real estate depreciation over twenty-five to forty years.

When you sell, your profit on the house or condominium counts as a long-term capital gain, assuming you have owned the property for more than one year, or for more than six months if you bought it after June 22, 1984. That's another Tax Saver—remember, only 40 percent of a long-term capital gain is subject to income tax.

You can combine this investment Tax Saver with other family needs. Under the tax rules, you're allowed to use your own rental property up to fourteen days a year. For example, you might buy a ski condo or a beach cottage, use it for a two-week family vacation every year, and rent it out the rest of the time. As long as you don't exceed that four-teen-day limit, that's a perfectly legal use of your property; you still get all the tax deductions. Even if you use it more often, you can reap significant Tax Savers.

Let's say your parents are retired and want to move to Arizona, but they aren't eager to buy a house. The two of you can combine on Tax Savers, to your mutual benefit. They can sell their present house and pocket up to $125,000 of profit free of tax, assuming they have not previously taken advantage of this Tax Saver, which an individual can use only once in his or her life, from age fifty-five on. You can then travel with them to Arizona to look for a house, deducting your travel costs as an investment expense. You buy the house of your parents' choice and rent it to them. Your parents get the house they wanted, at a reasonable rent, from a friendly landlord. You get all the Tax Savers that go with rental property.

You can even offer your parents a good deal: The law allows you to charge them rent as much as 10 percent below the going rate in that area. Of course, your parents need not move; you can buy the house they already live in from them, rent it back to them, and reap the same Tax Savers.

In yet another wrinkle, let's say that your son or daughter is going to college. He'll need a place to stay, and you can combine that need with an investment Tax Saver. Buy a duplex or a small apartment building in the college town, renting one unit to your child and the rest to other students. Your child must pay a fair rent, but it's all in the family. And you get a raft of Tax Savers, plus an investment in a building that is likely to yield an eventual capital gain.

ALTERNATIVE MINIMUM TAX

Investment Tax Savers are so numerous and so generous that many wealthy Americans used to avoid income tax altogether. In response, Congress enacted the "Alternative Minimum Tax," a device to capture some income tax from even the most adroit and dedicated users of Tax Savers. Because of the Alternative Minimum Tax, it's wise to spread out your capital gains. Before you cash in big capital gains or take advantage of other Tax Savers, figure whether you'll be hit with the Alternative Minimum Tax and, if so, how much it will amount to. Here's the formula:

Start with your adjusted gross income, from the bottom of the first page of Form 1040. Then add these so-called tax preference items:

1. The 60 percent of your long-term capital gains that would not otherwise be taxed.
2. The dividend exclusion of $100 for an individual ($200 for a couple filing jointly).
3. If you own rental property, the difference between your deduction under the accelerated depreciation formula and the deduction you'd get under the old straight-line depreciation formula.
4. If you cashed in a stock option or are thinking of doing so, add the bargain element—in effect, the discount you're getting on the stock.
5. If you have invested in a tax shelter, you'll have to add various deductions and credits from the shelter. To figure that, you'll need the help of a tax professional.

From that total, subtract these itemized deductions (and no others):

1. Deductible casualty and theft losses.
2. Charitable contributions.
3. Medical expenses that exceed 10 percent of your adjusted gross income.
4. Interest on your home mortgage.
5. Other interest paid by you during the year, but only to the extent of your net investment income.

At this point, you have your Alternative Minimum Taxable Income (AMTI). If you're single, deduct $30,000 from your AMTI. If you're married filing jointly, deduct $40,000. If you're married filing separately, deduct $20,000.

Multiply the result by the flat rate of 20 percent.

That's your Alternative Minimum Tax. Now figure your tax bill the regular way, ignoring the Alternative Minimum Tax. Compare the two tax liabilities: You have to pay the higher of the two. If the Alternative Minimum Tax would sock you with, say, $10,000 of additional income tax, you might want to spread out or postpone a capital gain or cash in a stock option next year rather than this year.

(Beginning in 1985, you're required to pay quarterly estimated income tax on tax you'll owe for that year under the
Alternative Minimum Tax.)

If you plan wisely, the Alternative Minimum Tax
amounts to a pop gun compared to the cannons of investment Tax Savers. Whether your goal is short-term savings,
a dream house, or early retirement, you can reach it more
readily and more quickly by using the Tax Savers that accompany prudent investments. Remember to chart your
own course, toward your own goal, utilizing the investments and Tax Savers of your choice. You'll profit on your
investments and pay less tax on your profits—a very pleasant combination.

13

Tax Savers for the Retired

A ll of us want a comfortable retirement, and the federal tax code is peppered with generous Tax Savers to help us achieve it. In no other area of life are the Tax Savers so numerous or so bounteous. If you save and invest wisely, you can build a retirement nest egg while cutting your taxes by tens of thousands of dollars.

The government's generosity is deliberate. Americans are retiring earlier and living longer. The earlier people retire and the longer they live, the more they will need in the way of retirement savings. The government wants Americans to provide for their own retirement so they will not become wards of the state. To encourage retirement savings, Congress has chosen one primary vehicle: Tax Savers.

When we talk about retirement Tax Savers, we don't mean provisions that cut your taxes after you retire. Quite the contrary. Retirement Tax Savers cut your taxes during your working years. The payoff is double: less tax now, more income in retirement. But most retirement Tax Savers are not automatic. You have to be aware of them, understand them, tailor them to your own situation, and take steps to put them into effect.

Think of your retirement income as a stool with three legs. One leg will be provided by Social Security. A second, if you are fortunate enough to be in on a private retirement program, will be your company pension—or pensions, if you worked for more than one firm during your career. The third has to be carved by you from your own investments.

To a large extent, all three legs employ Tax Savers. While you work, your employer pays about half of the total Social Security contribution credited to your account, and you pay no income tax on that portion. (You do pay income tax, however, on the Social Security contribution that is withheld from your paycheck.) Once you start receiving Social Security benefits, they are largely tax-free.

Company pension and profit-sharing plans are larded with Tax Savers. If your employer funds a plan in your behalf, you are not taxed on that contribution. In addition, a relatively new kind of Salary Reduction pension plan lets you defer compensation and put the cash into a company plan; you pay no income tax on that money, or on the interest or dividends it earns, until you withdraw it.

If you are self-employed, you can establish your own pension plan, deducting your pension contributions from your taxable income. Once again, those contributions keep compounding, free of income tax, until you begin withdrawing the money in retirement.

That brings us to your own carefully selected investments of various sizes and shapes.

Starting with an IRA, you can build a portfolio of investment Tax Savers that will—for many people—make the difference in retirement between penury and luxury. That is no exaggeration; these Tax Savers can save you tens of thousands of dollars in taxes while building hundreds of thousands of dollars in your retirement accounts.

We will discuss all of these Tax Savers. We'll tell you how they work, so you can choose the ones that best fit your income and aspirations. We'll give you the pros and cons of various Tax Saver investments, so you can make intelligent choices. But first, let's go back to those three legs that will provide the foundation of your retirement security. To plan your retirement Tax Savers, you have to know the amount and source of income that will be coming to you automatically, so you can figure how much more you will need—or want—and take the necessary steps to make sure it will be there when you stop working.

SOCIAL SECURITY

Social Security is a firm, solid source of retirement income. You can count on your Social Security pension. Those who say that the system will collapse are wrong. Congress will not let that happen.

But Social Security alone will not pay you nearly enough money to live comfortably. The maximum Social Security pension for someone retiring in 1984 at age sixty-five was $703 a month, or $8,436 a year. If you and your spouse both worked, both earned the maximum Social Security pension, and both retired in 1984 at age sixty five, you'd get $8,436 each, for a total of $16,872. If one of you worked and the other did not, the one who worked would get $8,436 and the spouse would get half that much, or $4,218, for a family total of $12,654. Every year, that amount is boosted in line with increases in the cost of living.

That may sound like a nice pension, especially since it's largely exempt from federal income tax. (In Chapter 14, Tax Savers for Senior Citizens, we describe the conditions under which a portion of your Social Security income may be taxed.) But it's not enough for a comfortable retirement, and in all candor it wasn't designed to be.

Moreover, you cannot count on the annual cost-of-living increases to continue in full. As Social Security recipients make up a larger and larger segment of our population, Congress will simply have to trim benefits. It may do so by reducing the annual cost-of-living increases. That kind of pruning may be needed to keep the Social Security system solvent. Your Social Security pension will be secure, but it may not keep up with inflation.

PENSIONS

We cannot tell you what your company pension will amount to, but you can find out. Write to the plan administrator and ask for an individual statement of benefits. If you're thinking of retiring at, say, age sixty-two, ask the administrator what your benefits would be if you retire at sixty-two and what they would be if you retire at sixty-five, or even at some later age. Under law, the plan administrator is required to provide individual benefit statements upon request.

In many cases, it will pay you handsomely to stay on the job until age sixty-five. In fact, you may be shocked to see how much lower your pension will be if you retire early. On the surface, the difference may seem unfairly large. In fact, it results from the arithmetic of pension formulas. Those last few years are likely to be your years of highest salary, and pensions are based partly on that factor. In addition, the more you have in the pension pot, the more it earns, and those last few years are the period in which you have the most in the pot.

Many pension plans provide "integrated benefits." That means your company pension will be calculated in conjunction with your Social Security pension; in effect, the more your Social Security pension is, the less your company pension will be. Make sure you understand the connection, so you can figure what you will receive in total from Social Security and your company pension.

Remember, too, that although your Social Security pension will be largely exempt from income tax, your company pension checks are, for the most part, taxed just like your salary is today.

MULTIPLE PENSIONS

We've been talking about your company "pension," but we really mean "pensions." Many of us toil for several employers during our working years. You may be entitled to pensions from two or three employers, or even more. In fact, before quitting a job at any time during your career it's wise to check your pension eligibility. Your benefits "vest" after a maximum of ten years of employment. That means that if you work for a firm for ten years, you're entitled to a pension at age sixty-five. But some pensions vest more

---

quickly. The provisions vary a great deal from plan to plan. You may find that by staying on a few additional months, you will become entitled to a pension.

As you plan your retirement income, write to the pension plan administrator of every firm you have worked for and inquire whether you will be entitled to a pension, and if so, how much, and at what age. Don't expect the company to come looking for you.

Add up what you can expect to receive from Social Security and company pensions. Figure in variables having to do with your age when you retire. In other words, if you retire at age sixty-two, or even earlier, the amount you receive from Social Security and from the pension plan of your final employer will be less than if you had retired at age sixty-five—less the first year and every year thereafter.

Then calculate how much more money you'll need every month. And work with us on providing it, using Tax Savers every step of the way. Do you want to retire early? Tax Savers will help you do it, by building up savings that will produce retirement income from the third leg of your stool—your own investments.

IRAs

In the preceding chapter, we discussed a variety of Tax Saver investments. We pointed out the advantages of tax-exempt municipal bonds. We talked about annuities, tax shelters, and the tax-favored treatment of capital gains. Many of these investments will pay off in retirement, too. But in planning for retirement, you should start with the Tax Savers that are designed specifically for that purpose. The most prominent among these, and one of the best, is the Individual Retirement Account, or IRA.

Any American age seventy and a half or younger who earns money from work can contribute to an IRA. Beginning in 1985, you can contribute money you receive from alimony. Your eligibility for an IRA is not curtailed by your participation in other pension programs. You may be fortunate enough to benefit from pension and profit-sharing programs at work. You may be self-employed and contributing to a Keogh pension plan—a Tax Saver similar to an IRA. Even so, you can contribute to your IRA every year. The maximum IRA contribution is $2,000 a year. If you earn just five dollars during a calendar year, you can contribute all of it to your IRA. If you earn $2,000, you can contribute all of that.

But if your income is entirely from other sources— pensions, interest, dividends, capital gains—you cannot contribute to an IRA. Only money earned from work or alimony qualifies. On a talk show, Strassels was challenged on this point by a man who was planning to open an IRA with income he was receiving from a pension. "They say earned income qualifies, and I earned every penny of my pension," the man explained. He probably did, but nevertheless pension money does not qualify. "Earned income" means money earned on the job or from self-employment.

If your spouse earns no money, you can contribute an additional $250, for a total annual contribution of $2,250. It must be in two accounts—one under your name, the other under your spouse's name. You and your spouse can divide up that $2,250 any way you want, as long as neither account gets more than $2,000. You may want to split the $2,250 evenly between you. If your spouse is younger, you may want to put $2,000 in that account and only $250 in yours. That way you can postpone withdrawals—and taxes —longer, since your spouse won't reach the mandatory age for withdrawals as soon as you will. If you are seventy and a half or older, you can no longer contribute to an IRA account in your own name. But if your spouse is younger, you can contribute up to $2,000 to an IRA in your spouse's name, even though you earned the wages. We can think of a prominent couple who qualify for just such a maneuver: Ronald and Nancy Reagan.

One warning: If your spouse earns even a dollar of income, he or she becomes ineligible for this so-called spousal contribution of $250. That's available only for spouses who earn absolutely nothing.

The money you and your spouse contribute to an IRA is tax-deferred. That means it's exempt from federal income tax until you withdraw it—usually in retirement, when your tax bracket is supposed to be lower. You don't have to itemize deductions on Schedule A to take advantage of the IRA Tax Saver. You simply list the amount of your IRA contribution on the first page of Form 1040. Look under "Adjustments to Income." You'll see a line for your IRA deduction. It's that simple. In fact, it's one of the best and simplest of Tax Savers. Assuming your tax bracket is 35 percent, a $2,000 IRA contribution cuts your income tax by $700. If you and your spouse both work and contribute $2,000 each, you'll cut your joint taxes by $1,400—perhaps more, because that $4,000 deduction may drop you into a lower tax bracket.

That initial deduction is only part of the benefit. Your IRA contributions will earn interest or dividends, and every penny they earn is tax-deferred, too.

Two thousand bucks a year may not sound like much, but it sure adds up. For example, let's say that you contribute $2,000 at the first of every year, and your IRA account earns interest of 10 percent a year, compounded annually. Here's how your account will build:

After 10 years	$ 35,062
After 20 years	$126,005
After 25 years	$216,364
After 35 years	$596,254
After 40 years	$973,704

To paraphrase Albert Einstein, that's the magic of compound interest.

Now, how much of that nest egg resulted from Tax Savers? Let's say that you put aside the same amount of savings every year toward retirement but had to pay income tax on it. We'll assume that your tax bracket is 25 percent. So when you scrape up $2,000 a year, you have to pay 25 percent of it to Uncle Sam. That cuts your annual savings to $1,500. Furthermore, you have to pay income tax on the interest or dividends. So the 10 percent that your account earns every year is reduced by tax. Here's how your account would build:

After 10 years	$ 22,812
After 20 years	$ 69,829
After 25 years	$109,614
After 35 years	$248,731
After 40 years	$366,451

Quite a difference! And if your tax bracket happens to be higher than 25 percent, the difference will be even more pronounced.

In our example, you're contributing $2,000 a year—the maximum for an individual. But if you and your spouse both work, you can contribute $4,000 a year—$2,000 each. Even if only one of you works, you can contribute $2,250. So the IRA advertisements are not exaggerating when they say that you and your spouse can become IRA millionaires.

But let's not get carried away. Even if inflation remains moderate, a million dollars forty years from now will be worth a lot less than a million dollars today. Your IRA will not, all by itself, support you in your retirement years—unless, of course, you choose an IRA investment that produces an unusually high return. But we're not looking for a single Tax Saver to take care of retirement. We're in favor of stacking one retirement Tax Saver atop another. And your IRA is one of the biggest and best.

Unfortunately, relatively few Americans take advantage of this generous Tax Saver. In 1982 and 1983, the first years that every working American could contribute to an IRA, fewer than 15 percent took advantage of it. Participation is low—pitifully so, since those who do not participate are denying themselves a Tax Saver that would greatly enhance their retirement years.

If you are in your fifties or sixties, don't pass up the IRA on the grounds that you don't have enough working years left to build up much of an account. In the first place, our example shows that you can build up quite a bit—$35,062 in just ten years, based on annual $2,000 contributions compounding at 10 percent interest. Furthermore, most of us reach our peak earning years in our fifties and sixties. The higher your income, the more this Tax Saver will reduce your annual income tax. We pointed out that in the 35 percent bracket, a $2,000 contribution cuts your taxes by $700. In the 40 percent bracket, the tax saving reaches $800. In the 50 percent bracket, it hits $1,000.

Furthermore, once you're fifty-nine and a half years old, you can use your IRA as both a Tax Saver and a source of income. As long as you earn money, you can keep making contributions up to $2,000 a year and keep deducting that amount from your taxable income. You can also make withdrawals, realizing that every dollar withdrawn is a dollar of taxable income.

Let's say you make $50,000 a year, and your tax bracket is 40 percent. You retire at the end of the year at any age from fifty-nine and a half up. In retirement, your tax bracket is only 20 percent. You can make an IRA contribution for that final year of work, cutting your taxes by $800. In the first year of retirement, you can withdraw that same $2,000, and pay only $400 in income tax. You're $400 ahead. That sounds almost too good to be true. But it's perfectly legal. In fact, that's the principle behind the IRA: Encourage Americans to save during their working years, when they are in relatively high tax brackets, and use that money during their retirement years, when they are in lower brackets.

Does that mean that the IRA is a poor investment for those who expect to be in a high tax bracket in retirement? It does not, because the IRA's Tax Saver characteristics allow an IRA account to build up so much so quickly. Just look back at those tables comparing the growth of an IRA account and an identical account that lacks the IRA's Tax Saver characteristics. If you are in the 50 percent tax bracket in retirement, your IRA withdrawals will, indeed, be taxed heavily. But look at how much more you will have to withdraw. On balance, the IRA is still yielding you a superb payoff.

WITHDRAWING YOUR MONEY

At the other extreme, younger Americans often decide against an IRA because they don't want to tie up their money for so long. After all, they reason, withdrawals aren't allowed before age fifty-nine and a half, except in case of death or disability. But that's a misconception. Withdrawals *are* allowed, at any age. When you make a premature withdrawal, you pay income tax on it, and in addition you pay a penalty of 10 percent. For example, if you withdraw $5,000 from your IRA, you pay a penalty of 10 percent—$500. If your tax bracket is 35 percent, your tax will be $1,750, plus $500 penalty, for a total of $2,250. Of the $5,000 you withdrew, Uncle Sam will get $2,250; you'll get to keep (and spend) $2,750.

That's stiff, but not as stiff as it sounds. Because an IRA keeps compounding free of income tax, in a few years it will build up more than enough extra money to pay the penalty and the tax on your withdrawal. By "extra" money, we mean the Tax Saver portion of your IRA account—the money that results directly from the tax deferral.

For example, let's say your tax bracket is 35 percent. You start two savings accounts—one an IRA, the other a regular savings account. You put aside $2,000 a year for each account. Both accounts compound at 10 percent interest. Each year, you contribute $2,000 to the IRA account. Of the $2,000 that you've put aside for the other account, 35 percent, or $700, has to go for income tax; you save the remaining $1,300. Every year, you pay income tax on the interest earned by the other account. In the meantime, your IRA account compounds without tax. In six years, your IRA account will be so much larger that even if you withdraw money, pay the penalty and the tax, you'll still have more left over in your IRA than the total accumulated in the other account. The higher your tax bracket and the greater the yield, the more quickly the IRA outpaces the other account, even after paying the penalty and tax on an IRA withdrawal.

You should not start an IRA with money that you may

need within the next two or three years. But if you can put the money aside for six or seven years, the IRA will pay handsomely. Of course, we do not recommend that you withdraw money from your IRA for frivolous reasons. As we've demonstrated, the more money in the account and the longer it's kept there, the more savings you build, thanks to the combined benefits of the Tax Saver and compound interest. But you should not shy away from an IRA for fear that you might have to get at the money before age fifty-nine and a half.

WHEN TO CONTRIBUTE

Not only is the IRA generous in itself; so are the rules for contributing. You can set up and contribute to an IRA as late as the deadline day for your income tax return, without extension. For most of us, that's April 15. If you send in Form 4868 for an automatic four-month extension, the deadline is August 15 for your tax return—but still April 15 for your IRA.

Remember, that's your IRA contribution for the previous year. To make the timing even more generous, the IRS has instituted what amounts to an honor system. Let's say that you fill out your income tax return on February 20, but can't scrape together the money for your IRA contribution for that previous year. Nevertheless, you can list your IRA contribution on your tax return and mail in your return, as if you had already contributed the IRA money. You are promising the IRS that you'll make your IRA contribution by deadline time, and you're getting the deduction in advance.

If you have a refund coming, the IRS might help you out. Send in your tax return, claiming your IRA deduction. When you get your tax refund, use it to make your IRA contribution. Thank you, Uncle Sam. Thank you, and thank you again.

That's last-minute strategy. First-day strategy pays off more. You can make your IRA contribution any time from January 1 until fifteen and a half months later—that is, until April 15 of the following year. The sooner you contribute, the sooner your money starts compounding, tax-deferred. Over time, that can make quite a difference. Assuming annual $2,000 contributions earning 10 percent interest, here's how much *more* your account will have if you contribute January 1 of each year compared with December 31:

After 5 years	$ 1,200
After 25 years	$19,000

Here's another way of looking at the difference. We'll consider just one year's contribution. If you make the $2,000 contribution on January 1, 1985, and it earns 10 percent interest, it will accumulate $258 by April 15, 1986—the normal deadline for making the same contribution. In twenty years, that $258 will have grown to $1,547. In thirty years, it will be $4,013. That's all yours—and it's simply the difference between investing $2,000 in your IRA on January 1, the very first day of eligibility, and investing it on April 15 of the following year, the final day of eligibility.

With so much elbow room—or rather, calendar room—in the timing of your IRA contributions, you'll have to keep records not only of your contributions but also of the year for which they count. When you write a deposit check to your IRA custodian, write in the bottom left corner of the check, "IRA contribution for 1985," or whatever year is appropriate. Your IRA custodian will report your contributions to the IRS. You might make two years' worth of IRA contributions all at once, say on April 15—$2,000 for the past year and $2,000 for the current year. Take the precaution of writing separate checks, with a note on each as to the year for which the contribution counts. If you're audited, that will make it easy for you to prove that you did not contribute more than the $2,000 maximum for any single year.

AFTER RETIREMENT

When you die, your beneficiary inherits your IRA. If you become permanently and completely disabled, you can cash in your IRA without tax penalty. Otherwise, you can begin withdrawing money from your IRA as early as when you reach fifty-nine and a half. You must begin withdrawals by age seventy and a half.

That gives you a lot of latitude. Every dollar withdrawn is taxable, and every dollar left in your IRA continues to be a Tax Saver, accumulating interest or dividends on a tax-deferred basis. At age seventy and a half, you must begin withdrawing money according to an actuarial formula based on your life expectancy.

For example, at age seventy-one a man can expect to live 11.6 more years, and a woman can expect to live 14.4 more years. So a man would be required to withdraw at least 8.6 percent of his IRA savings that year (1/11.6); a woman would be required to withdraw at least 6.9 percent (1/14.4). If you are married and you want to withdraw as little as possible from your IRA, you can instead choose the life expectancy of the last survivor between the two of you. That will add several years to the formula and allow you to withdraw a smaller percentage each year. Be sure to ask your IRA plan administrator for the current formula. Life expectancies increase slightly every year, so the percentages in our example will be out of date.

If your withdrawals fall short of the formula, the IRS will slap you with a severe penalty—50 percent of the amount that you should have withdrawn but did not. If your IRA account is large, the withdrawals formula won't dent it; the account will build up more every year in interest or dividends than the amounts you withdraw.

YOUR ESTATE

By itself, an IRA can amount to a sizable estate. If you are married and you name your spouse as beneficiary, he or she

will inherit your IRA account at your death and won't have
to pay any estate tax on it. But if you are unmarried, or if
you are a widow or widower, the tax treatment of your IRA
account will depend partly on whether you had started taking withdrawals from it.

Let's say you're a widow and you name your daughter
as beneficiary of your IRA. You die at age sixty-two, without ever withdrawing any money from your IRA. Under the
law, your daughter will have to pay tax on that inheritance
within five years. On the other hand, if you had started taking withdrawals—even a token amount, like $20 a month
—the tax treatment will be much gentler. Your daughter
will be able to spread out the taxes over your actuarial life
expectancy at the time of your death.

MOVING IRAs

We've been talking about your IRA "account," but in fact
most of us should have more than one IRA account. You
can have as many as you want, and you can switch accounts from one custodian to another. Theoretically, you
could spread your $2,000 contribution for this year among
twenty accounts of $100 each. The law allows it, and plenty
of financial institutions welcome IRA accounts as small as
$100.

To transfer an IRA account from one custodian to another, simply ask the new custodian to give you an IRA
transfer form. The institution will be glad to provide it, because it wants your account. You fill out the form, sign it,
and turn it in, and your IRA will automatically be trans-
ferred. You can transfer your IRA money as often as you
wish. In a transfer, you never touch the money; it simply
moves from one custodian to another.

Why would you want to move an IRA account? Many
people do it for convenience. Let's say you have your IRA
with a local bank, and you move to a distant city. You may
prefer to switch your IRA to a bank in your home town.
Before doing so, however, check with your present custodian about penalties. Many custodians charge a transfer fee.
In addition, you may have your IRA invested in a savings

certificate that hasn't matured. If you transfer the account, that certificate will be cashed prematurely, and you'll give up some of the interest that you otherwise would have earned.

In our opinion, moving from one city to another isn't a good reason to switch your IRA account. It doesn't much matter whether your IRA is invested near home or 3,000 miles away. You can't use your IRA for collateral, so it won't help you get a loan from your neighborhood banker.

What matters is performance—how much your account earns. That matters a lot; the effect of compound interest means that a difference of 1 or 2 or 3 percentage points in yield can make tens of thousands of dollars' difference in the amount your IRA builds up over the years. So if you can get a better IRA yield out of town, don't hesitate to do your IRA shopping by mail.

Another way of moving your IRA money from one custodian to another is called a rollover. You close your IRA account, get the money, and within sixty days deposit it in another IRA account. That's right; you get the use of that money for sixty days. But if you go a day beyond—in other words, if you don't open the new IRA account until sixty-one days have elapsed—you must pay income tax on the entire withdrawal, and pay a penalty of 10 percent on top of that. You can roll over an IRA account once a year. If you have ten IRA accounts, you can roll over each one of them once a year. You may prefer a rollover to a transfer if you would like to use the money for a month or so—and if you're sure you'll get it into the hands of your new IRA custodian within sixty days.

WHERE TO INVEST YOUR IRA

With so much at stake, you cannot afford to be casual in your choice of an IRA custodian. You first must choose the *kind* of custodian you want, and then you must find the *best* of that kind. Remember that you can hedge your bets by spreading your IRA savings among two or three or a dozen custodians, and that you can move your IRA savings from one custodian to another.

Here are the different kinds of IRA accounts and investments that we consider worthwhile. Generally speaking, the lower the risk, the less the potential return; that's true of any investment. We'll start with the least risky and work up.

Money Funds

These pay current short-term interest rates. Rates vary day to day, but usually are 2 to 3 percentage points below the prime rate. If you put your IRA in a money fund at a bank, savings institution, or credit union, it will be insured up to $100,000 by the federal government. Money market mutual funds aren't federally insured, but the risk of loss is minuscule. Yields of money market mutual funds are listed in *The Wall Street Journal.* Yields paid by the money funds of various banks, savings institutions, and credit unions around the country aren't listed in the paper, but the best yields are listed in a weekly newsletter, *Savers Rate News* (phone 800-447-0011). In comparing one account with another, ask for the effective annual yield. That's more important than the interest rate, because some institutions compound interest daily, some annually—and some pay simple interest, which yields a lot less. Find out if you have to pay an IRA setup fee or an annual maintenance fee, and whether you'll be socked with a transfer fee if you switch the account elsewhere.

Certificates of Deposit

CDs are the most popular kind of IRA account. They are sold by banks, savings institutions, and credit unions; each account is insured up to $100,000 by the federal government. You can choose certificates of various maturities, such as twelve months, thirty months, or more. When your certificate matures, you can roll it over into a new certificate, shift to a money fund, or transfer your IRA money elsewhere. If you cash in a certificate before it matures, you pay a penalty. Certificates usually pay slightly higher interest rates than money funds. You can choose certificates that pay fixed rates of interest or ones paying interest rates that vary according to market conditions.

Once again, you should compare effective annual yields, not the interest rates advertised in the newspaper, and ask about setup fees, maintenance fees, and transfer fees. As a benchmark, compare the best IRA certificate you can find with the best listed in *Savers Rate News*.

Mutual Funds

These offer a variety of investments, from the very conservative money market funds that we discussed earlier to funds that are quite speculative. Through a mutual fund, you can invest your IRA money in U.S. Government bonds, corporate bonds, conservative stocks that pay high dividends, a mix of bonds and stocks, stocks with good potential for long-term growth in value, stocks of small companies with good prospects for growth, and stocks of firms in a particular industry, including high-tech, energy, health care, and public utilities. Although you cannot use your IRA money to buy gold coins (or collectibles), you can open an IRA account with any of several mutual funds that buy gold or stock in gold-mining firms.

Although many mutual funds are speculative in their objective, any fund gives you the protection of diversification. In other words, even an IRA investment of $500 will be spread among all the fund's holdings, which may include hundreds of stocks or bonds. In an IRA account, dividends or interest are automatically reinvested in additional shares. Some funds have been breathtakingly successful, doubling and tripling and even quadrupling in value. The majority have performed well but not spectacularly, beating the market averages. Some have been abject failures, losing money for their shareholders.

It's easy to transfer your IRA money from one mutual fund to another. Many investment companies manage a variety of funds, each with a different manager and a different objective. Within that "family" of funds, you can switch your money by letter or even by telephone. To transfer your IRA account to a new mutual fund company, you simply fill out and sign a transfer form provided by the new fund of your choice. "No-load" mutual funds, those that charge no sales commission, are sold by telephone and mail. "Load" funds charge sales commissions ranging from 2 percent to, more typically, 8½ percent. Some load funds are sold by mail, others through stockbrokers.

Because mutual funds are professionally managed, many IRA investors fail to keep an eye on their fund's performance. That's unwise. A fund that was doing well when you chose it a year ago, or five years ago, may have changed managers or may have failed to keep up with market trends. *Money* magazine runs a monthly "Fund Watch" column that lists the mutual funds that have been performing the best. Even better is a monthly newsletter, *Retirement Fund Advisory* ($55 a year, tax-deductible, from Schabacker Investment Management, 8943 Shady Grove Court, Gaithersburg, Maryland 20877). This newsletter tracks the comparative performances of about seventy mutual funds. Most of them are no-load funds and are within fund families so that you can transfer your IRA money from one fund to another by telephone. In addition, the newsletter analyzes the economic and market outlook and advises investors which portion of their IRA nest egg should be in equity funds—that means mutual funds that invest in stocks—and which portion should be in money market funds.

In other words, the newsletter's editors try to forecast the stock market. When they expect the market to decline, they advise subscribers to telephone their mutual fund family and have all or part of their money switched from equity funds to a money market fund. When they expect the market to rise, they advise subscribers to have their money switched back into a stock fund. Most mutual fund families make these transfers free of charge.

If you did that kind of switching outside an IRA, you would have to pay capital-gains tax every time you cashed in a profit, because a switch from one fund to another, even with the same fund family, counts as a sale of one stock and a purchase of another. But those profits aren't taxed in an IRA until you withdraw the money. On the other hand, investment losses outside an IRA are tax-deductible. Within an IRA, they are not.

On balance, *Retirement Fund Advisory* has a good forecasting record. But its forecasts are sometimes wrong, and some investors prefer to ride out market fluctuations rather than try to predict them.

In every issue, the newsletter also recommends an IRA Model Portfolio. In September 1984, it was recommending that investors divide their IRA about evenly among four mutual funds, all of which invest in stocks: Twentieth Century Select (phone 816-531-5575), Fidelity Discoverer (phone 800-225-6190), Vanguard Ivest (phone 800-523-7910), and Fidelity Select Technology (phone 800-225-6190).

Here's the performance of those four funds over the five-year period that ended August 31, 1984. In addition, we're listing four other funds with excellent records, including one fund that invests in gold and one that invests in bonds. "Performance" means the total gain—accumulated dividends, plus gains in share value.

Twentieth Century Select	up 201 percent
Fidelity Discoverer	up 112 percent
Vanguard Ivest	up 103 percent
Fidelity Magellan (phone 800-225-6190)	up 319 percent
Tudor Fund (phone 800-223-3332)	up 183 percent
United Services Gold Shares (phone 800-531-5777)	up 217 percent
Vanguard Fixed Income High-Yield Bond Fund (phone 800-523-7910)	up 60 percent

Fidelity Select Technology started operations in July 1981. In its first three years, shares gained 131 percent in value.

Self-Directed Accounts

These accounts, with a broker, let you pick your own IRA investments, choosing particular stocks, bonds, or other investments. Fees tend to be high, and in addition you pay brokerage commissions on your transactions. In any kind of IRA, fees and charges are deductible, and don't count toward the $2,000 annual limit. On the other hand, brokerage commissions count toward the $2,000 limit.

Among the investments tailored for self-directed IRAs are zero-coupon bonds—bonds that pay no annual interest, but instead are sold at a steep discount. For example, if you bought a zero-coupon bond paying 12¼ percent interest, you could triple your money in ten years. In other words, you'd pay about $333 for the bond; it would mature in ten years and pay you $1,000. Zero-coupon bonds pay about the same effective yield as bank certificates or regular bonds. But bank certificates pay interest once a year and regular bonds pay interest twice a year. Those interest payments go into your IRA account, and you have to figure how to invest that money. A zero-coupon bond eliminates that chore and locks in current interest rates. If you buy zero-coupon bonds outside an IRA, you have to pay annual income tax on the "imputed interest"—the interest that is built into the difference between the purchase price and the value at maturity. But in an IRA, you pay no income tax until you withdraw the money, usually in retirement.

In considering zero-coupon bonds, always ask for the effective annual yield, compounded to maturity. Without that figure the numbers can be tricky. For example, here are three zero-coupon bonds that Merrill Lynch was selling in April 1984. All three are safe. Which is the best?

1. An IBM bond selling for $630, maturing in four years and three months at $1,000
2. A Bank of America bond selling for $340, maturing in nine years and two months at $1,000
3. A Trans-America bond selling for $65, maturing in twenty-eight years and five months at $1,000

The winner is Number 2, paying an effective annual yield of 12.08 percent. Bond Number 1 pays an effective annual yield of 11.15 percent. Bond Number 3, despite what appears to be a spectacular gain in value, pays an effective annual yield of only 9.86 percent.

With a self-directed account, you can invest IRA money in real estate, through limited partnerships that are specially tailored for IRA accounts. In the previous chapter, we discussed real estate partnerships as tax shelters. Tax-shelter real estate deals take full advantage of deductions for depreciation, interest, and real estate taxes. In an IRA, those deductions would be worthless, because you're paying no income tax on the account. So the real estate partnerships for IRA accounts pay in full for the shopping centers, apartment buildings, or other properties, and generate income from rents and from profits on sale of the properties.

Annuities

Annuities are often sold for IRAs, but we don't recommend them. An annuity is a Tax Saver in its own right, and you may want to consider one as an investment outside your IRA. At retirement, you may want to roll your IRA money into an annuity that guarantees a certain amount of monthly income for the rest of your life. We discuss annuities in the previous chapter. For an IRA, an annuity offers little or nothing that you cannot get on better terms through a mutual fund, bank certificates, bonds, or some other form of investment. We don't recommend tax-exempt bonds for an IRA, because an IRA is tax-exempt anyway. For the same reason, we don't recommend annuities.

COMPARING RETURNS

An IRA is a long-term investment. In choosing the right investment for your IRA money, it's helpful to compare the relative performances of money funds, bonds, and stocks over long periods of time, and to see how each one has fared against inflation. Johnson's Charts, Inc., tracks that kind of data. The figures below trace the growth of $100 for twenty-two years, from 1962 through 1983. Bank certificates aren't included, but their performance depends on interest rates, as does the performance of bonds and money funds.

Long-term government bonds	$244
Corporate bonds	$251
Consumer price index	$321
Prime commercial paper, i.e. the equivalent of money funds	$409
Standard & Poor's 500, i.e. a gauge of the overall stock market	$484

If you go back even further—to 1926, before the Depression—the superior performance of stocks becomes even more pronounced. But that does not guarantee that stocks will continue to outperform other investments. In fact, no one knows what kind of investment will perform best in the years to come. You have to make your own decision. Here are four approaches to IRA investing, all of them perfectly logical:

1. Since you will eventually need your IRA money for living expenses, it would be foolish to speculate with tomorrow's grocery money. Stick to money funds and short-term bank certificates, insured by Uncle Sam.

2. Buy stocks that pay high dividends—maybe utilities or a mutual fund that specializes in high-yield stocks. The dividends will build up free of tax, and the stocks are likely to appreciate in value over the long haul. That will give the best of both worlds—high yields plus appreciation.

3. Use your IRA for speculation in mutual funds. With the privilege of telephone switching, you can move money from stocks to bonds to money funds and back again, without paying any income tax or any commission. For steady, secure income, invest outside the IRA in tax-exempt bonds.

4. Hedge your bets. Divide your IRA money, investing some in money funds, some in bank certificates, some in stocks, and maybe even some in a mutual fund that buys gold. That way you'll be able to ride out unforeseen waves in the economy.

EMPLOYER PENSION PLANS

With all its generous features and options, you might assume that the IRA is the best of all retirement Tax Savers. But some others are even better. Best of all is your employer's pension plan or profit-sharing plan, because your employer provides the savings toward your retirement.

Among retirement Tax Savers that you choose for yourself, perhaps the finest is a relatively new kind of plan that may be available through your employer. It's called a Salary Reduction Plan, or—in pension jargon—a 401(k) plan, after the section of the United States tax law that made these wonderful Tax Savers legal.

Salary Reduction Plans are being offered by more and more employers. In many ways a Salary Reduction Plan is like an IRA, but in some ways it's even better. Best of all, you can have both. Your Salary Reduction Plan in no way limits your freedom to build up an IRA, nor does your IRA cut into your tax-saving investment privileges under the Salary Reduction Plan. You can have both, in full.

To enroll in a Salary Reduction Plan, you simply ask your participating employer to hang on to a certain percentage of your pay. Your employer invests that money in the plan's pension fund. You may be given a choice of funds—for example, one investing in stocks, one investing in bonds, and one investing in money market securities.

You pay no income tax on those contributions or on the interest or dividends they earn, until you withdraw them. And although your contribution dollars come out of your salary, you pay no Social Security tax on those dollars either—an additional Tax Saver that you don't get with an IRA.

Under the law, your annual contributions can be as much as 25 percent of your salary or $30,000, whichever is less. However, each company has its own plan, and the actual amount you can contribute varies from plan to plan and company to company. Ten percent is more typical, and that's a lot. On a salary of $30,000, for example, that would mean $3,000 invested toward retirement. If you are in the

35 percent tax bracket, this nifty Tax Saver would cut your income tax bill by $1,050 a year.

Moreover, most companies partially match your contributions. For example, for every dollar you contribute your employer might contribute 50 cents. Using our example, your $3,000 contribution would be supplemented by $1,500 from your employer, for a total of $4,500, all invested toward your retirement, drawing interest or dividends, compounding and accumulating tax-free until you start withdrawing the money. And meantime your annual income tax bill is a lot less, simply because you are saving for your own good. Quite a combination.

With an IRA, remember, any money you withdraw before age fifty-nine and a half is taxed in full, with a 10 percent penalty socked on. With a Salary Reduction Plan, the normal age for withdrawals to begin is the same, fifty-nine and a half. But you're allowed to withdraw money in case of hardship, which may include college expenses, medical bills, or a down payment on a home. And if you leave the company, you get your built-up savings in full, with a choice of these two Tax Savers to protect them:

Choice 1

Within 60 days, roll that nest egg over into an IRA plan of your choice. That way you pay no tax at all, and the savings keep accumulating tax-free.

Choice 2

Pay a limited tax on the money, using a special ten-year averaging formula. This formula treats the money as if it were your only income, and as if it were being received in even amounts over the next ten years. For example, if you build up $50,000 in a Salary Reduction Plan and left the company, you could pay tax as if you were getting income of $5,000 a year for ten years. You'd pay tax at low rates, and your tax bill would be light.

When you reach fifty-nine and a half, you can start withdrawing money gradually, just as you can from an IRA. You pay regular income tax on your withdrawals. But if you

■■■■

prefer, you can withdraw the whole account in one lump sum. If you do, you get to use that same ten-year averaging formula—a Tax Saver on top of a Tax Saver. That's a big advantage. If you withdraw all your IRA money in a lump sum, it all counts as taxable income for that year.

Why would you want to cash in your Salary Reduction Plan nest egg in a lump sum? Perhaps you want to buy a business or a vacation home. If so, you can factor that purchase into your plans, earmarking your Salary Reduction Plan account for that purpose. Of course, you'll have to make sure that other parts of your retirement plan provide the income you'll need for a comfortable living.

Let's say you are taking full advantage of your IRA and your company's Salary Reduction Plan, and you would like to save still more toward retirement. Some companies will let employees contribute an additional percentage of their salaries—10 percent is the limit—to a thrift plan account. You have to pay income tax on that contribution but not on the interest or dividends that it earns. So it's a good Tax Saver—to be sure, not as good as an IRA or a Salary Reduction Plan, but nevertheless it's quite good. And since you have already paid income tax on your contribution, you can withdraw that money at any time, for any reason.

KEOGH

Self-employed Americans are entitled to use a special retirement Tax Saver called a Keogh Plan. It was named after Eugene J. Keogh, the Congressman who sponsored the concept years ago. In recent years, Keogh provisions have been made even more generous. Best of all, you can contribute to both a Keogh and an IRA. If you have a job and run a business on the side, you might even put money in a Keogh, an IRA, and your employer's Salary Reduction Plan, all in the same year. One plan does not infringe upon another in any way.

A Keogh allows annual contributions of up to 20 percent of your net self-employment income, with a ceiling of $30,000 a year. You pay no income tax on that money or on the interest or dividends it earns, until you withdraw it. As with an IRA, withdrawals can begin at age fifty-nine and a half, and must begin by age seventy and a half. To contribute the full 20 percent, you have to divide your Keogh contributions between two kinds of accounts. We recommend that you put as much as you can into a profit-sharing Keogh, and the remainder into a money-purchase Keogh. Those terms are pension jargon; they have nothing to do with the kind of investment you are making. Your investment options are precisely the same ones available for an IRA—money funds, bank certificates, mutual funds, self-directed brokerage accounts. Choose the investment you want, and ask the plan custodian to help you split your contributions between the two kinds of Keogh accounts. Although you can begin withdrawing money from a profit-sharing Keogh at age fifty-nine and a half, you cannot withdraw from a money-purchase Keogh until you retire, no matter what your age.

If you withdraw your Keogh money in a lump sum, you get to use the same ten-year averaging formula that we described for Salary Reduction Plans.

If your self-employment income is unusually high, you can adopt a more generous—and more complicated—kind of Keogh called a defined-benefit plan. "Defined benefit" means that you decide in advance how much annual income—benefit—your Keogh should provide for you in retirement, and you contribute as much as needed to build a nest egg that will yield that annual income. Your defined benefit—in other words, the annual retirement pension toward which you are contributing—can be as high as $90,000 a year. If you happen to be close to retirement age, and your net self-employment income is well into six figures, you might be able to contribute as much as $100,000 to a defined-benefit Keogh plan in one year—and deduct all $100,000 from your taxable income. To set up a defined-benefit Keogh, you'll need a skilled accountant.

With so many Tax Savers available, retirement can be the most financially comfortable period of life. You will get a Social Security pension and perhaps pension or profit-sharing money from a number of former employers. Beyond those sources of income, you can build a substantial retirement nest egg with your contributions pleasantly sheltered from income tax. Saving toward retirement is a Tax Saver that none of us should pass up.

Tax Savers
for
Senior Citizens

$\mathcal{R}$ etirement is a time of sudden change in many ways, including tax strategy. No other stage of life calls for such thorough overhauling of family finances. For senior citizens who plan ahead and take the proper steps, retirement is the time when all the Tax Savers planted during the working years come to full flower.

Although we talk of senior citizens, age has little to do with this change. From the standpoint of Tax Savers and family finances in general, the landmark event is retirement, when we give up our salaries and wages and begin living on income from other sources.

To be sure, full Social Security benefits still begin at age sixty-five. But the majority of working Americans retire well before their sixty-fifth birthday. At the same time, significant numbers of us work beyond age sixty-five. Most companies used to force employees into retirement at age sixty-five, but that's now against the law. This diversity and this freedom of choice are some of the great benefits of our economic system.

So if you have planned toward retirement and taken advantage of Tax Savers during your high-income years, your retirement can begin when you want it to begin, and it can be as rich as any other period of your life, financially and otherwise. Indeed, most American senior citizens are well off. On the average, their incomes compare respectably with those of younger working Americans. With judicious use of Tax Savers, your standard of living in retirement can be at least as high as it was during your working years.

If you're like most people, you may have to make a change in your financial thinking. For decades, you have used Tax Savers to hold down your taxable income. You have invested in Individual Retirement Accounts, and you have probably purchased stocks or mutual funds that pay little in dividends but grow in value. You have made monthly mortgage payments, taking advantage of the many Tax Savers that go with homeownership. Some of you have purchased second homes and rented them out, making little or no cash profit but building equity while benefiting from Tax Savers. The more venturesome among you have bought into tax shelters that invest in real estate, oil exploration, livestock, even motion picture distribution.

In short, you have taken advantage of the Tax Savers appropriate to the various stages of your life, from early adulthood through marriage, parenthood, and homeownership. By doing so, you have reduced your taxes as you built your wealth.

Now you are in a new stage of life. In this stage, for the first time, it becomes appropriate to cash in many of these Tax Savers.

Many retired Americans have difficulty grasping this reality. The change seems too sudden. Tax Savers, after all, fit in with habits of thrift and saving that are taught to us as virtues. Many retired people cannot bring themselves to cash in the assets that they have so carefully built. Instead, they pinch to get by on reduced incomes, leaving their nest eggs intact.

But they are ignoring a simple reality: Their income and their tax brackets are down, often sharply. Many Tax Savers that made sense in, say, the 40 percent tax bracket make no sense at all in the 25 percent bracket. Nor does it make sense to forgo income—to deny yourself the use of your own assets—when you need them or could enjoy them.

After all, what do we save for if not for our retirement years?

To be sure, you certainly won't want to spend your assets unwisely, leaving too little for your spouse when you die or failing to provide a cushion against emergency needs such as nursing home care. Beyond your own needs, you may want to leave money to your children or other heirs.

Those are logical goals. We're cautioning against the illogical goals—the clinging to habits and Tax Savers that no longer fit. They were tailored to previous stages of life. Let's tailor new Tax Savers for our retirement.

EXEMPTION FOR AGE

Senior citizens benefit directly from two Tax Savers: one small, the other quite significant. The small one is the additional $1,000 exemption we become entitled to at age sixty-five. If you reach sixty-five any time during the year—even on December 31—you get the additional $1,000 exemption. So if you and your spouse both reach sixty-five and file a joint income tax return, you get $4,000 in exemptions—the $1,000 each that everyone gets plus an additional $1,000 each for attaining age sixty-five. Beginning in 1985, the amount of the personal exemption will rise automatically every year, in line with the Consumer Price Index.

That's nice, but, of course, the payoff is modest. If your tax bracket is 35 percent, a $1,000 exemption saves you $350. Most retirees slip into lower tax brackets, so the benefit of this Tax Saver is dampened still more. Don't forget, the higher your tax bracket, the more you benefit from any exemption or deduction. The lower your tax bracket, the less you benefit.

A caution: If you are supported by someone else—say, a son or daughter—and that person claims you on his tax return as a dependent, he or she cannot take that additional $1,000 exemption. The additional exemption for reaching age sixty-five can be taken only by you. If you do not support yourself and do not file your own tax return, the additional exemption is lost.

━━━━━━

SOCIAL SECURITY

The other automatic Tax Saver for senior citizens is Social Security income. Social Security provides a bedrock for many retired Americans. The amount of income is indexed to inflation, and most Social Security income is exempt from federal income tax.

Until 1984, all Social Security income was exempt from taxation. But our Social Security system was on the verge of dipping into the red, so Congress adopted changes recommended by a bipartisan commission. One of those changes imposed income tax on some Social Security income, for the first time. At the same time it imposed an indirect tax on income from another source that had always been entirely exempt—the interest paid on state and municipal bonds.

Make no mistake, this new tax is aimed directly at retired Americans who enjoy comfortable incomes. Many retirees live on income from Social Security and interest on tax-exempt bonds. The change is not catastrophic; in fact, the tax is quite limited. But it illustrates the caprice of Congress, which, after all, has the authority to rewrite the tax laws any time, any way it wants. We don't bring that up to frighten you. As far as this particular change goes, a sound Social Security system is worth the price. But never count on a particular provision of tax law as a guarantee for the future.

Here's the formula for figuring your tax—if any—on your income from Social Security and municipal bond interest:

Write down these three items:

1. Your adjusted gross income
2. Your income from tax-exempt bonds
3. Half of your Social Security income

Now add 1, 2, and 3. The total is called modified adjusted gross income. If you are single and the total exceeds $25,000, you're subject to the new tax. If you are married, filing a joint return, and the total exceeds $32,000, you're subject to the new tax.

The amount that will be taxed is the lesser of two figures:

1. Half your Social Security income (number 3 above), or
2. Half of the amount by which the total exceeds these limits: $25,000 for singles; $32,000 for couples filing jointly.

For example, let's say you're single and your modified adjusted gross income totals $26,000, including $4,000 from Social Security—half of your annual $8,000 in Social Security benefits. You will be taxed on whichever is less: half your Social Security income ($4,000) or half of the amount by which your $26,000 total exceeds the $25,000 limit ($1,000). Half of $1,000 is $500. So you pay income tax on $500 of your Social Security income.

Don't let that long formula give you the idea that your Social Security income, or your municipal bond income, is going to get soaked by the IRS. Taxed, yes; soaked, no. Social Security and interest from tax-exempt bonds continue to be good sources of retirement income and good Tax Savers.

BONDS

However, that tax is another factor in the new equation that goes with retirement. If you own municipal bonds, should you keep them, or would you be better off swapping them for U.S. Treasury bonds or corporate bonds? Treasury and corporate bonds pay higher interest rates than municipal bonds, but the interest is taxable. Look to your tax bracket. If it's down considerably, you might be better off with higher-yielding Treasuries or corporates. In the 40 percent tax bracket, you're almost certainly better off with municipal bonds, even considering the new tax. But if your tax bracket has declined to 30 percent or less, you may be better switching to Treasury or government bonds. Check your old and new tax brackets, get out your calculator, and figure it out. The municipal bond Tax Saver, so valuable while you were working and earning a high income, may now be costing you money.

AND LITTLE ELSE

We've discussed two Tax Savers: the additional exemption at age sixty-five and Social Security income. Beyond those two, our tax laws have little respect for age. You may think you're slowing down, but the IRS doesn't. You face the same laws, the same rules, the same tax rates, the same deadlines, as do your children and your neighbors of all ages.

Perhaps because of wishful thinking, quite a few senior citizens seem unaware of this. On a recent call-in show, Strassels mentioned that the tax laws did not favor the elderly, and an irate caller told him that he didn't know what he was talking about. This caller, who was seventy-two, said that people his age and older were exempt from paying income tax.

Wrong.

In times past, lots of retired people didn't owe any income tax—not because of their age but because their taxable incomes were not high enough. That's still true for a good many couples. A married couple, both sixty-five or older, can have full Social Security income, plus as much as $7,400 in income from other sources, and still owe not a penny in income tax, based on 1984 rates. Here's how that works:

First, take the standard deduction of $3,400 for a married couple filing jointly.

Add four exemptions of $1,000 each—one for each of you, plus another one for each of you because you're sixty-five or older.

That's a total of $7,400. On top of that, add your Social Security income, which for some couples exceeds $16,000 a year. Don't forget, Social Security income isn't taxed unless your joint income breaks the $32,000 barrier described in the formula on pages 197 and 198. With $16,000 from Social Security plus $7,400 in other income, a couple can get along pretty well without owing a dime of income tax. And when you don't owe any tax, you aren't required to file a tax return.

During the past decade, inflation pushed many senior citizens back into the tax-paying ranks. Interest rates shot up, and senior citizens—like everyone else—moved their savings into money funds paying interest rates that reached heights of 16 percent or more. Even when rates declined, money funds were paying 8 or 9 percent. For a couple with $50,000 in savings, a yield of 10 percent means $5,000 in fully taxable interest.

As a result, many senior citizens suffered bracket creep. Their living standards were no higher; inflation was eating up the increases in their incomes and then some. But their incomes moved into the taxable zone. Thousands of them were unaccustomed to filing tax returns and still did not file. Some of them got caught. These days, more are getting caught, because the IRS's computers are becoming increasingly sophisticated.

Whether you owe income tax or not, we recommend that you prepare an annual tax return, sign it, and send it in. Consider it a precaution, like fastening your seat belt. All financial institutions that pay you income—your money fund, your bank, corporations in which you own stock— must report that income to the IRS. Those income figures are fed into the IRS's computers, and matched against the figures you report on your tax return. If they match, fine; the IRS will leave you alone. But if you haven't filed a tax return, the IRS's computers will clank and groan, and the agency will ask you why you didn't report the income that it knows you received. You can still win your case, but the correspondence can be difficult and protracted, certainly unnecessary. Better to file a tax return so the issue will never arise.

In fact, you'll save yourself money and trouble by sitting down early in the year, estimating what your income will be, and calculating the tax bite, if any. If your federal income tax is likely to be $500 or more, not counting any tax that is being withheld, you have to pay estimated income tax every quarter. The payments are due April 15, June 15, September 15, and January 15 of the next year. The form is called 1040ES; it is so simple that it amounts to a coupon. Although none of us likes to fork over money to the government, it's easy to pay the quarterly estimated tax once you get in the swing of it. If you fail to do so and wind up owing $500 or more when you eventually figure your taxes and file your tax return, the IRS will sock you with a penalty for underpayment of estimated tax. The penalty is a percentage of what you owe; the percentage is based on the prime interest rate. So many retirees were being unexpectedly hit with this penalty that in 1984, Congress enacted an exception. For the first two years after you retire at age sixty-two or older, or for the first two years after you become disabled at any age, the IRS may waive the penalty.

If you get income from pensions or annuities, you have a choice: Have the issuer withhold federal income tax, just as your employer used to withhold tax from your paycheck; or take the full payments and pay quarterly estimated tax on them. The withholding is a convenience; the quarterly estimated tax lets you keep the money a little longer. Either way, your tax comes out the same.

On income from interest or dividends, you must pay quarterly estimated tax. The Reagan administration tried to get Congress to impose withholding on interest and dividends, but Congress declined. Instead, Congress imposed a penalty system for those who refuse to provide their Social Security numbers to banks, corporations, and others that pay them interest or dividends. When an institution that pays you money asks for your Social Security number, provide it, even if you already did so some time before. Otherwise you could be subject to a fine of $50, plus mandatory withholding of 20 percent of your interest or dividend payments.

PENSION CHOICES

More than ever before, retirees are given choices of how their pensions will be paid. You might have a choice of taking your pension in a lump sum at retirement, or spreading it out in monthly payments. Indeed, you might have two or three or even four pensions coming, each from a different employer for whom you worked, and each operating under a different plan, with different choices and different tax considerations.

Incidentally, we strongly recommend that you go fishing at age sixty-five—fishing for additional pension income. Many retirees assume that they're entitled to a pension only from their last employer or the employer for whom they worked the longest. In fact, many pension plans vest—that is, entitle participants to benefits—after just a few years of work. Check with all your previous employers, reminding them of your precise years of service, advising them that you're now sixty-five, and asking whether you're entitled to a pension. Don't wait for an old employer to seek you out. That's like waiting for a fish to jump into your boat.

If you have choices as to how your pension or pensions will be paid, take advantage of them, with Tax Savers in mind. If you take your pension in a lump sum, you can average that income over the next ten years and pay tax as if that one tenth of your pension was your only income each of those ten years. If you won't need the pension money right away, you can roll over the lump sum into an Individual Retirement Account, thus deferring taxes until you start withdrawing the money. You must start making withdrawals by age seventy and a half. Figure the choice carefully; the lump-sum deal often is more profitable.

That's just one example. Pension and profit-sharing plans vary tremendously, and the tax you will owe on your pension income varies according to the plan. If your employer made all the contributions, you'll probably owe tax on every penny of your pension income. If you contributed toward your own pension, you'll get some portion of your pension free of income tax, at least for the first few years. Don't take a wait-and-see attitude. Find out ahead of time so that you can dovetail your pension income with your income from other sources in ways that provide for your needs and your happiness while lessening the tax bite. Sit down with your employer's pension coordinator, preferably a year or more before you retire, so you can plan wisely.

Once you start receiving pension income, your tax obligation will be spelled out for you. You'll get an annual Form W-2P listing your total pension income, the amount subject to federal income tax, and the amount withheld for federal income tax, if any.

Every choice having to do with income and income tax provides an opportunity for Tax Savers. If you have planned and saved ahead, retirement provides more opportunities than any previous stage of life. That's particularly true if you are an empty nester, with fewer family obligations and more freedom to live where you want and do what you want. Tax Savers can help you pay the bills and enjoy your retirement.

SAVINGS AND INVESTMENTS

We touched on savings and investments in our discussion of tax-free municipal bonds versus corporate and Treasury bonds, on which the interest is taxable. The key always is to look at your new tax bracket, not your old one, and to remember that you're no longer saving toward retirement. You've arrived. Enjoy it.

If you have invested in anything that has appreciated in value, you are in line to cash in one of the most generous Tax Savers of all. That's the favorable tax treatment of long-term capital gains. If you sell anything that you have owned for more than one year, or for more than six months if you bought it after June 22, 1984, three fifths of your profit is exempt from income tax. Your profit is a long-term capital gain, and only 40 percent of it counts as taxable income.

Let's say you own stock that you bought for $40,000. It's now worth $80,000. It pays annual dividends of $2,400. That's a yield of only 3 percent, and dividend income is all taxable, except for the first $100 a year, or $200 for a couple filing jointly. Still, the stock is a sound investment; you expect the shares to continue appreciating in value. Should you sell it? And if you do, what should you do with the money?

That depends on your needs, your tax bracket, and your alternatives. We'll mention a few, but remember that we are only suggesting choices. You must make your own decision, tailored to your own situation.

If you sell the stock all in the same year, you'll have a long-term capital gain of $40,000. Of that, $16,000—40 percent—is taxable. Sixteen thousand dollars would push you into a higher tax bracket. Why not sell the stock gradually instead—spaced over two or three or four years—to spread out that capital gain, so you can keep your bracket down?

On the other hand, you may need the cash. Or you may want to invest that money in bonds or some other kind of security paying a high yield. Here's a sample formula, assuming you sell the stock all at once, and assuming the sale pushes you into the 35 percent tax bracket:

Proceeds	$80,000
Capital gain	$40,000
Taxable portion of capital gain	$16,000
Income tax, at 35 percent	$ 5,600
Balance after taxes	$74,400

Let's assume you invest that $74,400 in bonds yielding 12 percent interest.

Income on bonds	$8,928
Previous dividend income from the stock	$2,400
Gain in annual income	$6,528

Without spending a penny of your investment, you have improved your annual income by more than $6,000, even after paying the capital gains tax. Of course, that bond interest is taxable. You might be better off buying tax-exempt municipal bonds yielding a couple of percentage points less. Or you might prefer to keep your money liquid by investing in an insured money market account at a bank or savings institution or a money market mutual fund. In that case, the yield probably will be 2 or 3 percentage points less than the yield on taxable bonds.

The logic of this kind of change—from building the value of your assets to increasing your income—is not limited to investments in securities. If you own real estate and rent it out, you have been reaping the benefits of one of the best and most basic Tax Savers. By depreciating the property and deducting other expenses connected with it, you have sheltered a great deal of your other income from income tax.

In retirement, however, your tax bracket may be a good deal lower. That lessens the value of those real estate deductions. Besides, if your real estate deal is typical, you may not be making much profit, if any, on the cash flow. In other words, the rent you receive may barely cover the mortgage, property tax, and other expenses. To be sure, the property is probably continuing to increase in value. If you have plenty of income, you may want to hang on to the property as a hedge against future financial difficulty. But if you're short of income, a rental property with little cash-flow profit is a luxury you can do without. Why not sell it, taking advantage of the capital gains Tax Saver, and invest the proceeds in bonds, savings certificates, or a money fund? You will still have most of your capital; it will just be invested differently. And your income will be substantially higher.

If you plan to cash in a good deal of accumulated capital gains, look out for the Alternative Minimum Tax, Form 6251. It's designed to take a bite out of certain income that otherwise is not taxed, including the untaxed portion of capital gains. You can usually avoid the Alternative Minimum Tax by spreading your gain over several years rather than taking it all at once. If a capital gain balloons your taxable income for a single year, use Income Averaging, Schedule G. It lets you spread that income over the past four years, lowering your bracket and lessening the tax on that one year of unusually high income.

For most retirees, the capital gains Tax Saver comes

along just at the right time. It cushions your taxes while enabling you to change your investment portfolio from one aimed at restraining annual income (and taxes) in favor of capital gains, to one emphasizing high income. You're exchanging work and salary for retirement and investment income. Each one is a Tax Saver appropriate to its stage of life.

The IRA, or Individual Retirement Account, affords many retirees still another choice. Your IRA accumulates tax-free until you start withdrawing money from it. Normally, withdrawals cannot start before you are fifty-nine and a half years old, and must start by the time you're seventy and a half. So you have eleven years of latitude.

Let's say you're sixty-five and retired, and you need to start using some of your savings—after all, retirement is what you saved for. You could withdraw money from your IRA, or you could cash in some stocks that have appreciated in value, as in our previous example. Your natural impulse might be to withdraw money from your IRA.

But hold on. Any money you withdraw from your IRA is taxable as ordinary income. Even if half or three quarters of the money in your IRA built up as a result of capital gains, you cannot use the capital gains Tax Saver when you withdraw IRA money. The IRA is an entirely different kind of Tax Saver, with its own rules: A dollar withdrawn is a dollar of taxable income.

Given that choice, you would be wiser to sell some of your appreciated stocks, so you can take advantage of the capital gains Tax Saver. Remember, that way only 40 percent of your capital gain will be taxed. Let your IRA keep compounding. You have to start taking withdrawals at age seventy and a half, but by then the account may have gained appreciably in value. And as long as the money is in your IRA account, it accumulates tax-free. On the other hand, the dividends on your stock are taxable. So in every way you're better off cashing the stock and keeping the IRA. If you were self-employed and built up retirement savings in a Keogh account, the same is true; a Keogh is almost identical to an IRA in those respects. If you want to build up an estate to pass on to your heirs, consider your IRA or Keogh as an integral part. Although these accounts are designed for retirement, they can be passed on at death just like any other asset.

It's important to think of your IRA or Keogh (or both, if you are fortunate enough to have both) as an asset with its own opportunities. While you were working, it was a Tax Saver; your contributions were deductible and the interest or dividends compounded tax-free. Even though you're now retired, that's still true. If you keep on working, even part-time, you can keep on contributing, taking advantage of the tax deductions. Indeed, even if you work just a little, earning only $2,000 a year, you can contribute every penny of that to your IRA. That way you'll earn no taxable income at all. However, there can be no more contributions to your IRA once you reach age seventy and a half.

You say you need that $2,000 from a part-time job for living expenses? Fine. Spend it for that, and add to your IRA from your appreciated stocks instead, taking advantage of the capital gains Tax Saver. Put $2,000 of earnings from stock into your IRA, also taking advantage of the IRA Tax Saver. Your investment portfolio retains its value—$2,000 cashed from one account, $2,000 added to another account. And you've saved a tidy amount on taxes.

SELLING YOUR HOME

Many senior citizens move. If you move from a home that you own, you are entitled to a big Tax Saver. In fact, you are entitled to two of them.

If you sell a house or condominium in which you have lived for a number of years, you are likely to get a lot more for it than you originally paid. Profits of $100,000 or more are not unusual. With virtually any asset other than your home, you would have to pay capital gains tax on that profit. But if you buy another home that costs as much or more, you can defer taxation on your profit. You have to move into the new home within two years, and both the home you sell and the one you buy must be your principal residence; you can't use this Tax Saver on property that you rent out or on a vacation cottage that you use only two or three months a year. But as long as every move involves your principal residence, you can use this Tax Saver over and over again. You can defer the tax forever. Many senior citizens do.

But maybe you don't want to buy a home. Perhaps you're tired of the burdens of homeownership; you'd like to sell your house and rent an apartment in Florida. Another Tax Saver is waiting for you. Once in your life, at age fifty-five or older, you can pocket as much as $125,000 profit on the sale of your principal residence without paying a penny of tax. You get the exemption one time only, whether the profit is $1,000 or $125,000. If you sell at a $50,000 profit and elect to take this Tax Saver, you will lose out on the unused $75,000.

To qualify, you must have lived in the home for at least three of the previous five years. If you are married, only one of you has to be fifty-five; the other can be younger. But if either of you has taken advantage of this Tax Saver before— even in a previous marriage—you cannot do it again. Nor can the spouse who has not used this Tax Saver use it by filing a separate return. If you are married, this Tax Saver must be declared on a joint income tax return. That's the rule.

MOVING AWAY

Here's a Tax Saver that may surprise you, since we're talking about retirement. Your moving expenses are deductible if either you or your spouse goes to work full-time in a new location. The rule is this: You or your spouse must work in your new location at least thirty-nine weeks out of the fifty-two weeks immediately following your move.

Perhaps you're retiring, and you move to a friendly climate. Ten weeks after moving in, your spouse takes a store job. He or she keeps that job for a year. That work brings home money and earns a Tax Saver, too; your moving expenses are deductible.

SELF-EMPLOYMENT

Both Strassels and Mead are self-employed, and neither of us can resist the temptation to remind you of the bountiful Tax Savers that go with profitable self-employment, whether full-time or part-time. Perhaps you are looking forward to spending more time, in retirement, on an activity that was a hobby during your working years—photography, music, painting, rock collecting, whatever. If you are accustomed to business, you may enjoy that hobby more if you turn it into a business, however small. Perhaps you can set yourself up as the neighborhood photographer. You might teach piano, paint portraits, or polish and sell pretty rocks. You might work as a part-time consultant for your old firm or for other companies in the same business. By doing so, you can take advantage of numerous Tax Savers, starting with the deduction for moving expenses. To qualify, self-employed people need to work seventy-eight weeks of the two years following a move.

One way to pick up any slack in your finances during retirement years is for you to go back to work. There's not a thing wrong with bringing in a few extra bucks. It won't affect your corporate pensions, and it will keep you active. Senior citizens have a great deal of experience and expertise to share. Working a couple of hours a week or every day makes good sense.

In addition, don't ignore the possibility of becoming another Colonel Sanders or Grandma Moses. Start a new career now. Many of the same Tax Savers we discussed under Tax Savers for Young Marrieds in Chapter 6 apply now.

There are two Tax Soakers you should take into consideration before you go back to work. No matter what your age, your wages (or net earnings from self-employment) are subject to Social Security taxes. You can be eighty-five years old and working, and you'll have to pay Social Security tax. That's the rule.

In addition, for those receiving Social Security benefits each month, you will lose $1 in benefits for every $2 you earn once you exceed $5,160 in earnings. That's the level for those under age sixty-five. If you are sixty-five to seventy, you can earn up to $6,960 before you have your monthly Social Security benefit cut. And for those age seventy and above, you can earn unlimited amounts, and your benefit check will not be reduced. (These earnings limits were for 1984. The figures rise every year in line with average wage increases.)

WILLS

Our field is Tax Savers for the living. Your will certainly should be carefully drawn to restrain or eliminate estate taxes and to make sure your assets pass to whomever you want to receive them. You can leave an unlimited amount to your spouse without incurring any estate-tax liability. You can leave an estate of $400,000 in 1985, rising to $500,000 in 1986 and to $600,000 in 1987 and thereafter, without incurring any estate-tax liability. But you need a carefully crafted will, and you need a good lawyer.

Part Three

DEALING
WITH
THE IRS

15

Handling the Forms

A t just about Christmastime every year, the Internal Revenue Service mails an unwelcome present—your income tax forms, with instructions. If you use the IRS's package to pay your taxes, you're likely to overpay.

Not that these forms are crooked or slanted, or any different from federal income tax forms that you can pick up on your own. It's just that they are minimal. Many important Tax Savers require special forms—an additional page or an extra schedule—and the IRS's package is unlikely to include each and every form that could help you reduce your tax bill. You are entitled to use any form that will save you money, but the IRS does not feel obliged to call them to your attention. The government's idea of holiday spirit is to collect your taxes and spend the money. Help you save? Not Uncle Sam. That's up to you.

Usually, the IRS sends you a tax package loosely based on the tax forms you filed the previous year. That means some tax-saving forms will be left out, even if you happened to use them the previous year. It's nothing personal —the IRS won't include them in anyone else's package either.

Many taxpayers assume that they are supposed to use

the forms that the IRS sends them, but that is not necessarily so. Use those forms if you like, but also get every additional form that might save you money. We say "might," because you often can't tell whether a particular Tax Saver will help you until you see the form, read the instructions that go with it, and work out the numbers. But to stick with just the forms in the IRS package is to work in the dark.

THE LONG AND THE SHORT OF IT

By all means use the Form 1040, the so-called long form. The short form, 1040A, and the supershort form, 1040EZ, are for taxpayers who are unable or unwilling to take advantage of the hundreds of deductions, exemptions, and credits that we call Tax Savers. Every strategy that we recommend in this book, and every step that we will recommend in this chapter, is keyed to the Form 1040. Never, under any circumstances, can you pay less tax by using either of the short forms. Never, under any circumstances, can you pay more tax by using the long form, assuming you use it correctly.

If the short forms were abolished, a lot of Americans would groan, including the IRS Commissioner, the Secretary of the Treasury, and everyone else in the government who worries about collecting as much tax money as possible under the law. About 40 percent of American taxpayers use one or the other of the two short forms. The short forms save taxpayers time—and cost many of them money. Too many taxpayers are like ostriches, burying their heads in the sand, not even looking to see if they could save by using the long form. If you're wedded to either of the short forms, we're glad that you're reading this book. We have the opportunity to convince you that the long form will benefit your pocketbook. True, learning about all the Tax Savers you've missed in the past will depress you, because with the short forms you can't take advantage of most of them. But cheer up. We tell you how to get most of your money back from missed Tax Savers in the section in Chapter 17 on amended returns.

For example, in 1982, the first year Individual Retirement Accounts were available to all working taxpayers, only 11 percent of individual tax returns made use of that wonderful IRA Tax Saver. Many of those who didn't were short-form filers, since neither short form allowed the IRA. (Starting with 1983, you could claim the IRA deduction on form 1040A, although it's still not available on 1040EZ. Even so, only 14 percent of individual taxpayers took an IRA deduction.)

Lots of people think they can't use the long form unless they have enough deductions to itemize on Schedule A— covering charity, medical, tax, and interest payments. To itemize, you need these deductions to total $2,300 if you're single, $3,400 if you're married filing jointly, or $1,700 if you're married filing separately. (Beginning in 1985, those thresholds will rise annually in line with inflation.) But these deductions are just one of many reasons to use the long form. What if you bought storm windows? Whether you own or rent, that may entitle you to the residential energy credit (Form 5695). You can claim it, like most Tax Savers, only on the long form.

Some people have no choice about which form to file. You must use the long form if you have income from capital gains, trusts, partnerships, a business at home, or any of a variety of other sources. You must use the long form if your taxable income totals $50,000 or more, no matter what its source is.

ORDERING TAX FORMS

In ordering or picking up the forms you expect to need, don't count on your memory or your past experience. Some Tax Savers are once-in-a-lifetime opportunities, and others will fit your circumstances only occasionally. This may be the year. You won't know unless you consider them.

For example, how often do you move in connection with your career, spending more money on the move than you're reimbursed by your employer? Those out-of-pocket costs are deductible, but only if you file Form 3903. How often do you sell your principal residence? When you do, you're required to file Form 2119. How often is a house destroyed by a tornado (Form 4684, Casualties and Thefts)? We can't predict which particular Tax Savers will work for you at any given time—we can't say often enough that it's up to you to pick the right ones.

Only you can decide which forms you should use, or at least consider using. At the end of this book, in Part Four, we list the individual income tax forms and schedules you could need and the addresses of the IRS offices from which you can order them. Order any that might even remotely fit your circumstances. Whatever other forms you may decide upon, be sure to ask for Form 2210, which you'll have to include with your return if you owe additional taxes at filing time, and Form 4868, which we recommend that you have on hand in case you need it. Form 4868 automatically postpones your tax-filing deadline from April 15 to August 15. If you do any investing, or plan to, also get a copy of Schedule D, which runs you through the rules and procedures for figuring capital gains and losses. With Schedule D on hand as a guide, you can plan your investment moves to take best advantage of the capital gains Tax Saver.

Order your forms by mail in late December, and at the same time order the IRS instructional booklets that go with them. We list those in Part Four, too. Sure, that package of forms that the IRS sends you around Christmas includes instructions, but they're incomplete, and much of what they leave out is precisely what you need to cut your tax bill.

Whatever your tax situation, be sure to order IRS Publication 17, *Your Federal Income Tax*. This 170-page booklet doesn't go out of its way to emphasize Tax Savers—after all, it's published by the IRS—but it's a detailed and lucid guide to preparing your taxes, step by step. We think it's as good as many of the tax manuals for sale at bookstores. And it's free, as are all IRS publications. You don't even have to send postage. There is one major drawback to Publication 17—the tax schedules are missing. You'll find those in the instructions that come with the package in the Christmas mail. If you get the package of estimated income tax forms

━━━━━━

that the IRS mails out early in the year, it too includes the tax schedules.

With this book as an overall master planner, and with *Your Federal Income Tax* as a detailed guide to the lines on your tax return, you can intelligently figure your taxes to your best advantage. We hope you've already taken advantage of the Tax Savers that fit your situation—that you've worked them into your financial life during the year. Your tax return is your method of cashing in these Tax Savers.

Incidentally, getting all the forms and booklets you need can be a frustrating exercise. We recommend ordering by mail, but don't hold your breath; the forms may not get to you for several weeks. Even if you walk into an IRS office and ask, you may be told that certain forms won't be in stock until perhaps February or even later. If you hire a tax preparer, ask him or her for the forms you need. Many public libraries have master tax forms that you can photocopy. When you get forms, from whatever source, make two or three photocopies so you can try things first one way and then another—we'll get to that later in this chapter—and so you can throw away your mistakes.

MAILING LABELS

Your package of tax forms comes with a label, printed with your name, address, Social Security number, and a coded string of numbers and letters. The instructions tell you to stick that label on your tax return, but you don't have to. The label is purely for the convenience of the IRS. It may speed up the processing of your return, but that's to your advantage only if you've got a refund due and are eager to get it.

Some taxpayers suspect that the code on the label might earmark them for audit. Not so. Those codes only have to do with processing, not audit selection.

The printed instructions tell you that if something on the label is wrong, you should correct it, and the IRS will make that correction. Don't count on it. Several years ago, the Postal Service changed Mead's mailing ZIP code. For three years, he corrected the labels on every tax return and every quarterly estimated tax payment. The IRS stuck to his old ZIP code. That's par; IRS clerks are too swamped to bother with corrections jotted on little labels.

So use the label or don't use it, at your convenience. If anything on the label is wrong, by all means throw the label away and print or type the correct information on your tax form.

EARLY PREPARATION

Most Americans dread the annual chore of figuring their taxes, and understandably put off the task as long as they can. We hope you will become one of the fortunate few who tackle the job eagerly and early. Not because it's fun—the work is too detailed and time-consuming for that—but because it nails down your tax savings. Not until you prepare your tax return do you know exactly how much you've saved by using Tax Savers.

Anyway, it's wise to figure your taxes while your finances for the past year are fresh in your mind. The longer you wait the more you may forget and the more likely it is that you will confuse last year with the current year. Of course you'll be working from records, but those who take full advantage of Tax Savers are doing more than monotonously going from one receipt to the next. They're following a carefully constructed plan, and most of us can carry it through better if we don't put the whole thing aside for two or three months while beginning to organize the affairs—and Tax Savers—of the new year.

Most important, preparing your form early spares you the dreadful and risky ordeal of figuring your taxes under pressure at the last moment. Those conditions are hardly conducive to a thorough and careful job, by you or by a tax preparer. Five years ago, Mead roughed out his taxes on April 1 and turned them over to an accountant of impeccable reputation—so impeccable that the guy had hundreds of customers. The evening of April 15, the accountant delivered finished tax returns to Mead and dozens of other anxious taxpayers. Mead had barely an hour to look over the form. He hadn't filed Form 4868 for an extension of time (dumb), so he had to get his tax return to the post office. Later he went over it and found that his impeccable accountant had messed up; Mead had overpaid his taxes by nearly $400. He filed an amended return, got his money back, started doing his taxes earlier, and found a tax preparer who was good but not so well known.

We're recommending that you *prepare* your tax return early, but not that you *file* it early. When you actually file depends on your personal situation. If you have a substantial refund coming, you may want to file quickly so that you can collect your refund. Otherwise, you're probably better off filing just before the deadline.

Preparing your taxes early but waiting to file them only when they are due yields several advantages. It gives you time to think twice—to figure your taxes, put them aside, then look them over again. An overlooked Tax Saver may occur to you in the meantime, or you might catch an error or an omission.

If you owe money—that is, if your withholding and estimated tax payments don't cover your total tax bill—you'll know it in time to get the money together by April 15. Even if you already have the money, why give it to the IRS before you have to? The government will not reward you, or pay you interest, for filing and paying before the deadline. Instead, leave your money in the bank, where it will earn interest; pay the IRS just before the April 15 deadline.

By filing at the deadline you may actually reduce your chances of getting audited. The IRS contends that time of filing has nothing to do with its audit selection process. But the IRS decides ahead of time how many tax returns it will audit, and many knowledgeable tax people suspect that the agency starts to fill these audit quotas well before the last tax forms come in. After all, if you were running the IRS, would you wait from early January until August 15 before even beginning to process forms?

So we recommend this schedule for your tax return:

1. Prepare it early. The rest of this chapter will tell you how to prepare it right.

2. If you have a large refund coming, mail in your return soon, but not immediately. Let it sit for a couple of days and

then go over it again to make sure you haven't missed any Tax Savers and haven't made any mistakes. Then mail it in. Whether your refund is large or small, ask that it be mailed to you rather than applied to your estimated tax for the current year.

PROCRASTINATING

If you are a procrastinator or if you have a complex financial situation and doubt that you can meet the April 15 filing deadline, fill out Form 4868. It's a one-page, seven-question form that automatically grants you an additional four months, until August 15, to file your return. It doesn't postpone the April 15 deadline for payment, however. If you don't pay on time, you're assessed interest at the going prime rate. That's not a bad deal as interest rates go, but in addition the IRS is likely to sock you with a nondeductible penalty for late payment. So we recommend that you mail the amount you owe, along with Form 4868.

How can you figure what you owe if you aren't able to finish your return? The IRS gives you leeway of 10 percent. Write a check to the IRS for what you think your taxes will come to, staple it to your Form 4868, and mail it in about April 12 or 13—before the last-minute rush. As long as your Form 4868 is postmarked by April 15, and comes with a check for at least 90 percent of your finally and accurately computed tax liability, the IRS will be satisfied. Then, about August 12 or 13, write the IRS a check if you owe any remaining outstanding amount, staple it to your return, attach a copy of your Form 4868, and mail it in. If you owe, be sure to include a copy of Form 2210, calculating any underpayment penalty, or explaining why you didn't pay more in withholding or estimated taxes during the year. If you're due a refund, IRS will send it to you.

Form 2210 is called Underpayment of Estimated Tax. If you owe tax—that is, if your tax return shows a balance due after taking into account your withholding and estimated tax payments—you'll have to work out a formula on Form 2210 that often concludes with a cash penalty for underpayment. However, the form does give you several ways to exempt yourself from paying the penalty, so it's definitely to your advantage to include it with your return.

For example, you pay no penalty if:

1. The amount you owe is $400 or less for 1984—$500 for 1985 and thereafter.
2. The amount you owe is no more than 20 percent of your total tax liability.
3. Your withholding and estimated tax payments would have covered the tax bill on the return you filed a year ago.

The point is that if you owe, file Form 2210 to take advantage of any exemption from the penalty. With Form 2210, you may join the ranks of taxpayers who find an exemption that spares them any penalty.

If you do not itemize deductions, you can ask the IRS to compute your taxes for you; you fill out your own return but leave the final calculation to the IRS. Two to four weeks after you mail it in, the IRS will bill you and give you thirty more days to pay. So altogether you get an additional forty-five to sixty days before you have to cough up the cash.

FOREIGN TRAVEL

Actually, we have a more pleasant deal. Would you or your spouse like to travel abroad on April 15? If you're out of the country on April 15, you get two additional months to file and pay your income tax, although if you owe, you must pay interest on the unpaid balance. If you're married and filing a joint return, only one spouse need be out of the country that day. There's no printed form covering this cozy little deal, but you must attach a statement—a letter—to your tax form saying that you were out of the country that day, and we recommend that you have proof just in case the IRS asks for it.

You needn't go on much of a trip. On April 15 a couple of years ago, Strassels mentioned this deal during an interview on radio station WJR in Detroit—which is, of course, right across the Detroit River from Windsor, Ontario, Canada. Lots of Detroit people listen to WJR, and considering the bridge traffic that day, half of them must have jumped in their cars and driven to Windsor for lunch. In Detroit, April 15 is "Take Someone to Lunch in Windsor" Day. With lunch and bridge-toll receipts, you've got all the proof the IRS could demand: You were out of the country on April 15; you are entitled to file and pay two months late. If you like warm weather, we recommend Mexico and the Bahamas. But beware of Puerto Rico and the American Virgin Islands; they don't count as "out of the country."

You may be thinking that this doesn't make sense, that there's no logic to granting a two-month tax postponement simply for spending part of April 15 across the border. You're right, but don't let it trouble you. It's perfectly legal and—to the IRS—not even controversial. Ours is not a logical system of income tax laws. Instead it is an unwieldy collection of thousands of tax-law provisions, each enacted for its own sake without much thought about its effect on the overall tax system. Some provisions make sense, and some don't. Some help you, and some hurt you. The IRS enforces the ones that hurt you. It's up to you to take advantage of the ones that help you. As a citizen, you might want to write to your representatives in Congress and suggest that they try to close that foolish loophole allowing a two-month extension for people abroad. If you do, we suggest that you write the letter on April 15, over lunch at a nice restaurant in Canada or Mexico.

IMPORTANT MAIL

From late December through February, watch your mail. During that period you'll be receiving many important papers telling you of the numbers that you'll need for your tax return. Some will have to do with income, others with deductible expenses. Make sure you save them. Put them with the rest of the tax records you collected throughout the year. These reports—most of them mere slips of paper or sometimes just a line of information on a bill—are essential for preparing your return and for surviving an audit. Many of those having to do with your income have been sent to the IRS as well as to you; you'd better have your copies so that you can verify that the numbers you put on your tax return match the numbers that have been fed into the IRS computers. These reports of your income to the IRS by others are required by law; they're the IRS's way of looking over your shoulder to make sure you report all your income.

A surprising amount of useful data is voluntarily provided to taxpayers by stockbrokers, department stores, credit card companies, and the like. The spread of computerized systems has made it relatively easy for companies and agencies to produce individualized data, and as a result taxpayers are being fed more paper than ever. Don't shovel these reports into your wastebasket; they can help you figure your taxes and maybe even save you money. Don't automatically assume that all the facts you receive are correct. Check them against your records. If a number is wrong, it's up to you to catch the error and get the issuer to send out a correction, to you and to the IRS.

Here are some of the papers to look for:

Income

Your W-2 form—or forms, if you worked for more than one employer during the year. Employers are required to mail W-2s by January 31. Your W-2 tells you how much you were paid during the year and how much was withheld for federal income tax, state income tax, local income tax, and FICA (Social Security).

Your 1099 forms. These report dividends and interest. If you own stocks or bonds, each corporation must send you a 1099. If your cash deposits earned interest, the bank or savings institution must send you a 1099. Even your state government now sends 1099s to those who received tax refunds the previous year. Most 1099 forms simply report the total amount you were paid in dividends or interest. But some reports are more complicated, often to your advantage. If you own stock, particularly in a mutual fund, read— and save—correspondence from the company. Sometimes portions of dividend income are not fully taxed, for one reason or another. Mutual funds often pay dividends plus tax-favored capital gains distributions. By mail, companies will tell you how to report all this on your tax form. Hang on to that correspondence and use it.

If you receive money from a trust, the trust company will tell you just how much to report on your tax return and where to list it. You should get similar reports if you receive income from an annuity, a partnership, or any of a number of other sources. These reports are vital. For example, let's say you received $650 income from a trust and $2,500 from a partnership. The numbers on the year-end reports from the trust and the partnership may differ from the amounts you actually received. That's because you're taxed on your share of the income received during the year by the trust or partnership—regardless of whether more or less was actually distributed to you in cash.

Some stockbrokers will send you a summary of your transactions during the year. With these numbers you can quickly figure your capital gains and losses.

Deductions, Credits, and Exemptions

Many firms send you information that you can use to reduce your tax bill. You may get a year-end mortgage statement, listing how much you paid in interest and property taxes. The bank that handles our MasterCard and Visa cards includes a note at the bottom of the January bill telling how much we paid in interest during the past year. Many department stores and other credit-issuers do the same. It's handy. But they don't have to, and you shouldn't count on it. Deductions are Tax Savers, and it's up to you to make sure you keep track of your deductible dollars. Watch the mail, use what comes in, note the tax deductions and other Tax Savers that haven't been spoon-fed to you. Pull that information together. It should be in your records.

WORKING TOGETHER

If you are married, don't prepare your tax return alone. Drag your spouse to the table. It is no fun to prepare a tax return, but it is fun to save money, and you'll save more if you work together. The two of you should plan your Tax Savers together; the two of you should carry them through together.

The benefits go beyond tax savings and togetherness. In many families, only one spouse may have a real understanding of the family's finances. On a day-to-day basis, it's hard to bring the other spouse in; after all, you can't reasonably expect to sit down together every time you cash a check or make a deposit. However, income tax preparation is the single event of every year that brings together all the threads of a family's finances. It may not be a pleasant exercise, but it teaches you the details of your financial life.

That dreadful, detailed tax form demands that you look up and add up every source of income and many of your most significant expenditures. It forces you to review your savings and investments. How much are you earning in interest and dividends? How are you faring in the stock market or the real estate market or any other area where you might be in search of capital gains? How much have you put aside for retirement, what is it earning, and how well is it sheltered from current income taxes? How much do you spend every year on housing, medical expenses, debt payments, state and local taxes? How much are you giving to church and other worthwhile organizations? If either of you has a business at home, is it profitable? If so, just how profitable?

Many couples resolve from time to time to sit down together and educate each other on family finances, but they never get around to it. When only one spouse (or, in more cases than you might believe, neither spouse) really understands the family's financial picture, misunderstandings and arguments inevitably crop up. A wife who has left the finances to her husband can't help getting irritated when she's told that the $2,000 she had counted on for redecorating the living room will have to go instead to pay the balance due on income taxes. A husband who had looked forward to a fishing trip is unlikely to applaud when his wife, the family money manager, tells him that the $2,000 they saved should go into an IRA.

Counselors—and divorce lawyers—say that money, or the lack of it, is the leading cause of marital disputes. We

know an educated, sophisticated—socially, but not financially—couple who almost broke up over an event that
hardly sounds like a family tragedy: She inherited $35,000
from her father. Her husband had always handled the family finances, and she seized upon her inheritance as an opportunity to acquaint herself with the mysterious world of
money and investments, and to lessen her feeling of depen-
dence on her husband. So rather than pool her inheritance
with other family funds, she invested it for her own use.

She felt that her husband had always earned the income
and controlled the family purse strings, so it was about
time she had a little nest egg to control on her own.

He felt that everything he earned and saved had always
been used to support the family. He had no private nest egg,
so why should she?

The disagreement became increasingly heated and finally boiled over when he figured their income taxes—by
himself, as usual—and demanded $1,000 from her. She had
invested her inheritance in corporate bonds and had received $3,500 in interest during the year; he figured that her
interest income had boosted their taxes by about $1,000.

We didn't hear their conversation firsthand, but it must
have gone something like this:

SHE: "I don't have the $1,000. That's my money, and
I've spent it!"

HE: "You can't expect *me* to pay taxes on *your* private
income."

SHE: "You've *always* paid the taxes."

WE *(if we had been there):* "That's just the trouble."

We heard from another couple who seemed able to share
or divide most chores, but they could not get together on
their income tax. Neither volunteered to prepare the tax
return, and neither did it. They kept records crammed in
big coffee cans, a couple for each year, but for three years
they failed to file a return. The IRS sent letters, and finally
an agent came to their house. They were terrified but
lucky: They went to an accountant, had their taxes figured
for all three years, and found that instead of owing they had
overpaid every year, through withholding. They were not
penalized; if you do not owe taxes, you are not fined or oth-

erwise penalized for failing to file (but don't try it). In fact, they got refunds. They liked those refunds, and they now prepare their tax returns together. At least they told us that they do.

By working together on your taxes you'll save money, gain a common understanding of your family's finances, and become better able to work together toward your financial goals. That's the carrot. The stick, as usual, is wielded by the IRS. The vast majority of married couples save by filing a joint return. Both husband and wife must sign the return, and both are responsible for any errors—even for criminal tax evasion planned and carried out entirely by just one spouse. For more about this subject, see Chapter 6, Tax Savers for Young Marrieds.

YOUR WORK SHEET

A lot of people prepare their tax returns in one feverish night. That makes the job even more miserable—and more subject to error. If you've planned your Tax Savers and kept good records, you'll save time in tax preparation as well as money in taxes. But don't tackle the job when you're tired and under deadline pressure. Spread it over at least two days, preferably three or four. When you can't stand it anymore, stop until the next day. And when you finish your return, let it sit for at least a couple of days, then review it.

To begin, sit down with all your records at hand, and with all the tax forms you may need. Look them over to acquaint yourself—selves, if you are married—with each area that may fit your situation. Your first job is to identify and list every tax-sensitive item, whether it's on the income or expenditure side.

Start with your checkbook register. For most people, it serves as a master source of information. Make sure you know where every deposit came from. If the source isn't noted in your register, write it in now. If you fail to do so, and you are audited, the auditor may take the position that every unidentified deposit is taxable income unless you can convince him otherwise; your checkbook register is one of the first things an auditor looks at. Don't count on your memory; if you're audited, it won't be for about a year and a half after you filed your return. So note the source of every deposit—paycheck, bank loan, transfer from another account, gift from a relative, proceeds from a securities sale, whatever.

On the work sheet you're developing, write down deposits that may be taxable, either in full or in part, and those that are not taxed. Break the taxable ones into columns keyed to the categories of income on page 1 of your income tax return—wages, interest, dividends, refunds of state and local taxes, alimony, business income, capital gains, pensions, rents, and so on. If you are typical, you will have income from no more than four or five of these categories, although the more you have, the better the IRS likes it.

Make similar lists for expenditures. Your check stubs provide a chronology of your financial transactions for the year. You can make your income and expenditure lists simultaneously.

Again, make lists that correspond with categories of deductions and credits listed on the tax forms: from page 1, contributions to IRA or Keogh retirement accounts and alimony payments you made; from Schedule A, expenditures for medical treatment, state and local taxes, interest payments, union and professional dues; and so on.

It's easy to get frustrated. Form 1040 seems to have been conceived by the devil. Some lines make perfect sense, but others are imponderable. All of us know what's meant by "wages, salaries, tips," and most of us can come up with that figure pretty easily. But we may have trouble with "deduction for a married couple when both work."

Have patience. Pages 1 and 2 of Form 1040 are like a crossword puzzle; you can fill in some blanks easily, but others have to be painstakingly constructed from bits in other squares. The "other squares" of the tax form are the additional forms and schedules of Form 1040—such as Schedule W, Deduction for a Married Couple When Both Work, and so on.

You have to proceed one step at a time. At this stage, you're using the tax forms only for reference, as you put together your work sheets. So don't let the forms bother you. Make them work for you, providing reminders of ways to save, of bits of information that you will need or that your professional tax preparer can use.

After going through your check register, turn to other records that will help you flesh out your work sheet. Typically, these include your forms W-2 and 1099, various receipts, statements from your bank, mortgagor, broker, mutual fund. Your booklet of car-payment coupons may list the interest you paid for the year. Add them up. Don't copy the amount from last year's tax return; interest on car loans, mortgages, and many other kinds of loans will vary from year to year.

Scan your charge and credit card statements for tax-deductible items. It is quite common for a person to put business magazines and books, lunches, and other deductible expenses on a charge card.

Look through your personal and business calendars; they'll remind you of trips to the doctor, conventions, the Labor Day barbecue you threw for business associates, and other tax-related events. Make sure you list the cost of professional and tax books (don't forget this one) and magazine subscriptions related to your work or to family financial planning; those costs are deductible.

Do not succumb to the temptation to backdate documents or otherwise cheat. If you didn't take advantage of Tax Savers, do not pretend that you did; it's wrong, and it's risky. With the year behind you, only one Tax Saver can be exploited retroactively; and that's a retirement account. You can open an IRA and make your contribution for the past year as late as April 15. You used to be allowed to contribute to your IRA as late as August 15 if you mailed in Form 4868 for a postponement of your tax-filing deadline. But Congress outlawed that additional four-month IRA postponement as part of the 1984 tax law. If you are self-employed, full-time or part-time, you can take advantage of the same April 15 deadline for contributions to your Keogh account, although the account must have been opened before the year ended. If you file Form 4868, you can make your Keogh contribution as late as the date on which you file your tax return, which can be as late as August 15.

Look over your tax returns for the previous year or two and review the items you considered in your tax planning for the past year. Have you listed every Tax Saver? Did you remember to include loan prepayment penalties or penalties for cashing a certificate of deposit prior to maturity? How about business expenses not fully reimbursed by your employer? If you sold securities and mailed the certificates by express or insured mail, did you list the mailing expenses? On income taxes, little items like these add up—in fact, that's the essence of figuring your taxes to your best advantage.

As you go through your records, update your permanent House and Investment files, too. Anything you spent on home improvements should be noted for your House file. If you later sell your house at a profit, your Basis price includes your purchase price plus the cost of all capital improvements—bushes, storm windows, gutters and downspouts, a porch enclosure. The higher your Basis price, the lower your profit when you sell, and the less your potential capital gains tax will be.

When you sell stock, you have to report the price you paid for it as well as the price you got for it. So keep an Investment file with the transaction slips you get from brokers. Include your own notes on purchases and sales in the file. If you have stock or mutual fund dividends automatically reinvested, your Investment file should keep a running record of every transaction. You'll run across all that as you go through your records for the year. Take advantage of the opportunity to clear up two chores at once.

THE TWO-RETURN SYSTEM

With your work sheets completed, let's tackle the tax return. We recommend that you figure your taxes two ways. First, pretend that a nasty IRS agent is looking over your shoulder. Take nothing that you cannot absolutely prove.

Skip charitable contributions that were not made by check. Prepare a tax return so clean and provable that you would have no fear if called in for an audit.

Now, work out a second return, resolving gray areas in your own favor. If you think you dropped about a hundred dollars in the church collection plate and the Salvation Army pot, claim it. If you estimate that you spent roughly $30 on investment-related postage during the year, list it. Just as you resolved questionable areas in the IRS's favor on the first return, resolve them in your favor on this return. Don't cheat, but don't be timid either.

Now compare the two returns. What's the difference in your tax bills? Unless your situation is unusual, you'll be surprised at how little difference there is. That difference is the amount at stake just in case of an audit. If it's, say, $300, you would go into an audit knowing that at the very worst, you could not be socked for more than $300 in back taxes.

Our two-return system is reassuring and takes surprisingly little additional time. That's because once you've kept good records throughout the year, organized them to prepare your return, put together sensibly detailed work sheets, and taken advantage of every form and schedule that might help you, most of the rest of the work—the actual preparation of the tax return itself—is surprisingly cut and dried. To be sure, it's detailed, ponderous, and often aggravating. But you'll probably find that your two returns —both are thorough and honest but one is slanted to favor the IRS, the other is slanted to favor you—are twins on the vast majority of items and aren't terribly far apart on others. In tax preparation, there's much less elbow room than many tax preparers would have you believe. The elbow room—and the Tax Savers—are in tax planning, events that you put in place during the year.

FILING TIPS

Before we dissect the forms, let us give you a few general tips on the mechanics of handling your return.

1. Round numbers off to the nearest dollar, but no more.
2. Fill out your return in pencil or erasable ink so that you can make corrections easily. When you're finished, photocopy the return, sign the photocopy, and mail it to the IRS. You don't want to mail in an erasable return.
3. You may be tempted to attach notes or documents explaining items that, on their own, could look troublesome. Do it only if you can concisely and absolutely settle the potential question. For example, if you donate $4,000 worth of appreciated stock to a charity as a once-in-a-lifetime gift, by all means attach a letter from the charity acknowledging your gift. But don't raise issues that the IRS might not raise on its own, and don't argue tax law. If you do, you may cause yourself additional trouble.
4. Even if you rely on a professional tax preparer to fill out your return, you should still draft a preliminary Form 1040 and all its applicable schedules, as well as the work sheets that you'll turn over to him. That's the only way to discipline yourself fully, to make sure you give your preparer every scrap of information he might need. If he's thorough, he'll want your backup information as well, and that's fine. But use the tax return as part of your tax strategy.

Every year, reporters in one city or another take the same data to several tax preparers, ask them to figure their income tax, and come up with a funny story about six different preparers coming up with six different tax bills. That's supposed to prove that there's no such thing as an accurate tax return. In fact, it indicates that the six preparers were given somewhat different briefings or weren't told enough and, under the pressure of time, guessed here and there. During tax season, tax preparers are swamped; yours won't have time to call you and coax additional information out of you. Use the tax return and your work sheets, and you'll be forced to come up with the information *he* needs to save *you* money.

ANATOMY OF A FORM

From the top, let's go through the tax form. We aren't going to tell you how to write your name or where to put your salary income or how to add up your deductions. We'll stick to areas that aren't obvious, where a little additional insight can help you use your Tax Savers better, lessen your chances for audit, or otherwise benefit you. For the line-by-line details, we recommend that you get a copy of *Your Federal Income Tax*, IRS Publication 17.

Page 1, Item 1: Your Occupation and Your Spouse's Occupation

From experience, the IRS has learned that people in certain lucrative, high-visibility occupations tend to be more adventurous or aggressive in their approach to income tax. Strassels made this point on *The Phil Donahue Show* a few years ago. "Who's the most likely to be audited?" Donahue asked. "You!" Strassels replied. "Because you're an entertainer!"

If you are in a high-income occupation, don't flag yourself. Many doctors, dentists, and lawyers are incorporated and can legitimately list their occupation as "corporate officer." Be general, not specific. If you are retired and living off income from stocks and bonds, you could call yourself an "investor." But we'd recommend "retired." It's more peaceful, in many ways.

This isn't a risky area. We have never heard of the IRS taking a taxpayer to task for failing to be specific about his or her occupation.

Page 1, Item 2: Filing Status

Your filing status determines which tax table or tax rate schedule you use, and that affects the amount of tax you pay. So filing status is not an item to be casual about. Most of us have no choice. But if you are single and can qualify for Head of Household or Qualifying Widow(er) status, by all means do so; you'll pay less tax. If you are married, a joint return usually saves. If for some reason you are married and file separately from your spouse, or if you are separated or divorced, make sure your return and that of your spouse or former spouse dovetail. For example, you can't both claim the same child as a dependent.

For the rest of the form, follow the bullets—the little markers like this ▶ that point to certain lines on the tax return. The IRS computers scan those lines. Make sure you have them right.

Page 1, Item 3: Income

On Business income or loss and Farm income or loss, the IRS is particularly suspicious of a net loss. In the IRS's view, too many taxpayers call their hobbies businesses or their country homes farms, so they can take a loss and reduce their taxes. For a business, the rule of thumb is that it should show a profit at least two years of every five. To the IRS, a tiny profit doesn't look suspicious. A loss does. Better to profit by, say, $100 one year and lose $5,000 the next than to lose $2,000 five years in a row. Failing that, stand ready to prove that even if your business lost money year after year, you were operating it in pursuit of profit. For more on that subject, see Chapter 9, Tax Savers for the Self-Employed.

Page 1, Item 4: Adjustments to Income

The IRS is not particularly leery of these entries individually, but its computers are trained to compare your Total Adjustments with your overall income to make sure the ratio is not suspiciously out of line. Regardless, claim all your valid adjustments—and stand ready to back them up.

That's the key to prudent use of all Tax Savers. You do not want to arouse the IRS's suspicions unnecessarily and expose yourself to audit, but you certainly do not want to overpay your taxes simply to minimize your risk of audit.

To the IRS, one of the most important items does not even appear on the tax return. It's called total positive income, and it means your gross income, not counting any adjustments, exemptions, deductions, or tax-shelter write-offs. The IRS uses your total positive income figure to determine your income class for audit selection purposes. The greater your total positive income, the greater your chance of audit. But remember, even if you're flagged, you have every opportunity to prove your case.

Page 2, Item 1: Credits
This section is a taxpayer's delight. The items tend to be small but they add up, and they are rarely questioned. These include credits for political contributions, child care, and residential energy.

Page 2, Item 2: Other Taxes
Do not ignore the Alternative Minimum Tax, particularly if you are reporting a large capital gain or are taking large tax-shelter deductions. You'll need Form 6251. The Alternative Minimum Tax was enacted by Congress in reaction to public complaints about high rollers who paid little or no income tax.

Page 2, Item 3: Payments
If you worked for more than one employer during the year, check your W-2s and add up the amounts withheld for Social Security, sometimes called FICA. If more than $2,532.60 was withheld, in total, for 1984 (the amount goes up annually, and you can get it by calling your nearest Social Security office), claim the excess under "payments."

If you hired a preparer to work out your income tax, the IRS will check to see whether he or she is on the agency's list of "problem preparers"—professionals whom the IRS considers too aggressive, let us say, in their pursuit of tax savings. If your preparer is a problem preparer, you will very likely be audited, and you will be responsible for any questionable items, whether or not you fully understood what your preparer was doing. Sorry, the IRS will not tell you whether or not your preparer is under scrutiny.

The taxpayer, not the preparer, is always personally responsible for any deficiency in a tax return. A friend of ours had a nice profit on some stock and told his broker in mid-June to sell after the first of July; by that time he would have owned the stock long enough for the profit to qualify as a long-term capital gain. But the broker erred and sold the stock immediately. Too bad, said the IRS; it was your stock, you didn't hold it long enough before selling, so your gain is short-term; you pay income tax on the entire profit. The same is true if your preparer makes an error. As far as the IRS is concerned, you're responsible.

Schedule A, Itemized Deductions

Under medical and dental expenses, the IRS tends to cast a somewhat wary eye on line 4c, where you list "other" expenses such as the cost of glasses, false teeth, or hearing aids. The same is true under taxes; the IRS looks for your "other" expenses, such as personal property tax. Under Interest Expense, if you are paying interest to another individual under a creative financing mortgage, the IRS insists that you list his or her name and address and says it will check your deduction against that person's interest income to make sure they match.

Under Contributions, gifts of property valued at $5,000 or more arouse the computer. Under the 1984 tax law, you must attach to your tax return a written appraisal by a reputable appraiser. The IRS is also on the warpath against personal churches and foundations established by taxpayers for their own benefit—transparently phony tax dodges that, for some reason, continue to crop up.

Your total deductions are more important than your individual ones. As we have said before—and will say again—you should claim each valid deduction, no matter how outlandish it may appear. The IRS's computers will compare your deductions with average, or typical, deductions taken by others in your income class. It helps to know these IRS benchmarks, and here they are for 1981 returns filed by April 15, 1982.

Adjusted Gross Income	$20,000–$25,000	$25,000–$30,000	$30,000–$40,000	$40,000–$50,000	$50,000–$75,000	$75,000–$100,000
Medical Expenses	750	650	600	550	700	850
Taxes Paid	1,700	2,000	2,500	3,300	4,400	6,600
Interest Paid	2,900	3,100	3,500	4,300	5,600	8,300
Charitable Contributions	670	700	830	1,100	1,550	2,500
Miscellaneous Deductions	500	500	600	700	1,000	1,500
Total Tax Liabilities (Approx.)	$3,100	$4,100	$5,700	$8,500	$13,400	$23,300
Total Itemized Deductions as Percentage of Adjusted Gross Income	26%	23%	21%	20%	19%	19%

Schedule B, Interest and Dividend Income

Don't forget that the IRS has received data on your interest and dividend income, just as it has been told by your employer how much you were paid and how much was withheld. (The IRS is still fuming at Congress for killing the proposed 10 percent withholding tax on interest and dividends.) So don't be sloppy. You might guess how much you spent on a minor deductible item such as nonprescription drugs, but if you guess at your dividends from a stock, you'd better guess right. Otherwise the IRS will quickly correct you.

Answer Part III, at the bottom of the page, which has to do with foreign accounts and trusts. For most of us, the answer to both questions is no. But answer anyway. Failure to do so will hold up the processing of your return.

That does not hold true of every line of your tax return. If a line does not pertain to you, you can usually leave it blank. But when you are filing a particular form or schedule that includes an entire section not applicable to you, put down a zero on the line calling for a total. Again, watch those little marks. Get those numbers right, and if a marked line has nothing to do with you, put down a zero.

Schedule C, Profit (or Loss) from Business or Profession

As we said before, the agency is particularly wary of net losses. Among your business deductions, the IRS is most likely to challenge travel and entertainment expenses, if they seem high when compared to your reported income, and office-at-home deductions.

If you use a car or truck in connection with your business, keep receipts for actual expenses—gasoline and oil, repairs, insurance, depreciation. In most cases, the business share of your actual costs will provide a larger deduction than the simple mileage allowance of 20.5 cents a mile allowed and encouraged by the IRS. (That amount is subject to change.)

Toward the bottom of Schedule C is this mysterious question for taxpayers who report a net business loss: Do you have amounts for which you are not at risk in this business? The question has to do with tax shelters, and your answer most likely is no. Don't forget to answer; if you fail to answer, the IRS may bounce your tax return back to you.

Schedule D, Capital Gains and Losses

Make sure your dates and amounts are correct. If you lack the information, try to get it from your broker. The IRS is suspicious of very round numbers, so don't pretend that you paid precisely $10,000 for stock fifteen years ago.

Form 2441, Child and Dependent Care

If you paid an individual more than $50 a quarter to care for your children or for other dependents in your home so you can work, you have to pay withholding and Social Security tax on those wages. It's a small price to pay for the tax credit you get by using this form. If your children are cared for outside your home—for example, at a day-care center or

━━━━━

a summer camp—you don't have to pay withholding or Social Security tax.

Schedule G, Income Averaging
Legend to the contrary, this Tax Saver is not complicated,
nor is it restricted to show-biz types. Get the form and
you'll see; it's one page of aggravating but simple arithmetic.

Every year, you should work through the Income Averaging form to see if it pays. If it doesn't, put the form in next
year's tax file and try again. Then, you'll be glad you saved
the figures. If you haven't tried it before, ask a tax preparer
for copies of Schedule G for each of the past three years.
(You can't use this year's form in refiguring taxes for past
years.) Work through the formula for all three years, and see
whether you could have paid less income tax by Income
Averaging. If so, file an amended return—or returns, if Income Averaging would have helped you for more than one
of those three years. In fact, Income Averaging is more
likely to have helped you in past years. Congress tightened
the rules, effective for 1984, making it more difficult to
benefit from the Income Averaging Tax Saver.

Schedule E, Supplemental Income
This form covers vacation homes and many other tax shelters, plus income from royalties, partnerships, estates,
trusts, and other sources. As with a business at home, the
IRS will welcome any net income you report here and is
unlikely to question the details. But if you report a net loss,
stand ready to prove it. When asked to name the three
items most likely to spark an audit, one IRS official re-
sponded, "Tax shelters, tax shelters, and tax shelters."
Schedule E is where they usually show up.

MORE FILING TIPS
If you hire a tax preparer, compare the tax return he prepared for you with the one you prepared for yourself as a
work sheet for him. Look for Tax Savers that he found for
you—and for errors or omissions on his part.

If you owe, make sure—dead sure—that you have enough money in your account to cover your check. The IRS used to let checks sit around, but now it deposits them promptly.

A few years ago, a neighbor bought a six-month U.S. Treasury bill in October, maturing the next April, to cover his anticipated tax bill. That's a nice Tax Saver; when you buy a Treasury bill, you get the interest immediately, but the interest isn't taxable until the bill matures, which in this case was the following year.

Smart, eh? Well, the T-bill matured, the Treasury sent our neighbor a check, and he deposited the amount in his money market mutual fund. A couple of days later he wrote a check against the mutual fund, payable to the IRS for his taxes, and mailed it in with an application for an extension of the filing deadline.

The check bounced, marked "uncollected funds." The money market fund explained that it requires two weeks clearance time for all deposits, even, as in this case, checks from the U.S. Treasury.

If a check to, say, your doctor bounced under those circumstances, you could explain it with a little chuckle. But the IRS has no sense of humor. It denied the extension of the filing deadline, imposed a penalty of 5 percent a month for filing late, tacked on a 1 percent penalty for paying with a bad check, and added interest. Under the law, our stricken taxpayer had no kick coming.

Arrange your tax return in order, first by schedule letter, then form number. Staple your W-2 form and your check to the first page. Use stamps, not a postage meter; the IRS is aware that meters can be backdated. Take it to the post office a couple of days before the deadline. Take pleasure in the Tax Savers you used and start putting new ones in place for the current year.

16

Tax Professionals

$\mathcal{B}$y now, you are probably feeling more in charge of your finances and tax situation and more aware of the Tax Savers you can use now and the ones you will want to use in the future. Nevertheless, we recommend that you consult a tax professional, at least occasionally. Depending upon your financial circumstances and your personal preferences and outlook, you should sit down with a tax professional as often as four times a year or as infrequently as once every three years. We believe in self-help taxpaying—and tax saving—but no layman can keep on top of every detail of tax law, much less every change. The 1984 Tax Reform Act was the eighth major package of tax-law changes enacted by Congress in the past ten years. Even before President Reagan signed that bill into law, leaders in Congress and the administration were talking of further changes. So all of us need to lean on a tax professional now and then.

Among tax professionals, some are *tax advisers*. Others are *tax-return preparers*.

A good tax adviser will look over your tax returns for past years, talk with you about your prospects and your tax and financial goals, and recommend appropriate Tax Savers. This book is a tax adviser of sorts; we tailored its chapters to fit individual circumstances. If you want and need tax advice on an even more individualized basis, by all means hire a good tax adviser. To make good use of an adviser, see him on a regular basis. Ideally, make it four times a year. In Chapter 3, we outline our recommended four-looks-a-year program for year-long tax planning.

A tax preparer is just that—someone who fills out tax returns. Once you bring him your records and receipts in, say, February or March, it won't do much good for him to tell you what you should have done the previous November to reduce your taxes. All he can do is prepare your return on the basis of the information you supplied. Of course, you can learn from his work, and if he has good ideas, you can apply them for subsequent years.

Most tax preparers will promise to accompany you to an audit, and most will promise to pay any penalties and interest that are their fault—those assessed by the IRS because of an error in the preparation of your return.

Two points here are important to keep in mind: First, ask your preparer about his policy on audit representation and on paying penalties and interest. Second, remember that no preparer we've ever heard of will take care of penalties and interest if the taxpayer has supplied incomplete or inaccurate information. In other words, if you fail to tell the preparer about all your income, and the IRS later calls you in, you should not expect the preparer to pay your fine.

It is up to you to make sure that your tax preparer takes full advantage of all the Tax Savers you have put in place. That's your job; don't leave it to him. For one thing, he probably won't know about all of them unless you tell him. For another, a tax preparer doesn't have the time or the inclination to scratch around looking for every possible way to cut your tax bill. He's preparing hundreds of returns during a very tight and hectic tax filing season.

Too often, taxpayers make their preparers work at cross purposes with them. They want their taxes kept to the absolute minimum, but they don't want to risk an audit. No one can have it both ways.

If you want at all costs to avoid an audit, you'll most likely end up overpaying your taxes. If you want to keep your taxes down, your audit risk will go up. Preparers rarely bill clients at a full rate for time spent representing them during an audit of a return they prepared; they feel clients would consider a big bill to be heaping insult on top of injury. That's one of a number of reasons that so many preparers tend to be quite conservative—perhaps more conservative than you would like yours to be.

By following the advice and recommendations in this book, you will be playing a big part in handling your taxes. When you do take your returns to a good professional, ask the professional to look over your returns for the past three years and see if you may have missed any Tax Savers that were available to you. If so, amended returns may be in order. Generally, you can send in amended tax forms for the three previous years. You can't amend a return that's older than that because of the three-year statute of limitations; neither can the IRS go after a return that is more than three years old except in the most extraordinary circumstances.

Your need for a tax professional is determined more by the complexity of your financial affairs than by the size of your income. Even if you have an income of $150,000 a year, preparing your tax return can be a cut-and-dried affair, although an income in that range certainly suggests opportunities for Tax Savers. On the other hand, we know of fledgling entrepreneurs who struggle to net $25,000 after expenses, yet have fairly complicated tax returns and tax plans.

You may need a tax professional who deals regularly with others in your particular line of work. For example, Strassels appears regularly on television, and as a result, TV people often ask him, off-camera of course, how they can personally save on taxes in connection with video equipment they buy on their own, special wardrobes, and travel. One TV news director has gone so far as to equip his camper with sophisticated receiving equipment so he can monitor all three networks even when he is in the wild. Many occupations raise specific questions like these. A tax professional familiar with particular situations that arise in your line of work can be invaluable.

WHAT TO LOOK FOR

We use the term "tax professional" because it describes what you are looking for—someone who devotes his or her career to helping people with their taxes. A good tax professional may or may not have an impressive degree. What's most important is his skill, his philosophy, and whether he makes his living helping people like you with their taxes.

For example, Strassels' brother is an excellent and successful certified public accountant, but we don't recommend him to friends seeking tax help because he doesn't specialize in taxes. His field is management accounting, planning, and troubleshooting work for small businesses. CPAs can specialize in many different areas besides taxes. In fact, many won't even prepare their own taxes, much less anyone else's. They go to a tax specialist.

Anyway, unless your affairs are very complex—for example, if you are running a complicated business venture or investing in delicate tax shelters—you probably don't need a CPA, much less a tax attorney. Both tend to charge high fees, and there's no sense in paying more than you need to. To be sure, the income tax laws and regulations are complicated. But you don't need a particular degree to understand them.

It's not difficult for a person to call himself a tax expert and hang out a shingle. So how do you choose a good tax professional? We recommend that you ask friends and colleagues. You want someone who handles taxes for individuals or families whose income and circumstances are much like yours. If your family income is primarily from wages and amounts to, say, $40,000 a year, don't ask your millionaire boss whom he uses for tax help. A co-worker or neighbor would be more appropriate. In fact, ask several people whose income you estimate is close to yours and whose judgment you respect. Another person to ask is someone who makes less than you do but lives better. That's the one who may have discovered how to apply Tax Savers—or has a tax professional who knows how.

Philosophy is also important. If you are conservative by

nature, you won't want a tax professional who will try to steer you into speculative tax shelters. If you are willing to accept risk in exchange for potential financial rewards, you won't want a tax consultant who dedicates his life to avoiding disagreements and conflicts with the IRS.

Besides lawyers and CPAs, there are others who work as tax professionals. The label doesn't tell everything, but it helps.

Enrolled agents

Far and away the best pond to fish in as you look for good, solid professional help. To become an agent enrolled to practice taxes before the IRS, a person has to pass a difficult test on the federal income tax, administered by the IRS. As with any other profession, some are good, some are bad, and some are indifferent. But all of them at least went to the trouble to learn about the income tax laws and have passed an examination. Chances are they are full-time tax professionals. How do you find one? Check the yellow pages, now that they are permitted to advertise their services. Look under Tax Preparers.

Public accountants

People with undergraduate accounting degrees. That's plenty of education to provide a good foundation for tax work, and many public accountants are superb tax professionals. Some of them have gone to the additional trouble of becoming enrolled agents. On the other hand, some may not know any more than you do about income taxes. They may, like many CPAs, specialize in other areas of accounting.

Former IRS agents

Many former IRS agents switch to the other side. Strassels got his training by spending five years as a tax-law specialist with the IRS. Former employees generally have a pretty fair understanding of the laws and regulations, and many have become excellent tax professionals on the outside. However, some cannot bring themselves to go against their training and advocate a taxpayer's interests over the IRS's.

To its credit, the IRS is an agency with a very strong sense of mission. Many former agents retain that feeling, making it difficult for them to use (we didn't say *twist*) the laws and regulations to produce Tax Savers for their clients.

Unaffiliated individuals

These people have no degree or certificate, but they have become tax professionals nevertheless. The lack of a degree, specialized experience, or training should sound a note of caution on your part. However, if an unaffiliated individual is strongly recommended to you, you should talk with him. If you like him, you should consider using his services. Mead's father ran his own successful small business for years, and along the way he became adept at preparing its tax returns. After he retired, he began to handle tax work for other small businesses. Almost by accident, he had become an "unaffiliated individual," specializing in the tax matters of small firms. And he was darned good at it.

Storefront preparers

Many of these are chain operations. The preparers generally do an adequate job of filling out relatively straightforward, basic returns. They do their job quickly and in great volume. And they are inexpensive. They are strictly preparers, not advisers.

YEAR-ROUND PROS

Whatever classification of tax professional you choose, we think you should make sure he or she is in the tax business year-round and available to you in case of an audit. In fact, the worst time to look for a tax professional is during the tax filing season. That's when the best ones are too busy to sit down for the kind of get-acquainted interview that both of you need to establish a working relationship. The good tax professionals have a year-to-year clientele, and they may not have time to add someone coming in off the street.

If you are reading this during tax filing season and are looking for a tax professional, you may find that the best way to accomplish this is to agree to file for an automatic four-month extension of time to get your return in for this year. That way, your newly acquired tax adviser will have sufficient time to review your tax situation after the traditional April 15 filing deadline.

Ideally, look for your tax pro between May and November. The professionals you interview will appreciate your consideration, and, more importantly, they will have the time to go over your financial situation in detail.

SALESPEOPLE

These days, unfortunately, many tax professionals double as investment brokers, tax-shelter salespeople, and financial planners. Tax-shelter promoters bombard tax pros with literature about their offerings, hoping the tax people will steer their clients toward the investment. Often, the tax pros collect healthy commissions for selling tax shelters to clients.

Frankly, we consider that to be bad form—a conflict of interest. Before you sign up with a tax professional, tell him that you'll welcome his advice on Tax Savers, including recommendations about various shelters, but that you would prefer to keep your investments separate from your taxes. You'll buy shelters from someone else. Any decent and honest tax professional will understand that.

By the same token, don't let your stockbroker become your tax adviser. Brokers hawk tax shelters. Don't let a broker pretend that he knows what you need by way of Tax Savers. It's your job to decide that, perhaps with the aid of a tax professional. No one knows your affairs as well as you do, or cares as much. Buy advice if you want to, but keep your advisers in their respective places. Tax advisers talk about taxes, investment advisers about investments.

As you interview prospective tax professionals, here are some red flags to look out for:

1. If he hints that he'll get you in on some mysterious-sounding deal, he's softening you up so he can sell you a tax shelter.
2. If he makes your tax situation sound so complicated that only he and other supernatural beings can deal with

it, he's blowing smoke. It's his job to explain your taxes to you so you understand them and participate in handling them.

3. If he promises that he will keep you from getting audited, he's really saying that he will decide each and every issue in the IRS's favor, not yours. Ask yourself whom your tax preparer is working for—you or the IRS. Furthermore, he's lying; some returns are audited strictly at random.

4. If he guarantees an annual refund, he's advocating a foolish tax plan. As we've said before, you and the IRS should break even at the end of the year, or you should end up owing a little. The larger your refund, the poorer your tax planning.

These days, many tax preparers don't actually prepare your return. Computers do that job. Preparers who use computers have become detailed interviewers. They take the information, organize it, and turn it over to a computerized tax preparation company.

That's perfectly okay. Actually, there are even some advantages. For example, the computers are programmed automatically to try certain Tax Savers that a preparer may be too busy to use, such as Income Averaging. Although a tax preparer should be meticulous, the pressure of the filing deadline might cause a Tax Saver to be missed now and then.

If your tax pro does use a computer and an error shows up on your return, don't let him blame the computer. That's part of the service he's selling.

There are no hard-and-fast rules on the cost of tax advice or tax-return preparation. But the more work you do on your taxes yourself, the less time your tax professional will have to devote to mundane bookkeeping tasks and organization. He can spend more time on Tax Savers, and less time filling out your return. It's just another example of the advantages of taking charge of your own finances and your income taxes. And remember: The expense of hiring a tax professional is deductible.

17

Cash In Your Old Tax Returns

$\mathcal{A}$ s you have read this book, you've probably kicked yourself for failing to take advantage of our Tax Savers in past years. Good news: You may get to reach back and make use of some of them after all.

You are allowed to file an amended federal income tax return for any (or all) of the past three years. The tax form is called 1040X, Amended Return. It runs a single page, front and back. Honestly, it's not complicated. You simply explain why you are amending your return—the Form 1040X gives you a big blank space for that. In three columns, you list first the figures you reported on your original tax return, second the change—perhaps a deduction that you overlooked—and third the new correct amount. You attach the appropriate forms and schedules (for example, Schedule A, Itemized Deductions), and you sign the 1040X and mail it in. The IRS will scan your amended return to make sure it looks all right. Assuming it passes muster, and most of them do, the IRS will mail you a check for the amount you are claiming.

The amended return is one of the most widely overlooked Tax Savers in America. If every taxpayer reviewed his or her tax returns for the past three years and claimed every dollar that he had overlooked the first time around, it would amount to a raid on the U.S. Treasury.

But that isn't likely to happen, for a number of reasons. Most people don't know they can amend old returns. Of those who do, many never get around to it. And still others fear that an amended return would arouse the suspicions of the IRS and spark an audit.

FEAR OF AUDIT

Let's deal first with that fear. To the IRS, an amended return is routine. Sophisticated taxpayers file them all the time. Assuming your claim is valid and your form is filled out properly, you will be paid without question. You will not be pegged for an audit because you file an amended return. Of course, if your amended return makes a claim that looks suspicious or unusual, you might indeed get audited; that's true of any tax return you file. If your claim on an amended return fails to pass muster, the IRS most likely will just turn you down. There is nothing about the act of filing an amended return that raises your audit profile. In fact, you can amend your return for a past year time after time if necessary. The idea is to report your income and deductions accurately. If it takes more than once, so be it. And if each claim looks right, you'll get your money.

Look at it this way. If you worked for the IRS, you certainly would be fully aware of how complicated our income tax system is, how often the rules change, and how difficult the tax forms are for most citizens. You would know that taxpayers make mistakes and miss opportunities for Tax Savers. Knowing all that, you wouldn't get suspicious when a taxpayer caught up with himself and filed an amended return. You would probably wonder why more taxpayers didn't do the same.

FINDING THE NUGGETS

Looking for Tax Savers in old returns can be like looking for nuggets at an old mine; the untrained eye has a hard time telling gold from worthless rock. Besides, there's that problem of finding the time. That's why we're advocating that you spend more time on your taxes, and we hope we've convinced you that you'll be well paid for every minute you spend. But for some of you, poring over returns from years past may be a bit much.

For those reasons, we recommend that you go to a tax professional at least once every three years. Bring him or her the tax forms you've just prepared, with the backup data, as we outlined in Chapter 16. At the same time, bring your tax returns for the past three years. By following our Tax Savers, you've provided a thorough picture of your tax situation. Knowing that, the professional can quickly look over your past returns and determine whether it would be worthwhile to amend your tax returns for any—or all—of the past three years. Bring along your state and local income tax returns, too. In many cases, if you have a valid reason to get money back on an old federal income tax return, it will apply also to your state and local income taxes, since most states and localities gear their tax formulas to the federal system. So you can shine up that old Tax Saver and cash it in twice or even three times.

By all means suggest to your tax pro areas in which you think an amended return might be worthwhile. In fact, if you see an opportunity on your own to amend a past return, do it; you certainly don't need to wait three years. Use your tax professional as a fail-safe measure. Even if you've filed amended returns on your own, let him look over your return and your amended return before the opportunity expires to file one last amendment.

THREE-YEAR LIMIT

The precise rule is that you can file an amended return within three years from the date you filed your original return, or within two years from the time you paid your tax, whichever is later. A return filed early is considered to be filed on its due date, usually April 15.

So your 1981 tax return was due April 15, 1982, and can be amended as late as April 15, 1985. If for that year you filed a Form 4868 for an automatic extension of time (now four months, but then two months), then the deadline for an amended return is three years from that extended deadline. For your 1981 tax return, the extended deadline for filing an amended return is June 15, 1985. For your 1982 return, and returns filed thereafter, Form 4868 provides a four-month extension of time for filing. So, the extended deadline for filing amended returns is August 15, three years after the due date—for example, August 15, 1988, for your 1984 return.

Incidentally, you and the IRS have the same deadline for getting back at each other. If the IRS wants to audit a past return of yours, it has to let you know within three years. The specific dates are just like those for amended returns, outlined above.

You cannot go back and take tax-saving steps retroactively. For example, say you intended to invest $2,000 in an Individual Retirement Account for 1982, the first year it was available to all workers. But you didn't get around to it. You are not permitted to make that contribution at this late date, designate it for 1982, file an amended return, and receive a refund.

Nevertheless, lots of Tax Savers can be found. Here are the best and most common ones:

1. Did you use either of the short forms,
1040A or 1040EZ?

If so, you probably paid more taxes than you had to. See if you could have saved by filing the long form, 1040. If the answer is yes, file an amended return. For example, could you have reduced your taxes by itemizing deductions on Schedule A? Could you have claimed moving expenses in connection with your line of work or job-related expenses for which your employer did not reimburse you? Did you buy storm windows, insulate your house, or take any other steps that might qualify you for the residential energy credit? All of these are good Tax Savers, and you can use them now, for past years, by filing amended returns.

2. Did you try Income Averaging?

It can never cost you money to try this Tax Saver, and if you didn't work out the formulas for those three past years, you should do it now, or have your tax pro do it. You'll need your income tax returns going back four years plus the return you're reviewing. For example, if you're checking to see whether you could have saved by filing Schedule G (the Income-Averaging form) for, say, 1983, you'll need your tax returns for 1983, 1982, 1981, 1980, and 1979. You don't have to send in those old returns, but Schedule G requires you to list numbers copied from them. Beginning with 1984 tax returns, you can average only four years, not five.

3. Did you and your spouse file separate tax returns?

In most cases, a joint return saves you money. Even if you didn't get married until December 31, you can file a joint income tax return covering that entire year. So if you and your spouse filed separately, work out a joint return and see if it would have cut your tax bill. If so, file an amended return. (If you filed jointly, you cannot amend and switch to separate returns. But you can switch from separate to joint, and usually a joint return is to your advantage.)

4. Did you take full advantage of the deduction for sales tax?

Sure, you probably looked in the table that's printed in the tax instructions and deducted the amount listed under your adjusted gross income level. If you stopped there, you probably cheated yourself. Let's say you own municipal bonds that pay you $2,000 a year in tax-exempt interest. In addition, you sold some stock or a piece of land at a long-term capital gain of $10,000. Even though your municipal bond interest doesn't even appear on your income tax return, you should add it to your adjusted gross income to get the total income figure that you use when referring to the sales tax table in the instructions. You can also add the untaxed portion of your capital gain. Only 40 percent of that profit was taxed. So you've got $2,000 in bond interest and $6,000 in untaxed capital gains—$8,000 worth of income, all of it qualifying for the sales tax deduction. Look in the table and see what that's worth. (The amount varies, depending upon the sales tax in your state or city.) It's almost surely worth the time and trouble of filing an amended tax return.

Other examples of unreported income to add in for sales tax computation purposes include untaxed Social Security payments, veterans' benefits, workmen's compensation, the dividend exclusion, and even the untaxed part of unemployment compensation. Along the same lines, you can deduct the sales tax you paid on big-ticket purchases such as cars, trucks, motor homes, motorcycles, boats, even the building materials for a new home.

5. Did you keep up with the changes in the tax law?

Here's a Tax Saver that illustrates the capriciousness of the tax law and the reason it's wise to lean on a tax professional at least occasionally. Let's say you have belonged to the same social, athletic, or sports club for years, using it mostly—but not entirely—in connection with your business. At one time, dues and fees paid to these clubs were not deductible under any circumstances. Then, Congress changed the law—retroactively—to make legitimate business expenses deductible. To get that deduction for past years, you would have to file amended tax returns.

FORM 1040X

The Form 1040X doesn't change from year to year. You just fill in a blank stating the year for which you're amending your old return. That's important. You have to attach the forms or schedules that provide the details of the amendment. Those do change from year to year, and you have to use the forms or schedules that were printed for the year you're amending. For example, if you're amending your 1982 tax return in order to take advantage of Income Averaging, you have to attach Schedule G for 1982—not Schedule G that the IRS distributes for the year just past.

You also have to know the tax law that was in effect for that past year, and remember, *the law changes*. Let's say you neglected to take advantage of the deduction granted to married couples when both work. Well, in 1981 that deduction didn't even exist. In 1982 it was pegged at 5 percent of the secondary salary—your salary or your spouse's, whichever was lower—with a maximum deduction of $1,500. In 1983 the deduction was raised to 10 percent of the secondary salary, with a maximum deduction of $3,000. That's where it stands now—unless Congress has changed the law since we wrote this book.

Do people really neglect to take advantage of Tax Savers like that? You bet. The IRS surveyed use of that very deduction for 1982 and found that 15 percent of married couples who qualified for the deduction didn't take it. No, the IRS did not tell them about it. But we are telling them, and until April 15, 1986, all of them can reach back and get that deduction by filing amended returns.

In addition to knowing the old tax law, you have to know the old tax rates. You wind up Form 1040X, your amended return, by figuring what your income tax should have been, taking the amendments into account. And you can't do that unless you have the tax tables or tax rate schedules for that year. They, too, change frequently. How frequently? Well, they changed in 1981, again in 1982, yet again in 1983, and—yes!—also in 1984.

Your friendly regional IRS office probably does not have this past material for you. In most cases, it will tell you that it does not have the past forms, the past instructions, or the past tax rates. But tax professionals keep them—another reason to lean on your tax pro for this one important part of your Tax Saver strategy.

From now on, you should keep old forms. When you finish your tax return for the previous year, you file away a copy of your tax return, along with records, receipts, and other pertinent papers. Add to that file a complete batch of blank tax forms for that year, a copy of instructions that accompanied the forms, the tax tables, and a copy of *Your Federal Income Tax*, IRS Publication 17. You may never need them, but if you get a chance to reach back and pull some money out of those musty old tax returns, having the forms, instructions, and tax tables will help.

18

Surviving an Audit

$\mathscr{P}$ icture this situation: Your income tax return is completed, signed, sealed, and ready to be mailed. Now think about how you feel. If you are a typical taxpayer, you are left with one overriding fear: Is the IRS going to audit this return?

That fear—not the audit itself but the fear of being audited—is the IRS's most effective enforcement weapon. It is also the taxpayer's greatest enemy—in two ways. First, in planning their taxes and preparing their returns, many people purposely skip legitimate Tax Savers. You'll hear them say, "I won't take this deduction because I don't want a hassle with the IRS," or words to that effect. They are intimidated by the possibility of an audit. To avoid one, they will even overpay their tax.

Don't do that. Take advantage of every Tax Saver that's coming to you. Just keep records to support your claims.

As we described in Chapter 15, we suggest that you prepare two tax returns, one resolving every gray area in the IRS's favor, the other resolving gray areas in your favor. Then compare the two. The difference is probably the most you could lose in an audit. In most cases, the amount is surprisingly small. Go ahead and file the second return—

the one claiming all your Tax Savers. You'll know precisely how much money is at stake. The unknown fear will be replaced by a known and manageable amount.

Many taxpayers go into their audits ready to give away the store. They're scared. Big Brother is confronting them, demanding money, accusing them of cheating. They fear they'll be thrown in jail. They pay, almost eagerly, even if they know the IRS's position is wrong. They'll do anything to send the auditor away with a smile.

Don't fall into that trap. An audit is no fun, but it rarely implies a threat of criminal prosecution. An audit simply means that the IRS thinks you might have underpaid your taxes and is asking you to prove otherwise—or pay up. To the IRS, your audit is routine. The more you exaggerate in your mind its clout and intention, the less likely you are to handle the audit coolly and methodically. And that's too bad, because a cool and methodical taxpayer is the most likely to come out of an audit unscathed. Believe it or not, 25 percent of taxpayers who are audited come out clean— owing nothing more or, in some cases, getting an additional refund.

To remain cool and methodical you have to control your emotions, and fear is not the only emotion aroused by an audit notice. Many taxpayers react with anger. They interpret an audit notice as a personal affront, an assault on their integrity. They bellow that the IRS has singled them out—an honest little guy like me!—while letting millionaires and multinational corporations get by. They resolve to show up the auditor, to strike a blow for the rights of the tormented middle class. They'll fight all the way to the Supreme Court for the principle at stake.

An angry reaction is even more harmful than a timid one. Shout around the house, complain to your neighbors, growl at the cat. But when it comes to dealing with the reality of an audit, take things calmly and coolly. Resolve to get your audit over with as quickly and as easily as you can, at the lowest possible cost and with a minimum of anguish.

WHY YOU'RE AUDITED

Virtually every taxpayer who receives an audit notice wonders why. In perhaps 75 percent of all cases, an audit notice means that something on your tax return triggered a response in the IRS's computers, which are programmed to catch variations that exceed the norms. Maybe your itemized deduction for contributions to charity significantly exceeded the average for people of your income range (see the average itemized deductions, by income class, on page 237). Perhaps you used Tax Savers to shelter a substantial proportion of your income. Neither of these is illegal, but they may be unusual enough so that the IRS wants you to prove them.

Never—absolutely never—will the IRS audit you because your deductions were unusually small or because you failed to avail yourself of Tax Savers that would have reduced your tax bill. The IRS is in the business of collecting taxes and enforcing our system of voluntary self-assessment. It is not responsible for keeping your tax bill to a minimum. That responsibility is yours.

Your audit notice may provide you clues as to why your return was selected. Most audit notices list the items that the IRS is questioning and ask you to bring along records that support those items. Even so, you might sometimes wonder why the IRS singled you out or singled out a particular item on your tax return. You might never find out. Some audits are part of IRS surveys. Some returns are selected strictly at random.

But most result from a pretty sophisticated classification system that concentrates on tax returns most likely to yield the government significant amounts of additional money. The audit selection system has to be sophisticated to make up for the small number of returns that are actually audited. Most Americans don't know it, and the IRS would just as soon it remain that way, but the IRS audits a smaller percentage of returns every year. When Strassels joined the IRS in 1970, the agency was auditing nearly 2 percent of all individual income tax returns. Now only 1.5 percent are being audited.

But the IRS is now much better at selecting promising returns than it was ten or fifteen years ago, thanks to the sophistication of computers. Fewer returns are picked at random. The IRS concentrates more on people with high incomes and complex financial affairs. It has also developed a more accurate method based on real income levels. The computers used to scan your adjusted gross income, listed at the bottom of page 1 of Form 1040. Now instead it computes a figure that the IRS calls total positive income. That means all your income, before deductions and exemptions. Why the change? Because a high roller with large tax-shelter investments might wind up with the same modest adjusted gross income as a wage earner with no outside income. Now the computers hone in on people who take in large incomes, regardless of how well they use Tax Savers to shrink it on their tax returns.

YOUR AUDIT PROFILE

Three things raise your likelihood of being audited—what we call your audit profile. One is illegal tax protest—arguing on your return that the government has no right to tax your income. The second is to invest in tax shelters that the IRS determines to be "abusive." That means shelters that provide a much larger tax deduction than your investment and that seem designed purely for tax savings rather than for legitimate investment. The third is a high income, from whatever sources. We recommend that you avoid illegal tax protest and abusive shelters. As for a high income, by all means go after it and use legitimate Tax Savers to lessen the tax bite. But if you attain a high income, you must be all the more prepared for an audit.

Even among these ripest of candidates, however, relatively few are audited. If your income is $50,000 or less, your chances of being audited are about 1 in 25. If your income is $100,000 or less, your chances aren't that much higher—1 in 17. Even if you are heavily invested in tax

shelters, your chances are a mere 1 in 4. Only those identi-
fied as illegal tax protesters face a 100 percent audit risk.

But the possibility of an audit exists for everyone every
year, and you would be foolish to gamble on getting by
without one forever. To maintain its presence—to preserve
that widespread fear that serves it so well—the IRS audits
at least some returns from every income level. Even a few
short forms are audited. No taxpayer, in any category, at
any level of income, can safely assume that he or she is
immune from audit.

CHEATING

Let's be straightforward about the delicate subject of cheating on your tax return. In the overwhelming majority of
cases, the IRS calls for an audit in hopes of collecting more
taxes. No criminal activity is suspected. But if you are
caught in outright cheating—particularly in deliberately
failing to report a significant amount of income—the IRS
will not hesitate to put on its police hat and prosecute you.
We almost hate to bring that up. For one thing, we assume
you're honest, and for another we want to calm your fears,
not arouse them. But we don't want you to have any false
illusions either.

ANTICIPATE AN AUDIT

To make sure an audit will not upset you, financially or
emotionally, we recommend that you assume, every year,
that your tax return will indeed be audited. That means you
have to take the proper precautions, of which we emphasize
three: (1) Keep records, (2) keep records, (3) and keep
records.

Auditors tend to be unimpressed by taxpayers' arguments unless they are supported by records. That means
receipts, checkbook stubs, canceled checks, financial statements, W-2 and 1099 forms, personal and business calendars—anything that supports the figures listed on the tax
returns. In Chapter 2, we outline a simple record-keeping
system.

An audit normally is a civil proceeding, and the burden of proof is on you. We have reviewed hundreds of cases in which the courts have ruled in favor of the IRS and against the taxpayer, solely because the taxpayer lacked records to support his or her Tax Savers.

If you're audited, you will need those records to refresh your own memory, as well as to persuade the auditor. By the time a tax return is selected for audit, it's old stuff, largely forgotten. The process of picking returns for audit takes the IRS a year or so. For example, if you get an audit notice in mid-1985, it will almost surely be to check your 1983 return. You filed that return fifteen months earlier, and it covered events that occurred the year before that. The actual financial events can be two and a half years old. You can't depend on your memory to reconstruct the happenings of that year. Your auditor won't believe you, and you're likely to forget, or to confuse that year with the following or preceding years. Depend instead upon your written records. Without them you're stuck, both in putting together your case and in proving it to the IRS.

REACTING TO YOUR AUDIT
Even for the taxpayer who considers himself well-prepared, an audit notice is unsettling. It arrives suddenly in the mail, and it is a stiff, formal letter, usually one page printed on both the front and back. The language is firm—very official and bureaucratic. You are instructed to appear for audit and to bring records bearing on the areas checked—perhaps your charity and interest deductions, or the deductions that resulted from your investment in a tax shelter, or both.

Put aside your emotions and resolve to play by the IRS's rules. You really have no choice. It is very unlikely that you can persuade the IRS to cancel the audit. One exception: If you were audited on the same issue last year or the year before and got the issue resolved in your favor, by all means write to the IRS and remind them. If this year's questions look like more of the same, your audit may be canceled.

Otherwise, grit your teeth and cooperate, and don't let fear or anger affect your response. You will have to go through the audit. If you refuse, you face serious trouble. The tax laws give you every opportunity to prove your case, and even to appeal the auditor's findings if you disagree, but if you resort to outright stubborn resistance, the IRS will pin you to the mat. The agency has extraordinary powers. It can garnishee your wages, even sell your house and other possessions, without proving you owe as much as 10 cents. In a test of wills or a test of power you will lose. We all occasionally read stories about taxpayers who are devoting their lives to a bitter contest with the IRS. Well, the tax agency will outlive them, and it almost surely will get what it wants from them.

We recommend that you hire a tax professional to work with you in preparing for your audit, as well as to represent you at the audit itself. The fee is money well spent; besides, it's deductible. Of course, you can do your preaudit planning alone, and you can walk in unattended, but we think you shouldn't unless you can answer yes to each of these three questions:

1. Have you been audited before? It takes experience to handle an audit smoothly.
2. Are you absolutely sure that you can prove every item questioned in your audit notice? If there is any doubt, you're better off with a professional preparing and arguing your case.
3. Can you go through an audit with a cool head and an impersonal attitude? The auditor won't go in angry, but if you are hostile, he or she is likely to react in kind. That's no way to win the close points.

If a professional prepared your tax return and you are satisfied with his work, call him and ask him to represent you. Many storefront tax preparers say that they will accompany you to an audit, but not as your legal representative. That's not good enough. If the preparer isn't your legal representative, the auditor won't let him speak in your behalf. You'll have to answer the important questions. You want someone who can speak for you.

If you prepared your own tax return, or if you are not satisfied with the professional who prepared it, hire someone else. Get recommendations from friends or colleagues whose income and financial philosophy are much like yours. A tax professional will not be surprised to be brought in at this stage, but you'll have to spend time bringing him up-to-date on your tax situation.

An important point to note here: Don't feel that the preparer who filled out the tax return necessarily did an incompetent job simply because you're being audited. In fact, the opposite may be true—returns that are never challenged are probably prepared too much in the IRS's favor. An audited return, on the other hand, could mean that the preparer is calling the close ones in your behalf.

However, if the IRS is looking at your return because of extreme positions taken on tax issues, or because of negligent work on your preparer's part, then by all means go elsewhere.

THREE KINDS OF AUDITS

While the precise reason your return has been picked for audit doesn't make a great deal of difference at this point, the type of audit you will be undergoing does. Essentially, the IRS conducts three kinds of audits, each one implying a greater degree of severity than the one before. You can usually tell which one you are involved in from your audit notice itself.

1. Correspondence audits

In relatively simple cases with no more than a few thousand dollars at stake, the IRS may send you a notice asking you to reply by mail rather than appear in person. These notices usually include work sheets detailing the items that the IRS is challenging and automatically claiming additional amounts of tax for each one. The IRS always assumes you owe unless you prove otherwise. You are invited to reply, to pay up, or to enclose verifying receipts and other records.

The notice will tell you that if you would prefer to be audited face-to-face, you can be. Just call or write, it will say. It even gives you the name and phone number of someone to call. That sounds chummy, but it is not. In fact, you almost surely will not be able to reach that person by phone, and if you ask for a face-to-face audit, your request will almost surely be ignored. The IRS won't flatly say no; the rules supposedly grant you the right to an audit in person. Instead, the IRS will send you a deficiency notice, telling you to pay within a certain period of time—usually ninety days—unless you can first explain why you should not. And the explanation, you will be told, had better be mailed.

Mead recently went through this frustrating experience. He ended up pounding his desk, cursing his fate—and finally replying by mail. Once he had done so, he realized that it was a safer procedure for him anyway. In a correspondence audit, you can carefully phrase your response. An auditor isn't present to surprise you with loaded questions, and there is no danger that you will say something that might harm your case.

Even if you write your own reply and pack up your own receipts, funnel it through your tax professional. He can review material, make additions or changes if necessary, and be in a position to back up your word that you did indeed respond to the IRS. The IRS is notoriously slow in acknowledging receipt of your material. Even if you send your material by certified mail, the IRS can contend that your receipt shows only that it received an envelope from you; the receipt says nothing about the contents. Keep a copy of everything you send to the IRS and a log of any telephone conversations. Get the name of the person you talk to and note the time and substance of the conversation.

It's not impossible for the deficiency deadline to pass while your material is still sitting in some clerk's in-basket. Keep pressing the IRS, by mail, until your case is resolved.

2. Office audits

Most audits of individual taxpayers are held at one of the IRS's numerous local offices. Your audit notice will give you the address, suggest a date and time, and offer you the opportunity to choose an alternate date and time more convenient for you. Feel free to do so, but don't use this right as an excuse to postpone your audit indefinitely or to change the time repeatedly. Find a time that's mutually convenient. After all, you need time to prepare for the confrontation. You can postpone your audit meeting for a month or six weeks with no problem.

You can expect to deal with an auditor of limited experience who will ask you to verify a handful of items on your return. Office audits usually cover the basics, not highly complex areas. In most situations, office audits are routine, causing few serious problems.

3. Field audits

These tend to be the most detailed audits with the most money at stake, although that is not always the case; some random audits of short-form tax returns can be held in the field.

Your auditor will be a revenue agent—a more experienced and higher ranking official than those who handle office or correspondence audits. "Field" usually means at your home or someplace else you suggest. We recommend that you try to hold it at the office of your tax professional—a neutral site for you and the auditor, and the home ground of the person on whom you will be depending to carry the case in your favor.

No matter where the field audit is held, the auditor may want to come to your house. In fact, he may insist upon doing so. If he does, he will be checking whether your lifestyle is consistent with your tax return. If you are claiming three children as dependents, where are the toys and bicycles? If you are reporting only $25,000 in income, how did you come to own two Mercedes?

Strassels was summoned for a field audit a couple of years ago, without being told what part of his tax return looked questionable. Even with his background, he was apprehensive, and his wife was downright nervous. The auditor recognized him as a former IRS tax-law specialist who had become a writer and television spokesman specializing in taxes.

But none of this made the audit procedure unfair or particularly difficult. As things turned out, the auditor didn't bother checking deductions; he was interested only in making sure Strassels had reported all of his income. The session was held at the office of Strassels' accountant, and it lasted two hours. It was followed by this impersonal form letter, the kind all taxpayers would like to get after an audit:

Internal Revenue Service
District Director

Department of the Treasury

Date:

Return Form Number:
1040

Tax Periods Ended:
8012

Person to Contact:
W. Kachinsky

Contact Telephone Number:
703-756-6668

We are pleased to tell you that our examination of your tax returns for the above periods shows no change is required in the tax reported. Your returns are accepted as filed.

If you have any questions, please contact the person whose name and telephone number are shown above.

Thank you for your cooperation.

Sincerely yours,

Charles E. Roddy

District Director

400 N. 8th St., Richmond, VA

PREPARING FOR AN AUDIT

Whether you are facing a correspondence, office, or field audit, your preparations will be the same. They must be thorough. The audit notice will tell you the areas at issue, but in fact the IRS has the right to challenge anything in your return.

Few taxpayers know it, but they have the same right. During the audit, you can claim Tax Savers that you may have failed to include on the tax return when it was originally filed. If you have the evidence to back them up, the auditor will allow them. They certainly make for a nice bargaining chip. Some taxpayers emerge from an audit smiling, with a net gain, using this strategy.

So you and your tax professional should go over your entire tax return. Show him the records that support the items at issue and listen to his advice. He may suggest that you yield, at least partially, on some issues, while holding fast on others. If you lack documentation of some important items, now is the time to get it. For example, let's say you deducted the costs of attending a business convention, but have nothing to prove that your time was indeed spent on business. Get a copy of the convention program or a letter from a colleague or organizer summarizing your business activities while you were there. Whatever the issue, don't let recent changes in the tax laws confuse you. Remember, for the audit, you're working under the laws that were in force two years before.

You have to remember that the audit process is entirely impersonal and that errors and misunderstandings are bound to crop up in a tax system as detailed and complex as ours. Don't focus on the idiocy or frustration of your problems; focus instead on their prospective cost. For example, if it appears that your audit will primarily involve $1,000 in deductions, calculate how much tax you will have to pay if the auditor refuses to allow a single dollar of the thousand. If you are in the 35 percent tax bracket, the amount at stake is $350. Are the time, effort, and frustration you would have to spend trying to obtain documentation for those deductions worth more or less than $350? If your time is more valuable, go into your audit prepared to yield. Even then, your tax professional may persuade the auditor to allow a portion of the $1,000.

Lean hard on your tax professional as you prepare for your audit and make sure he is familiar with every detail that might affect your tax obligation for the year at issue.

Remember the burden of proof is on you. But on many issues you simply can't get the kind of proof that would stand up in a courtroom. Your presentation must be logical, meticulous, and supported with records. If it is, the auditor is more likely to believe you in areas where your documentation is slim. You cannot charm your way through an audit, but if your records are detailed and orderly, you are likely to come across to the auditor as an honest and meticulous taxpayer, and that impression is likely to affect his judgment on close calls.

DECIDING WHETHER TO GO

As you and your tax professional discuss your audit strategy, you have to decide whether to accompany him to the audit or send him in alone. We think most taxpayers should attend but should leave most of the talking to their hired professional. You'll learn a lot. Many taxpayers find their first audit almost calming; it isn't fun, but it isn't nearly so horrible as they anticipated. Besides, a question may arise that your professional cannot answer. If you are married and filed a joint tax return, it might be helpful for both you and your spouse to attend, provided both of you have gone through the preparations with your tax professional.

Stay home only if you are a frightened white-knuckler, a chatty Cathy who can't resist telling the auditor things he shouldn't know, or a vengeful citizen unable to control anger.

Don't worry that the auditor might suspect that you are bringing a professional because you have something to hide. In fact, the auditor will be glad to deal with a fellow tax pro. They can talk tax shorthand and whip through the session more quickly than if you were representing yourself.

COMPROMISING

Auditors aren't supposed to negotiate, and an auditor is unlikely to negotiate with an unrepresented taxpayer. But between fellow professionals, a good deal of informal negotiation goes on.

The IRS is now auditing tax returns for the early 1980s. Let's say for 1983 you deducted $30 a day, five days a week, for entertaining customers at lunch but have few receipts to prove it. Your tax professional will almost surely advise you that the auditor isn't likely to take your word; the deduction is out of the question. But he'll probably ask you to give him whatever you can to prove that your business requires a lot of luncheon entertaining. He can present that material during the audit and may persuade the auditor to allow a portion of your entertainment deductions.

In tax circles that sort of compromise is called an exercise of the "Cohan rule," named after George M. Cohan, the great composer and actor whose career spanned the beginning of the income tax in the 1920s. Cohan entertained lavishly, but he never bothered to keep receipts. He estimated his professional entertainment expenses, and the IRS challenged that deduction. The case went to court. Cohan argued that the IRS and the judges knew very well that he entertained a lot in connection with his work; his parties were regularly written up in the society pages. The IRS demurred, but the court ruled in Cohan's favor and allowed a good portion of Cohan's deduction.

You are always better off with records. In fact, for tax returns beginning with 1985 you are required to maintain records backing up any deductions having to do with entertainment, business travel, and business use of personal equipment such as a car or a computer. If a professional prepares your tax return, you will have to sign a form certifying that you have the records; otherwise the preparer cannot allow the deductions. If you prepare your own tax return, you'll have to certify to the IRS that you have such records. If you say you have the records but fail to produce them at an audit, you face a heavy penalty.

If you lack records for years before 1985, the IRS may let you retreat to a "safe harbor." For example, if you can't document all your automobile expenses related to your business, the auditor will let you deduct the standard mileage rate. If you lack receipts for meals eaten while you were on a business trip, the IRS will let you deduct $14 a day. But these safe harbors still cost you some money. Furthermore, your auditor may take a stiff stance and refuse to compromise.

As you and your tax professional wind up your preparations for the audit, make sure both of you are fully aware of the amount of money at stake and the items and amounts you are prepared to yield on. Make sure your records are neatly arranged. For example, if the audit notice lists interest income as one item at issue, get your 1099 forms together, separating those reporting interest from those reporting dividends. You may not benefit from making the auditor's job easy, but you surely will not benefit if you make his job hard. Bring along only the records that the audit notice asks for. Don't bring records for other years or for other areas of your tax return.

THE CONFRONTATION

No one goes into an audit with a light heart. You tend to feel something like a draftee reporting for a preinduction physical: Big Brother has called you in to probe you, expose you, and seize part of your life—in this case, your financial life.

But the better you are able to contain your apprehension and resentment, the more likely your audit will go smoothly. To the auditor, it is a routine meeting. Try to perform as if you approached it the same way. Dress as you would dress for any business meeting. Show up a little early and ask your tax professional to get there early, too. If the audit is at an IRS office, it helps to get familiar with the place. Besides, you and your professional can use that time to go over your plans.

███████████

Don't go into the audit with a preconceived picture of your auditor. The stereotype calls for a mean and sour middle-aged man with an encyclopedic knowledge of the tax laws and a laserlike eye for flaws on your return or in your presentation. In fact, many auditors are young, many are women, many are minorities, and many are still learning the tax laws. These are midlevel civil servants. The IRS does not get many MBAs from Stanford or Wharton. It gets run-of-the-mill accounting graduates from run-of-the-mill universities.

But you can be sure that your auditor has done his homework on your return and that he is familiar with the laws and regulations covering the areas at issue. Only one person at the audit knows more than the auditor, and that's your tax professional. He knows the laws as well as the auditor does (maybe better), and he knows details about your taxes and your finances that the auditor does not know.

At an IRS office, you will be ushered into a partitioned cubbyhole, not an office. Exchange the usual pleasantries. You and the auditor are cast in somewhat adversarial roles, but keep in mind that there is nothing personal about it.

Get down to work promptly. If your tax professional can begin the audit with an item that you can cleanly and quickly prove, so much the better; it will put you in a positive light and set a businesslike, efficient tone.

Be prepared to answer some questions yourself, if the auditor asks you to and if you are confident of the answers. Early in the interview, the auditor may ask you who prepared your tax return, whether your preparer (if you used one) gave you a copy, and whether your refund (if you were entitled to one) was mailed to you rather than to your preparer. These questions have to do with the IRS's program of identifying tax preparers who are out of line—so-called problem preparers.

As the audit continues, keep alert for signs that most of the issues resulted from the way your tax return was prepared, rather than from the material you provided to your tax preparer in the first place. If it was, you might consider changing preparers.

The auditor is likely to ask whether you received any

income that you did not report on your tax return. You and your professional will have gone over that. If you found some taxable income that you inadvertently did not report, make a clean breast of it. If you did not, say so—or, better, let your tax professional answer—that you're not aware of any unreported income. That's a better answer than a flat no, because the IRS may have come across some income that you did not report and still are unaware of.

Here are three defenses you should never use in an audit:

1. "But I've taken that deduction for years!"

That invites the auditor to order a review of your past returns. Under the statute of limitations, the IRS can audit returns as far back as three years. So if your audit is being held in mid-1985, reviewing your 1983 tax return, the auditor can get your 1982 and 1984 returns looked over for the same deduction. Nearly all audits cover just a single year.

2. "But everyone takes that!"

To an auditor, that is the lamest of all excuses, and it implies that you believe in cutting corners. Besides, it's a line that doesn't work. If the auditor has caught a deduction that you were not entitled to take or some income that you failed to report, let your tax professional deal with him. Of course you have friends who were not audited, and perhaps they got by with questionable items. But that doesn't mean that the IRS gave its blessing to their tax returns, only that they were lucky enough to escape audit. Their time will come.

3. "You want my records? Okay, here's every scrap of paper, mixed up in this grocery bag!"

This paper-dumping ploy succeeds only in stiffening the auditor's resolve and ruining the rest of your day. Typically, your auditor will excuse himself, tell his supervisor that he's stuck with one of those boneheaded paper dumpers, and get the rest of his schedule cleared so that he can, indeed, go over every scrap of paper. You'll have to go over it with him. He's earning his salary, whether he spends all day with you or sees half a dozen taxpayers. What do you get from spending the whole day with him? He certainly isn't going to give you a break on your taxes. If you were in his shoes, would you?

Although you and your tax professional prepared for this session, you do not want to sound as if you rehearsed lines from a script. We heard of an audit that was going smoothly until the auditor asked about a deduction for moving expenses. "What's my answer to that?" the taxpayer asked, turning to his preparer. The auditor was incensed. "I want the truth, not some rehearsed answer," he said. The rest of the audit was rough; that question cost the taxpayer.

If something comes up that you are uncertain about or that your professional may not be familiar with, politely ask the auditor if you and your professional can step outside for a minute. He'll let you. Get your heads together and decide how to respond. If the auditor has brought up an area of your tax return not listed on the audit notice, respond to his question only if you are sure you can handle the issue. We recommend that you bring records only for those areas listed on the audit notice. That way, you'll be in a position to tell the auditor that you're not prepared to deal with something new. Ask for another appointment. If the audit has been going in your favor, he may decide to skip the issue rather than keep your return open.

Your auditor may well lack financial sophistication and may have difficulty grasping areas of your work or your investments affecting your tax return. We have a friend in the international arms trade whose deductions included $2,400 for a dinner for twelve in Paris. He had all the records—a receipt, a list of his guests with their business affiliations, a summary of the business they discussed. Nevertheless, the auditor balked. He couldn't believe a dinner could cost $200 per person, much less that anyone would pick up a check for twelve guests at that price. With the help of his tax professional, our friend explained that lavish entertaining was expected in the arms business.

When an issue is worth it, do not hesitate to stand your

ground. When a taxpayer and an auditor reach an impasse on a cloudy issue, the auditor may say that he'll keep the audit open while checking with his superiors. Tax shelters are most likely to cause a delay. We know a couple who deducted $25,000 in losses on an equipment-leasing shelter. The auditor refused to allow any of the deduction; the couple refused to back down. Finally, the auditor said he would write to IRS headquarters for a ruling—a process that takes about a year. If you think you are right and you can stand the uncertainty and the delay, hold your ground. You can suggest that every area of your tax return be closed except the question at issue. That way the IRS could not reopen some other issue, nor could you.

By the way, this taxpayer used a little-known technique that made sure he wouldn't have to pay unnecessary penalties and interest in case the IRS decided against the claimed tax deductions. The taxpayer made a payment in lieu of bond, meaning that he paid the money to a sort of IRS escrow account. If the IRS decided against him, it would take the money from the account without charging additional penalties or interest. If the decision went the taxpayer's way, the money would be returned, although the IRS would not pay interest on it. On balance, payment in lieu of bond protects you from the accumulation of large penalties while the IRS decides your case.

You have the right to resist the auditor on every point, to appeal to his or her supervisor, and if that fails, to appeal further up the IRS hierarchy. You also have the right to appeal to the U.S. Tax Court. But we lean against that unless you have a lot of money at stake and a good chance of winning. Don't get carried away with the notion that your case will have a far-reaching effect on the American system of tax enforcement. The IRS wins the large majority of appeals. The IRS keeps lawyers on the payroll to handle appeals; you, on the other hand, have to pay for your professional help.

You pay your taxes in dollars, and you should decide how hard to press your case based on the dollars involved. We have a friend who swallowed his pride and his anger and paid $1,500 to settle a point he was sure he could win in court. To him, it just wasn't economically worth it to press an appeal.

THE AFTERMATH

At this point, you probably know why you were audited and if your preparer was at fault. Your auditor probably can tell you how you have fared and how much additional tax, if any, you will owe. But his decision is tentative. He has to write a report for review by his superiors. If you have persuaded him to yield on some points, he has to persuade his superiors. So close your audit session on a cordial note.

The IRS will mail you a bill or a notice that the audit was closed with no additional tax due. If you owe, you have ten days to pay. While waiting for your note from the IRS, you can weigh the prospects of appeal. If a tax shelter is the issue, you can call the sponsor of the shelter and ask for advice; other investors probably have faced the same difficulty.

Assuming your audit did not result in a heavy assessment, look upon it as a valuable experience. Unless you did something to arouse the auditor's suspicions, you are unlikely to be audited next year; one audit does not put you on a list of suspects.

But it could happen again, and some day it probably will. When it does, gnash your teeth, curse your cat, and complain to your neighbor. But remember, to the IRS it's all in a day's work.

Do we expect to be audited again? You bet. But we're not worried. We both have tax plans, good records, and lots of Tax Savers.

Part Four

FORMS, MAILING ADDRESSES, AND OTHER ESSENTIALS

Tax Glossary

Adjusted gross income—All your income from taxable sources, minus eight specific "adjustments," which amount to deductions. They're listed at the bottom of the first page of Form 1040.

Alternative minimum tax—A backstop tax imposed on high-income taxpayers whose income would otherwise be largely sheltered from income tax.

Audit—A review of your tax return by the IRS.

Basis—Your cost, used in figuring gain or loss, when you sell a house or other property. On real estate, Basis includes the price you paid plus the cost of improvements.

Capital gains and losses—Profit or loss on the sale of real estate, stocks, or anything else of value. If you bought the asset after June 22, 1984, and sell after owning it for six months or less, you have a short-term capital gain (or loss). If you have owned it for more than six months, your capital gain or loss is long-term. For assets purchased earlier, the holding period is one year. Long-term capital gains qualify for favored tax treatment.

Casualty loss—A loss resulting from a sudden or unusual event, such as lightning destroying your prize oak tree or a thief making off with the family jewels. A casualty loss is deductible to the extent that you do not collect insurance and the loss exceeds 10 percent of your adjusted gross income.

Credits—Dollar-for-dollar subtractions from the income tax you would otherwise pay. For example, the credit for child and dependent care expenses, and the partial credit for political contributions. Tax credits are more valuable than tax deductions, but deductions are more plentiful.

Deductions—Expenses subtracted from your taxable income. For example, state and local income taxes; charitable contributions; union and professional dues.

Deficiency—Additional income tax that you owe.

Depreciation—A deduction reflecting the gradual wearing out of a business asset, such as a salesman's car.

Earned income—Money you earn from working, as opposed to unearned income from interest and dividends.

Estimated tax—The income tax that you anticipate paying for the current year.

Exemption—All your dependents—everyone you support, including yourself—are exemptions, and every exemption cuts your taxable income by $1,000. At age sixty-five, you get an extra exemption. Blind taxpayers also qualify for an extra exemption.

Filing status—Your family situation, most typically "single" or "married filing joint return." Your filing status determines the tax table, or tax rate schedule, that you must use.

Gross income—All your income from taxable sources. After calculating your gross income, you can then take off adjustments, then deductions, and finally exemptions.

Holding period—The length of time you own a piece of property, such as a house or a hundred shares of AT&T stock.

Imputed interest—Interest that you don't actually receive but that is taxed anyway. For example, zero-coupon bonds pay no annual interest; instead, they yield a big gain at maturity. The IRS calls that gain a form of gradual, year-by-year "imputed interest" and taxes it.

Income Averaging—A Tax Saver that lets you average your income over the past four years, lessening the tax that you otherwise would pay if one year's income took a big jump.

Individual Retirement Account (IRA)—A tax-deferred savings account. One of the most extraordinary Tax Savers available.

Itemized deductions—Deductions from your taxable income, listed on Schedule A, Form 1040.

Keogh Account—Like an IRA, but more generous. Only for the self-employed.

Penalty—Additional money you're assessed by the IRS for filing your return and/or paying your tax late, not paying enough estimated income tax, or breaking other IRS rules.

Principal residence—The home you live in, as opposed to a vacation home or a home you rent out.

Subchapter S Corporation—A corporation that pays no tax itself, because it passes all profits and losses to its shareholders. Subchapter S Corporations are used by many self-employed individuals.

Tax Reform Act of 1984—The eighth major revision of the income tax laws in the past ten years. The act contains more than 250 revisions, many of them altering the rules that determine what is a good Tax Saver and what is not.

Tax Saver, Tax incentive, Tax loophole, Tax shelter—Synonymous terms, referring to the various ways you can reduce your income tax burden. We prefer "Tax Saver" because it doesn't carry the emotional and political implications of the other three terms.

Taxable income—Your income after taking off adjustments, deductions, and exemptions.

Unearned income—Taxable income from sources other than work, such as interest and dividends.

Wash sale—The sale of a stock or bond at a loss and the repurchase of that investment within thirty days.

Withholding—Money your employer takes out of your paycheck and pays to Uncle Sam. Through withholding, you pay income tax on your salary gradually, all year long.

20

Primary Tax Forms and Schedules

Income Tax Return	Form 1040
Itemized Deductions	Schedule A
Interest and Dividend Income	Schedule B
Profit (or Loss) from Business or Profession	Schedule C
Capital Gains and Losses	Schedule D
Supplemental Income Schedule	Schedule E
Farm Income and Expenses	Schedule F
Income Averaging	Schedule G
Credit for the Elderly	Schedule R & RP
Computation of Social Security Self-Employment	Schedule SE
Deduction for Married Couples When Both Work	Schedule W
Employee Withholding Allowance Certificate	Form W-4
Amended U.S. Individual Income Tax Return	Form 1040X
Computation of Foreign Tax Credit—Individual, Fiduciary, or Non-Resident Alien	Form 1116
Employee Business Expenses	Form 2106

Sale or Exchange of Principal
Residence .... Form 2119
Multiple Support Declaration ..... Form 2120
Underpayment of Estimated Tax
by Individuals .... Form 2210
Credit for Child and Dependent
Care Expenses .... Form 2441
Application for Extension of
Time to File (for a specific reason) . Form 2688
Computation of Investment Credit Form 3468
Moving Expense Adjustment ...... Form 3903
Computation of Social Security Tax
or Unreported Tip Income .... Form 4137
Request for Copy of Tax Return ... Form 4506
Depreciation and Amortization .... Form 4562
Casualties and Thefts .... Form 4684
Gains and Losses (Supplemental
Schedule) .... Form 4797
Application for Automatic
Extension of Time to File U.S.
Individual Income Tax Return ..... Form 4868
Investment Interest Expense
Deduction .... Form 4952
Special 10-year Averaging Method . Form 4972
Residential Energy Credit .... Form 5695
Alternative Minimum Tax
Computation .... Form 6251
Computation of Installment Sale
Income .... Form 6252
Report of Foreign Bank, Securities,
and Other Financial Accounts ..... Treas. Dept. Form
90-22.1

21

Free IRS Instructional Booklets

Pub. No.	Title	Principal Related Forms
17	Your Federal Income Tax	Forms 1040, 1040A
54	Tax Guide for U.S. Citizens Abroad	Form 2555
225	Farmer's Tax Guide	Schedule F Form 1040
334	Tax Guide for Small Business	Schedule C Form 1040, Forms 1065, 1120, 1120S
448	Federal Estate and Gift Taxes	Forms 706, 709
463	Travel, Entertainment, and Gift Expenses	Form 2106
501	Exemptions	Form 1040 Form 2120

502	Medical and Dental Expenses	Schedule A, Form 1040
503	Child and Disabled Dependent Care	Forms W-2, W-3, 940, 942, 1040, 2441
504	Tax Information for Divorced or Separated Individuals	
505	Tax Withholding and Estimated Tax	Forms W-4, W-5, 1040-ES, 2210
506	Income Averaging	Schedule G Form 1040
508	Educational Expenses	Form 2106
509	Tax Calendar	
513	Tax Information for Visitors to the United States	Form 1040NR
514	Foreign Tax Credit for U.S. Citizens and Resident Aliens	Form 1116
515	Withholding of Tax on Non-Resident Aliens and Foreign Corporations	Forms 1042, 1042S
516	Tax Information for U.S. Government Civilian Employees Stationed Abroad	
517	Social Security for Members of the Clergy and Religious Workers	Form 4361

535	Business Expenses and Operating Losses	
539	Withholding Taxes and Reporting Requirements	Form 940
541	Tax Information on Partnerships	Forms 1065, 4797
542	Tax Information on Corporations	Form 1120
544	Sales and Other Dispositions of Assets	Schedule D Form 1040 Form 4797
545	Interest Expense	Schedule A Form 1040 Form 4952
547	Tax Information on Disasters, Casualties, and Thefts	Form 4684
548	Deduction for Bad Debts	
550	Investment Income and Expenses	Schedules B and D Form 1040
551	Basis of Assets	
552	Recordkeeping Requirements and a List of Tax Publications	
554	Tax Benefits for Older Americans	Schedules E, R Form 1040
555	Community Property and the Federal Income Tax	

556	Examination of Returns, Appeal Rights, and Claims for Refund	Forms 1040X, 1120X
557	How to Apply for and Retain Exempt Status for Your Organization	Forms 1023, 1024
558	Tax Information for Sponsors of Contests and Sporting Events	Form 1099-MISC
559	Tax Information for Survivors, Executors, and Administrators	Form 1041
560	Tax Information on Self-Employed Retirement Plans	Forms 5500-K, 5500-R
561	Determining the Value of Donated Property	
564	Mutual Fund Distributions	Form 1099-DIV
567	Tax Information on U.S. Civil Service Retirement and Disability Retirement	
570	Tax Guide for U.S. Citizens Employed in U.S. Possessions	Form 4563
571	Tax-Sheltered Annuity Programs for Employees of Public Schools and Certain Tax-Exempt Organizations	Forms 5500, 5500-C

572	Investment Credit	Forms 3468, 4255
575	Pension and Annuity Income	Schedule E Form 1040 Form 4972
583	Recordkeeping for a Small Business	
584	Disaster and Casualty Loss Workbook	Schedule A Form 1040
585	Voluntary Tax Methods to Help Finance Political Campaigns	
586A	The Collection Process (Income Tax Accounts)	
587	Business Use of Your Home	Schedule C Form 1040
588	Condominiums, Cooperative Apartments, and Homeowners Associations	
589	Tax Information on Subchapter S Corporations	Form 1120S
590	Tax Information on Individual Retirement Arrangements	Form 5329
593	Income Tax Benefits for U.S. Citizens Who Go Overseas	

596	Earned Income Credit	Forms W-5, 1040, 1040A
721	Comprehensive Tax Guide for U.S. Civil Service Retirement Benefits	
724	Favorable Determination Letter	
903	Energy Credits for Individuals	Form 5695
904	Computing the Interrelated Charitable, Marital, and Orphans' Deductions and Net Gifts	
905	Tax Information on Unemployment Compensation	
907	Tax Information for Handicapped and Disabled Individuals	Schedule A Form 1040 Form 2440
1004	Identification Numbers Under ERISA	

$\mathcal{IRS}$
Service Centers

$\mathcal{Y}$ ou can order federal tax forms and publications from the IRS Forms Distribution Center for your state at the address below. Or, if you prefer, you can photocopy tax forms from reproducible copies kept at many public libraries. In addition, many libraries have reference sets of IRS publications that you can also read or copy—on the spot.

ALABAMA—Caller No. 848, Atlanta, GA 30370
ALASKA—P.O. Box 12626, Fresno, CA 93778
ARIZONA—P.O. Box 12626, Fresno, CA 93778
ARKANSAS—P.O. Box 2924, Austin, TX 78769
CALIFORNIA—P.O. Box 12626, Fresno, CA 93778
COLORADO—P.O. Box 2924, Austin, TX 78769
CONNECTICUT—P.O. Box 1040, Methuen, MA 01844
DELAWARE—P.O. Box 25866, Richmond, VA 23260
DISTRICT OF COLUMBIA—P.O. Box 25866, Richmond, VA 23260
FLORIDA—Caller No. 848, Atlanta, GA 30370
GEORGIA—Caller No. 848, Atlanta, GA 30370
HAWAII—P.O. Box 12626, Fresno, CA 93778
IDAHO—P.O. Box 12626, Fresno, CA 93778

PART FOUR: FORMS, ADDRESSES, ETC.

ILLINOIS—P.O. Box 24711, 1500 E. Bannister Road, Kansas City, MO 64131
INDIANA—P.O. Box 6900, Florence, KY 41042
IOWA—P.O. Box 24711, 1500 E. Bannister Road, Kansas City, MO 64131
KANSAS—P.O. Box 2924, Austin, TX 78769
KENTUCKY—P.O. Box 6900, Florence, KY 41042
LOUISIANA—P.O. Box 2924, Austin, TX 78769
MAINE—P.O. Box 1040, Methuen, MA 01844
MARYLAND—P.O. Box 25866, Richmond, VA 23260
MASSACHUSETTS—P.O. Box 1040, Methuen, MA 01844
MICHIGAN—P.O. Box 6900, Florence, KY 41042
MINNESOTA—P.O. Box 24711, 1500 E. Bannister Road, Kansas City, MO 64131
MISSISSIPPI—Caller No. 848, Atlanta, GA 30370
MISSOURI—P.O. Box 24711, 1500 E. Bannister Road, Kansas City, MO 64131
MONTANA—P.O. Box 12626, Fresno, CA 93778
NEBRASKA—P.O. Box 24711, 1500 E. Bannister Road, Kansas City, MO 64131
NEVADA—P.O. Box 12626, Fresno, CA 93778
NEW HAMPSHIRE—P.O. Box 1040, Methuen, MA 01844
NEW JERSEY—P.O. Box 25866, Richmond, VA 23260
NEW MEXICO—P.O. Box 2924, Austin, TX 78769
NEW YORK—
    Western New York, P.O. Box 260, Buffalo, NY 14201
    Eastern New York (including New York City), P.O. Box 1040, Methuen, MA 01844
NORTH CAROLINA—Caller No. 848, Atlanta, GA 30370
NORTH DAKOTA—P.O. Box 24711, 1500 E. Bannister Road, Kansas City, MO 64131
OHIO—P.O. Box 6900, Florence, KY 41042
OKLAHOMA—P.O. Box 2924, Austin, TX 78769
OREGON—P.O. Box 12626, Fresno, CA 93778
PENNSYLVANIA—P.O. Box 25866, Richmond, VA 23260
RHODE ISLAND—P.O. Box 1040, Methuen, MA 01844
SOUTH CAROLINA—Caller No. 848, Atlanta, GA 30370
SOUTH DAKOTA—P.O. Box 24711, 1500 E. Bannister Road, Kansas City, MO 64131
TENNESSEE—Caller No. 848, Atlanta, GA 30370

TEXAS—P.O. Box 2924, Austin, TX 78769
UTAH—P.O. Box 12626, Fresno, CA 93778
VERMONT—P.O. Box 1040, Methuen, MA 01844
VIRGINIA—P.O. Box 25866, Richmond, VA 23260
WASHINGTON—P.O. Box 12626, Fresno, CA 93778
WEST VIRGINIA—P.O. Box 636, Florence, KY 41042
WISCONSIN—P.O. Box 24711, 1500 E. Bannister Road,
    Kansas City, MO 64131
WYOMING—P.O. Box 2924, Austin, TX 78769

Foreign Addresses—Taxpayers with mailing addresses in
    foreign countries should send requests for forms and
    publications to IRS Distribution Center, P.O. Box
    25866, Richmond, VA 23260.

Puerto Rico—Director's Representative, U.S. Internal
    Revenue Service, Federal Office Building, Chardon
    Street, Hato Rey, PR 00918.

Virgin Islands—Department of Finance, Tax Division,
    Charlotte Amalie, St. Thomas, VI 00801

23

Addresses for Filing Your Return

U se the addressed envelope that came with your return. If you do not have an addressed envelope, or if you moved during the year, mail your return to the Internal Revenue Service Center for the place where you live. No street address is needed.

If your address is located in	Use the following Internal Revenue Center address:
New Jersey, New York City, and counties of Nassau, Rockland, Suffolk, and Westchester	Holtsville, NY 00501
New York (all other counties), Connecticut, Maine, Massachusetts, New Hampshire, Rhode Island, Vermont	Andover, MA 05501

Alabama, Florida,
Georgia, Mississippi,
South Carolina ......   Atlanta, GA 31101

Michigan, Ohio ......   Cincinnati, OH 45999

Arkansas, Kansas,
Louisiana, New
Mexico, Oklahoma,
Texas ....   Austin, TX 73301

Alaska, Arizona,
Colorado, Idaho,
Minnesota, Montana,
Nebraska, Nevada,
North Dakota,
Oregon, South Dakota,
Utah, Washington,
Wyoming ....   Ogden, UT 84201

Illinois, Iowa,
Missouri, Wisconsin .   Kansas City, MO 64999

California, Hawaii ...   Fresno, CA 93888

Indiana, Kentucky,
North Carolina,
Tennessee, Virginia,
West Virginia ....   Memphis, TN 37501

Delaware, District of
Columbia, Maryland,
Pennsylvania ....   Philadelphia, PA 19255

American Samoa ....   Philadelphia, PA 19255

Guam ....   Commissioner of Revenue
and Taxation
Agana, GU 96910

Puerto Rico ....   Philadelphia, PA 19255

Virgin Islands: Nonpermanent resident	Philadelphia, PA 19255
Virgin Islands: Permanent resident ..	Bureau of Internal Revenue Charlotte Amalie St. Thomas, VI 00801

APO or FPO
address of:

Miami	Atlanta, GA 31101
New York	Holtsville, NY 00501
San Francisco	Fresno, CA 93888
Seattle	Ogden, UT 84201

Foreign country: U.S. citizens and those excluding income under section 911 or 931 or claiming the housing deduction under section 911	Philadelphia, PA 19255

24

Tax Tables

SINGLE TAXPAYERS
FOR TAX YEARS BEGINNING IN 1984

Taxable Income				
Over	Not Over	Pay	+ Tax Rate %	On Excess Over
. . . . . .	$ 2,300	. . . . . .	. .	. . . . . .
$ 2,300	3,400	. . . . . .	11	$ 2,300
3,400	4,400	$ 121	12	3,400
4,400	6,500	241	14	4,400
6,500	8,500	535	15	6,500
8,500	10,800	835	16	8,500
10,800	12,900	1,203	18	10,800
12,900	15,000	1,581	20	12,900
15,000	18,200	2,001	23	15,000
18,200	23,500	2,737	26	18,200
23,500	28,800	4,115	30	23,500
28,800	34,100	5,705	34	28,800
34,100	41,500	7,507	38	34,100
41,500	55,300	10,319	42	41,500
55,300	81,800	16,115	48	55,300
81,800	. . . . . .	28,835	50	81,800

JOINT RETURNS
FOR TAX YEARS BEGINNING IN 1984

For Use Only by Married Individuals Filing Joint
Returns and Certain Surviving Spouses

Taxable Income				Tax	On Excess
Over	Not Over	Pay	+	Rate %	Over
. . . . . .	$ 3,400	. . . . . .		. .	. . . .
$ 3,400	5,500	. . . . . .		11	$ 3,400
5,500	7,600	$ 231		12	5,500
7,600	11,900	483		14	7,600
11,900	16,000	1,085		16	11,900
16,000	20,200	1,741		18	16,000
20,200	24,600	2,497		22	20,200
24,600	29,900	3,465		25	24,600
29,900	35,200	4,790		28	29,900
35,200	45,800	6,274		33	35,200
45,800	60,000	9,772		38	45,800
60,000	85,600	15,168		42	60,000
85,600	109,400	25,920		45	85,600
109,400	162,400	36,630		49	109,400
162,400	. . . . . .	62,600		50	162,400

MARRIED FILING SEPARATELY
FOR TAX YEARS BEGINNING IN 1984

Taxable Income				Tax	On Excess
Over	Not Over	Pay	+	Rate %	Over
. . . . . .	$ 1,700	. . . .		. .	. . . . . .
$ 1,700	2,750	. . . .		11	$ 1,700
2,750	3,800	$ 115.50		12	2,750
3,800	5,950	241.50		14	3,800
5,950	8,000	542.50		16	5,950
8,000	10,100	870.50		18	8,000
10,100	12,300	1,248.50		22	10,100
12,300	14,950	1,732.50		25	12,300
14,950	17,600	2,395.00		28	14,950
17,600	22,900	3,137.00		33	17,600
22,900	30,000	4,886.00		38	22,900
30,000	42,800	7,584.00		42	30,000
42,800	54,700	12,960.00		45	42,800
54,700	81,200	18,315.00		49	54,700
81,200	. . . . . .	31,300.00		50	81,200

HEAD OF HOUSEHOLD
FOR TAX YEARS BEGINNING IN 1984

Taxable Income				Tax	On Excess
Over	*Not Over*	*Pay*	+	*Rate %*	*Over*
. . . . . .	$ 2,300	. . . . . .		. .	. . . . . .
$ 2,300	4,400	. . . . . .		11	$ 2,300
4,400	6,500	$ 231		12	4,400
6,500	8,700	483		14	6,500
8,700	11,800	791		17	8,700
11,800	15,000	1,318		18	11,800
15,000	18,200	1,894		20	15,000
18,200	23,500	2,534		24	18,200
23,500	28,800	3,806		28	23,500
28,800	34,100	5,290		32	28,800
34,100	44,700	6,986		35	34,100
44,700	60,600	10,696		42	44,700
60,600	81,800	17,374		45	60,600
81,800	108,300	26,914		48	81,800
108,300	. . . . . .	39,634		50	108,300

Index

Index